A LITTLE TREASURY OF LOVE POEMS

A LITTLE
TREASURY OF
LOVE POEMS

FROM CHAUCER TO DYLAN THOMAS

Edited with an Introduction
by
JOHN HOLMES

Decorations by
JOHANNES TROYER

CHARLES SCRIBNER'S SONS
NEW YORK

COPYRIGHT NOTICES
AND ACKNOWLEDGMENTS

Copyright Notices & Acknowledgments

Copyright Notices & Acknowledgments

CONTENTS

I LOVE'S RIDDLES:
Definitions of Love

CONTENTS

II   I HEREBY SWEAR:
Dedication to Love

III   NEVER TOLD CAN BE:
Heights & Depths of Love

IV ENDEARING YOUNG CHARMS:
Youth, Beauty, Grace

V A ROSY WREATH:
The Tokens of Love

VI IN NEW SURPRISE:
World Transformed by Love

VII LOVE WILL FIND OUT THE WAY:
Courtship

CONTENTS

VIII GATHER YE ROSEBUDS:
Make Haste, Sweet Love

IX ALL THE PLEASURES PROVE:
Erotic, Sensuous

X FALLING STAR:
Doubt, Infidelity, Hurt

XI   BITTER CHILL:
Ballads, Sorrow, Revenge

XII   THE SECRET WOUNDS:
Renunciation, Resignation

CONTENTS

XIII   KISS AND PART:
Separation, Absence, Loss

XIV   WHOSE HOLY FIRE:
Married Love, Domestic

xviii

CONTENTS

XV THE ONE BELL ONLY:
Love's Elegies

CONTENTS

XVI TILL A' THE SEAS GANG DRY:
Love Eternal

XVII THE GREAT LOVE SONGS

XVIII LOVE: *The Light Side*

CONTENTS

APPENDIX:

NEVER TOLD CAN BE

I

THE shortest and most important love-letter ever written said, "Tonight, same place, same time." Was the language of that miniature classic Latin, or Babylonian, or was it pencilled and pushed into a Brooklyn mailbox? A girl in Nebraska knew where to find it, and a lady in Elizabeth's court; both, in some secret place. It was the message on page 231, on a scrap of paper passed in the drawing-room, it was a word in a telephone-booth. The urgent and universal language of love, speaking of the most powerful attraction in human experience, says, as the language of love always says, more than the words it uses.

One of the shortest love-poems of our times is by an unknown poet, apparently of the 1920's, who echoes the Elizabethans by speaking of the turtle-dove, a term of endearment because those birds were affectionate, and, I might say, because the English language is poor in rhymes for important words like death, silver, and love. Here is the simplest of all expressions of love, that fullness and all-giving, in the largest metaphor the lover could call up.

I love you more than the gilder his gilding,
  And more than the turtle his dove,
And more than the people in the Woolworth Building
  Love all the people they love.

That would be a great many people, and a great flood of love, though there is never a way of saying it that is full enough. There are buildings in New York now so much bigger than the Woolworth Building. What a lover's metaphor it might be to say Empire State,

Rockefeller Center, or United Nations. Love being what it is, someone has no doubt already said so, and better than the variation which follows, on a tender and exuberant modern love-poem.

> *I love you more than the conductor his stations,*
> *Or the stamp-collector his trove,*
> *And more than the delegates to the United Nations*
> *Love all the people they love.*

> *I love you more than all doorways marked Enter,*
> *Or planes pilots spot up above,*
> *And more than the people in Rockefeller Center*
> *Love all the people they love.*

Which, as an experiment in improvisation, delights the writer as much as the original must have delighted its author—and the one for whom it was written. It is to be remembered that a gathering of love poems involves twice as many people as it seems to, because every poet in it wrote his poem *to* someone. Shadowy and immortal, the beloved inspirers of the poem stand like a great gallery above and behind the poets, all the Celias and Antheas, the Margarets and Carolines, lads and lasses, husbands and wives. Though for the most part nameless, they yet live in that eternal life poetry confers, forever loved as warmly as when the poet first set down his lines. The only lonely people in a book of love-poems are those separated from their lovers, and even they once knew that sweetest and fullest of human relations.

The poet in love makes any name beautiful. Herrick's girls have symbolic or equivalent names, because it was the fashion—the wench might have been called Miggie, or Babs, by her brothers and sisters, and what could a poet do with that?—but Herrick had partly to disguise his sweethearts, partly to make their names me-

xxiv

lodious. One age smiles at the names of another age, and Ermyntrude and Maude seem ridiculous to us, breathed fervently into a sonnet. But the poetry of love takes each generation's fashion in stride, and the Amelias, Annes, Sheilas, and Jeans, the Biblical names and the nicknames, the parents' mistakes and the proud family traditions, can all shine and turn, in love poems, to the most beautiful sound in the language. Dorcas. Kitty. Marilyn. Ethel.

A collection of love poems is read by people in love, first of all. It is not quite true that they are the only people who read it; such a book is read by those who are almost in love, almost out of love, long past love, and sworn never to be in love again. But for the first kind, the people in love, a book of poetry about it is part of the paraphernalia of courtship. The young man takes it out of his coat pocket of an evening, and reads from it to the girl. Or he packs it with the picnic lunch, and on a summer afternoon reads to her, turning the pages under the trees. All that he cannot say he may read; some poet has said it for him, but his own voice speaks the lines to her ears, and she knows all the passion is his. An anthology of love poetry is a great convenience, an aid to communication, and in every way a powerful forwarder of civilization. It seems likely that two or three young men would read love poetry aloud, each of them being in love with a woman somewhere, than it does for girls to read to one another, their men being away from them. Men have a proud kind of secrecy about love; women are as secret and as proud, yet they can share the fact of being loved. Men will pack a book of love poems to a fishing camp, in a barracks bag, out over the Pacific, and never show it to the man next them. Women, from such reading, find communion and understanding, the mood and the music of the poems going only incidentally to the nearer listeners in apartment rooms and college dormitories; it is the faraway listener to whom the girl is really reading.

It is certainly true that, as often as not, love poems are read in solitude. If the solitude is by reason of separation not in spirit but in distance, then it is also certain that the lover will hunt through the pages till he or she finds a poem saying what the other must hear, and it is copied into a letter. Often and often the lover becomes the poet. The author may be John Donne, or E. E. Cummings, but the letter-writer is to all real purposes composing the poem as he copies it out. The poet is Cyrano under the balcony in the dark, making ardent phrases for Roxane to hear, who thinks the wordless Christian speaks them.

And two people in love, reading the poetry of love, by no means choose only poems that speak of their own tentative, early fondness. They are quite as likely to turn and to taste the sweet-bitter sadness of love ended or ending—Rupert Brooke's "The Hill," or Michael Drayton's "Parting," that sonnet of hopeless hope that in all English poetry says best what lovers know of loss. Some pity and terror will stir at William Morris's "The Haystack in the Floods," as if these lovers want to imagine all the experiences of love, even the brutal. They will think they could know what it means to love in silence, as Mark Van Doren says it, in "Private Worship." Secure and close, and at ease, having each other, they will read A. E. Housman's "Bredon Hill,"

> *Here of a Sunday morning*
> *My love and I would lie,*
> *And see the coloured counties,*
> *And hear the larks so high*
> *About us in the sky.*

> *But when the snows at Christmas*
> *On Bredon top were strown,*
> *My love rose up so early*
> *And stole out unbeknown*
> *And went to church alone.*

Or John Crowe Ransom's "Parting Without a Sequel," a poem of another kind of separation, and somehow all or any of these will tell the listener how well, how very well she is loved. "It could not happen to us," he is saying, as they lie there in the sunlight under the trees. "We are the only truly happy ones, we are the only two who really know," he is saying, as he reads the sad, the dark and tragic poems, what it would mean to lose one another.

He will turn to the poems of married love, exploring that part of content and loyalty, patterned and habituated, about which neither lover knows anything at all. "This," he is saying, and she knows it as he reads, "this is what we could have." Or he will read Cummings—gay, healthy, ribald—or Donne, in his mixed devotion and defiance, or Emily Dickinson, or the Brownings or Millay, or Herrick—in the poetry of love we always come back to the seventeenth century. "This, too," he says. Somehow one lives in love poetry all that has not yet been lived—foresees, foreknows, the worst and best.

To be in love is to be most newly alive and aware, as nothing else will ever bring it about again, except perhaps grief. And even grief will move these two readers, the grief of love before they know it, the truth of grief after they know it. All those poems on the incommunicability of love, all those poems of death and mourning, of vows of eternal faith! What dolor, and what truth. Brightest, best, and most immediate is the poetry of new surprise, of the outer world transformed, since in love that is the way the world looks.

The old can be ignored, the poor are poor indeed, the past is gone, done, and dead; but the two in love are together and alive, and nothing else matters. Love makes all the difference to the poets, whether John Donne sings his "Good Morrow," or John Cleveland muses "Upon Phyllis Walking," or Robert Frost, in "Two Look at Two," sees the world changed. Nothing else matters. For the first time the young male human animal knows the warming care of thinking of someone else more than himself. This is a consuming emotion, both terribly selfish and utterly unselfish, a contradiction that accounts for the turmoil of love. Desire, though not yet wholly understood, is a little way beyond him in consummation. Small griefs are large; the tone of a word, a minor thoughtlessness. Children, when they are hurt, hurt all over, unable to localize or rationalize the pain. The young (but everyone is young in love) also ache throughout the newly sensitized nerves and skin and understanding. If the male animal suffers in his deep wordless way, the female of the species has the greater difficulty: she knows that he knows that she knows he knows, but she finds it a painfully slow and far too polite manoeuvering to get him to admit it. It is little wonder that most of the love poetry is written by men, who want to but never do speak up, and less by women, who could speak up, but must not. Yet there is a pure wholeness in love, an avowal and a devotion which the marriage ceremony merely confirms, about which the woman can hardly speak, and has hardly ever spoken. Only the man she loves knows how far beyond any words it goes. The fact remains, in English literature, that men have written more great love poems than women have written.

What the young man learns in time, if he ever learns what it is to be loved by a woman, is humility; that this creature, desired and delicate and unique, should by miracle return his animal desire and his unselfish love; that she should wish to serve him as he would serve her. Humility; and generosity; two lessons of love, and not often represented in the poetry of love.

In love, the two most beautiful devotions are those of the very young to the young, and of the old to the very old. Only the very old know, and few of them, what it is to have found accord. There seems to be a peace, all faults long since known, and all acquaintance made, that the middle-aged and the heartier younger lovers have not reached. They come to look alike, we say, and to think alike. The way the mind of one works may be no surprise to the other, but it is a pleasure, and there is forever the shared pride, the shared good, the shared trouble. It is much the same with the very young in love and marriage. The wars of our times have brought men and women together in love and marriage at an age earlier than anything except pioneering has ever done. No one has yet said in poetry or in prose what a great new force this is and is to be. The loyalty, the effort, the clenched joy of these young marriages is most moving; the qualities they show are those of courage and durability, and the world will endure because of them. Their trouble and pride and love are usually not so early expected of the young, but these veterans and their wives have met and compassed the demands. They have found their peace early, and happily, that acquaintance of body with body, and growing mind with mind, which makes life and poetry go.

II

The poems in this book have been arranged in a sequence from the first awareness of love, to love's focus on one person, its urgency, its consummation, the pain of love—doubt, parting, renunciation—to that lasting love through all of marriage, and after death. There are added a group of love songs, and a group of poems on the lighter side of love.

"Love's riddles" are not so much puzzles as definitions; they answer the very questions they ask. Some of these poems ache with the early sweetness of love, and some like Sandburg's "Explanations of Love," or Louise Bogan's "Men Loved Wholly Beyond Wisdom," were written by poets looking backward at love. The poems of this sort testify to the infinite variousness of love, sometimes hinting at its pain, more often celebrating its fullness and its wonder. "I feed a flame within," says Dryden. To Samuel Daniel, "love is a sickness," but Elizabeth Barrett Browning, in what is probably the best-known of modern love-poems, speaks for all lovers, saying, "How do I love thee? Let me count the ways," and Christopher Marlowe cries out, "Who ever loved that loved not at first sight?" In one way or another, the poets find words for all that comes in love.

One of Elinor Wylie's sonnets, from the beautiful sequence called "Angels and Earthly Creatures," dedicates her not only to love itself, but to the beloved, taking the vow,

> *I hereby swear that to uphold your house*
> *I would lay my bones in quick destroying lime*
> *Or turn my flesh to timber for all time;*
> *Cut down my womanhood*

It is from this sonnet that the title for the second experience of love comes, *I Hereby Swear.* Carew, Meredith, Sedley, Jonson, Herrick, indeed all the poets in love have at one time or another made this selfless surrender.

"Never seek to tell thy love," sings William Blake,

"love that never told can be." There comes a time when the lover knows he knows beyond any words a thing that has made him greatly happy. Fortunately for all lovers, the poets are articulate, and compelled to speak the experience of love. They seek any device to report that they have found something too marvelous to be reported. Archibald MacLeish, in one of the finest of all love poems in our language, says, "Therefore I will not speak of the undying glory of women," and yet he communicates that glory.

I shall say you were young and your arms straight and your mouth scarlet
I shall say you will die and none will remember you
Your arms change and none remember the swish of your garments
Nor the click of your shoe

Not with my hand's strength not with difficult labor
Springing the obstinate words to the bones of your breast
And the stubborn line to your young stride and the breath to your breathing
And the beat to your haste
Shall I prevail on the hearts of unborn men to remember

This is the poet in love, making symbols speak, not in words, of the unspeakable.

I will say the shape of a leaf lay once on your hair
Till the world ends and the eyes are out and the mouths broken
Look! It is there!

Poets can do this, as Shakespeare had done it in the sonnet from which MacLeish took his title.

Not marble, nor the gilded monuments
Of Princes shall outlive this powerfull rime,
But you shall shine more bright in these contents
Than unswept stone.

And Sidney said, "Look in thy heart, and write," but what is written, Spenser said, is written on the sands. Time and tide may wash away the name and the words, yet never the memory of all the words stand for, the unforgotten beloved.

A time comes in love, as lovers know, when the name, the sight of the loved one, walking, dancing, sleeping, is its utmost beautiful embodiment. Praise crowds the poet's mind, and he cries out, "There be none of beauty's daughters," as Byron did; or, like Yeats, he sings of the one and only yellow head—in an ardent chorus all but drowned out by Marlowe, Shakespeare; and always Herrick.

As the lover comes close and closer, things associated with the beloved are exciting in themselves—a glove, a book, her clothes. The glove was certainly a mild and satisfactory symbol a hundred years ago, and her clothes are always. One or two love-poems about my love in dungarees, or "On Returning—" ski-boots, car-keys, or camera, would bring things up to date, but no one has written them, in this decade. "The rosy wreath" of which Ben Jonson sang, the token, becomes part of what the lover loves. The two send gifts back and forth, whether letters or small gifts, flowers. All is precious. Attire and possessions, the telephone number, long-lost toys and rooms and schools—all simple associations become part of the lover's haste in love, to enter another life-story. But it comes to pass also that a packet of old letters, or dresses in a closet, or "the gold pen she gave me," can be in time the most painful of reminders. The risk in sending a rosy wreath is that it fades, but who quibbles with the wreath-seller? Gifts are one of the best first delights of love.

There is still wonder and joy to come. *"In New Surprise"* the lover looks at the world as it never was before.

The very air is different, voices and the hours of day come to him and to her, with a not quite intolerable beauty, because for once in life all is open, and all is possible. The best within matches the best in the world without; there are to be few later times of such ecstasy, such selfless identification. All giving, all humility, and understanding now open into this love, such a blooming as one had not thought possible. It gentles and somehow unselves the lover. It is an old, a common beautiful thing, and like all such things comes to be said in easy old phrases. All the world loves a lover. But the lover loves all the world, which is truer, and more wonderful, and what the old saying tries to say.

The poetry of love is truer than legal, military, or scientific history. We think we know little about the three-hundred-years-ago world, but we know what it is to be in love. It was the same then. Wyatt, with "How like you this?" and Drayton's "Since there's no help, come let us kiss and part," tell us how life was. Treaties wither and monuments fall, but the love-poems of an age endure. The nameless young man, exulting in an Elizabethan lane, or prison-cell, had as good a chance of being remembered as his king, and Shakespeare said, "Haply I think on thee," and made that moment of time immortal.

The lover's increasing eagerness brings about still another sort of poetry. Escape me? Never. Love has come far from its definitions of itself, and even of sending the rosy wreaths. It is determined now to find out the way, and to claim the second kiss. It is a time of happy company, too, and sharing hours of sky and music and talk. The persuasions to love are as quick as ever, and Marvell can say for all, "Had we but world enough, and time—" All his ironic patience! Then the firm and famous lines, "But at my back I always hear/ Time's

winged chariot hurrying near," and the sober if Elizabethan graveyard thought, "But none, I think, do there
embrace." This tender irony gathers in the final image of
this great poem, lust delayed, time urging on, and resistance to death, the three great themes of all poetry all
in one poem.

The poetry of physical love is not rare in English
poetry, yet is not often satisfying; there is probably in
existence a poetry of consummation far larger than exists
in print, and without doubt more beautiful. What is to
be said can so easily be said so very badly. The more
explicit poems are often either embarrassing or unprint-
able. They should be, too, because this is the time of
two alone together, and perhaps the only real reason for
writing about it would be for one to remind the other.
But the very best poems on this aspect of love, have
shadowy behind them the other poem, the one that tells
what may not be told. This ghostly poem one creates as
he reads. It is made of memory and imagination, and
rightly only by lovers.

The cycle that began with definitions of love and
rhymed its way through vows, tokens, persuasions, and
consummation ends sometimes in separation, or doubt,
or faithlessness. The bitter sharpens the sweet now. The
sense of time's swift passing all but overcomes the
exultant timelessness of the gradual approach to consummation. And the poet can be more specific, being
alone, and needing more the help of poetry. Shut away
from his beloved to whom he could say his heart, now
he must say it to the poem, and hope somehow to heal
himself. Indirectly, of course, he is saying his hurt to the
lost one who will not listen, though he hopes she hears.
The story-poems about love seem so often to be of the
cold and lonely part of love that they become almost a
separate part of the literature. In *"Bitter Chill"* are the

I

Love's Riddles:

Definitions of Love

A book of Verses underneath the Bough,
A Jug of Wine, a Loaf of Bread—and Thou
   Beside me singing in the Wilderness—
O, Wilderness were Paradise enow!

Rubaiyat of Omar Khayyam
EDWARD FITZGERALD

LOVE'S INFINITENESS

If yet I have not all thy love,
Dear, I shall never have it all,
I cannot breathe one other sigh, to move,
Nor can entreat one other tear to fall,
And all my treasure, which should purchase thee,
Sighs, tears, and oaths, and letters I have spent.
Yet no more can be due to me,
Than at the bargain made was meant;
If then thy gift of love were partial,
That some to me, some should to others fall,
  Dear, I shall never have thee all.

Or if then thou gavest me all,
All was but all, which thou hadst then;
But if in thy heart, since, there be or shall
New love created be, by other men,
Which have their stocks entire, and can in tears,
In sighs, in oaths, and letters outbid me,
This new love may beget new fears,
For, this love was not vowed by thee.
And yet it was, thy gift being general;
The ground, thy heart, is mine, whatever shall
  Grow there, dear, I should have it all.

Yet I would not have all yet;
He that hath all can have no more,
And since my love doth every day admit
New growth, thou shouldst have new rewards in store;
Thou canst not every day give me thy heart,
If thou canst give it, then thou never gavest it:
Love's riddles are, that though thy heart depart,
It stays at home, and thou with losing savest it:

3

But we will have a way more liberal,
Than changing hearts, to join them, so we shall
  Be one, and one another's all.

JOHN DONNE

TO HIS MISTRESS

My light thou art, without thy glorious sight
My eyes are darkened with eternal night;
My love, thou art my way, my life, my light.

Thou art my way, I wander if thou fly;
Thou art my light, if hid, how blind am I!
Thou art my life, if thou withdraw'st I die.

Thou art my life, if thou but turn away,
My life's a thousand deaths. Thou art my way;
Without thee, love, I travel not, but stray.

JOHN WILMOT, *Earl of Rochester*

LOVE IS A SICKNESS

LOVE is a sickness full of woes,
  All remedies refusing;
A plant that most with cutting grows,
  Most barren with best using.
      Why so?
More we enjoy it, more it dies;
If not enjoyed, it sighing cries
      Heigh-ho!

Love is a torment of the mind,
   A tempest everlasting;
And Jove hath made it of a kind,
   Not well, nor full, nor fasting.
          Why so?
More we enjoy it, more it dies;
If not enjoyed, it sighing cries
          Heigh-ho!   SAMUEL DANIEL

GO, LOVELY ROSE

   Go, lovely rose,
Tell her that wastes her time and me,
   That now she knows,
When I resemble her to thee,
How sweet and fair she seems to be.

   Tell her that's young
And shuns to have her graces spied,
   That hadst thou sprung
In deserts where no men abide,
Thou must have uncommended died.

   Small is the worth
Of beauty from the light retired;
   Bid her come forth,
Suffer herself to be desired,
And not blush so to be admired.

   Then die, that she
The common fate of all things rare
   May read in thee;
How small a part of time they share
That are so wondrous sweet and fair.

                  EDMUND WALLER

5

THE DEFINITION OF LOVE

My love is of a birth as rare
As 'tis for object strange and high;
It was begotten by despair
Upon impossibility.

Magnanimous despair alone
Could show me so divine a thing,
Where feeble hope could ne'er have flown
But vainly flapt its tinsel wing.

And yet I quickly might arrive
Where my extended soul is fixt,
But fate does iron wedges drive,
And always crowds itself betwixt.

For fate with jealous eye does see
Two perfect loves, nor lets them close;
Their union would her ruin be,
And her tyrannic power depose.

And therefore her decrees of steel
Us as the distant poles have placed,
(Though love's whole world on us doth wheel)
Not by themselves to be embraced.

Unless the giddy heaven fall,
And earth some new convulsion tear;
And, us to join, the world should all
Be cramped into a planisphere.

As lines, so loves, oblique may well
Themselves in every angle greet;

But ours so truly parallel,
Though infinite, can never meet.

Therefore the love which us doth bind,
But fate so enviously debars,
Is the conjunction of the mind,
And opposition of the stars.

ANDREW MARVELL

SONG

Love and harmony combine,
And round our souls entwine
While thy branches mix with mine,
And our roots together join.

Joys upon our branches sit,
Chirping loud and singing sweet;
Like gentle streams beneath our feet
Innocence and virtue meet.

Thou the golden fruit dost bear,
I am clad in flowers fair;
Thy sweet boughs perfume the air,
And the turtle buildeth there.

There she sits and feeds her young,
Sweet I hear her mournful song;
And thy lovely leaves among,
There is love, I hear his tongue.

There his charming nest doth lay,
There he sleeps the night away;

7

There he sports along the day,
And doth among our branches play.

WILLIAM BLAKE

O NEVER SAY THAT I WAS FALSE OF HEART

O NEVER say that I was false of heart,
Though absence seemed my flame to qualify,
As easy might I from myself depart
As from my soul, which in thy breast doth lie.
That is my home of love; if I have ranged,
Like him that travels, I return again,
Just to the time, not with the time exchanged,
So that myself bring water for my stain.
Never believe, though in my nature reign'd
All frailties that besiege all kinds of blood,
That it could so preposterously be stain'd
To leave for nothing all thy sum of good;
For nothing this wide universe I call
Save thou, my rose; in it thou art my all.

WILLIAM SHAKESPEARE

WISHES TO HIS SUPPOSED MISTRESS

WHOE'ER she be—
That not impossible She
That shall command my heart and me:

Where'er she lie,
Lock'd up from mortal eye
In shady leaves of destiny:

Till that ripe birth
Of studied Fate stand forth,
And teach her fair steps to our earth:

Till that divine
Idea take a shrine
Of crystal flesh, through which to shine:

Meet you her, my Wishes,
Bespeak her to my blisses,
And be ye call'd my absent kisses.

I wish her Beauty,
That owes not all its duty
To gaudy tire, or glist'ring shoe-tie:

Something more than
Taffeta or tissue can,
Or rampant feather, or rich fan.

A Face, that's best
By its own beauty drest,
And can alone commend the rest.

A Face, made up
Out of no other shop
Than what Nature's white hand sets ope.

A Cheek, where youth
And blood, with pen of truth,
Write what the reader sweetly ru'th.

A Cheek, where grows
More than a morning rose,
Which to no box his being owes.

Lips, where all day
A lover's kiss may play,
Yet carry nothing thence away.

Looks, that oppress
Their richest tires, but dress
And clothe their simplest nakedness.

Eyes, that displace
The neighbour diamond, and outface
That sunshine by their own sweet grace.

Tresses, that wear
Jewels but to declare
How much themselves more precious are:

Whose native ray
Can tame the wanton day
Of gems that in their bright shades play.

Each ruby there,
Or pearl that dare appear,
Be its own blush, be its own tear.

A well-tamed Heart,
For whose more noble smart
Love may be long choosing a dart.

Eyes, that bestow
Full quivers on love's bow,
Yet pay less arrows than they owe.

Smiles, that can warm
The blood, yet teach a charm,
That chastity shall take no harm.

Blushes, that bin
The burnish of no sin,
Nor flames of aught too hot within.

Joys, that confess
Virtue their mistress,
And have no other head to dress.

Fears, fond and slight
As the coy bride's, when night
First does the longing lover right.

Days, that need borrow
No part of their good-morrow
From a fore-spent night of sorrow.

Days, that in spite
Of darkness, by the light
Of a clear mind, are day all night.

Nights, sweet as they,
Made short by lovers' play,
Yet long by th' absence of the day.

Life, that dares send
A challenge to his end,
And when it comes, say, "Welcome, friend!"

Sydneian showers
Of sweet discourse, whose powers
Can crown old Winter's head with flowers.

Soft silken hours,
Open suns, shady bowers;
'Bove all, nothing within that lowers.

Whate'er delight
Can make Day's forehead bright,
Or give down to the wings of Night.

I wish her store
Of worth may leave her poor
Of wishes; and I wish—no more.

11

Now, if Time knows
That Her, whose radiant brows
Weave them a garland of my vows;

Her, whose just bays
My future hopes can raise,
A trophy to her present praise;

Her, that dares be
What these lines wish to see;
I seek no further, it is She.

'Tis She, and here,
Lo! I unclothe and clear
My Wishes' cloudy character.

May she enjoy it
Whose merit dare apply it,
But modesty dares still deny it!

Such worth as this is
Shall fix my flying Wishes,
And determine them to kisses.

Let her full glory,
My fancies, fly before ye;
Be ye my fictions—but her story.

RICHARD CRASHAW

MY DELIGHT AND THY DELIGHT

My delight and thy delight
Walking, like two angels white,
In the gardens of the night:

My desire and thy desire
Twining to a tongue of fire,
Leaping live, and laughing higher:

Thro' the everlasting strife
In the mystery of life.
Love, from whom the world begun,
Hath the secret of the sun.

Love can tell, and love alone,
Whence the million stars were strewn,
Why each atom knows its own,
How, in spite of woe and death,
Gay is life, and sweet is breath:

This he taught us, this we knew,
Happy is his science true,
Hand in hand as we stood
'Neath the shadows of the wood,
Heart to heart as we lay
In the dawning of the day.

ROBERT BRIDGES

A BIRTHDAY

My heart is like a singing bird
    Whose nest is in a water'd shoot;
My heart is like an apple-tree
    Whose boughs are bent with thick-set fruit;
My heart is like a rainbow shell
    That paddles in a halcyon sea;
My heart is gladder than all these,
    Because my love is come to me.

Raise me a daïs of silk and down;
  Hang it with vair and purple dyes;
Carve it in doves and pomegranates,
  And peacocks with a hundred eyes;
Work it in gold and silver grapes,
  In leaves and silver fleurs-de-lys;
Because the birthday of my life
  Is come, my love is come to me.

CHRISTINA GEORGINA ROSSETTI

THE NIGHT HAS A THOUSAND EYES

THE night has a thousand eyes,
  And the day but one;
Yet the light of the bright world dies
  With the dying sun.

The mind has a thousand eyes,
  And the heart but one;
Yet the light of a whole life dies
  When love is done.

FRANCIS WILLIAM BOURDILLON

SONG

How many times do I love thee, dear?
  Tell me how many thoughts there be
    In the atmosphere
    Of a new-fall'n year,

Whose white and sable hours appear
   The latest flake of Eternity:—
So many times do I love thee, dear.

How many times do I love again?
   Tell me how many beads there are
      In a silver chain
      Of evening rain,
Unravelled from the tumbling main,
   And threading the eye of a yellow star:—
So many times do I love again.

                THOMAS LOVELL BEDDOES

SOMEWHERE I HAVE NEVER
TRAVELLED, GLADLY BEYOND

somewhere i have never travelled, gladly beyond
any experience, your eyes have their silence:
in your most frail gesture are things which enclose me,
or which i cannot touch because they are too near

your slightest look easily will unclose me
though i have closed myself as fingers,
you open always petal by petal myself as Spring opens
(touching skilfully, mysteriously) her first rose

or if your wish be to close me, i and
my life will shut very beautifully, suddenly,
as when the heart of this flower imagines
the snow carefully everywhere descending;

15

nothing which we are to perceive in this world equals
the power of your intense fragility: whose texture
compels me with the colour of its countries,
rendering death and forever with each breathing

(i do not know what it is about you that closes
and opens; only something in me understands
the voice of your eyes is deeper than all roses)
nobody, not even the rain, has such small hands

E. E. Cummings

LOVE IN MY BOSOM LIKE A BEE

Love in my bosom like a bee
    Doth suck his sweet;
Now with his wings he plays with me,
    Now with his feet.
Within mine eyes he makes his nest,
His bed amidst my tender breast;
My kisses are his daily feast,
And yet he robs me of my rest.
    Ah wanton, will ye?

And if I sleep, then percheth he,
    With pretty flight,
And makes his pillow of my knee
    The livelong night.
Strike I my lute, he tunes the string;
He music plays if so I sing;
He lends me every lovely thing;
Yet cruel he my heart doth sting.
    Whist, wanton, still ye!

Else I with roses every day
   Will whip you hence,
And bind you, when you long to play,
   For your offence.
I'll shut mine eyes to keep you in,
I'll make you fast it for your sin,
I'll count your power not worth a pin.
Alas, what hereby shall I win,
   If he gainsay me?

What if I beat the wanton boy
   With many a rod?
He will repay me with annoy,
   Because a god.
Then sit thou safely on my knee,
Then let thy bower my bosom be;
Lurk in mine eyes, I like of thee.
O Cupid, so thou pity me,
   Spare not, but play thee.

THOMAS LODGE

17

WHO EVER LOVED, THAT LOVED NOT AT FIRST SIGHT?

It lies not in our power to love or hate,
For will in us is overruled by fate.
When two are stripped, long ere the course begin,
We wish that one should lose, the other win;
And one especially do we affect
Of two gold ingots, like in each respect:
The reason no man knows; let it suffice
What we behold is censured by our eyes.
Where both deliberate, the love is slight:
Who ever loved, that loved not at first sight?

CHRISTOPHER MARLOWE

HOW DO I LOVE THEE

How do I love thee? Let me count the ways.
I love thee to the depth and breadth and height
My soul can reach, when feeling out of sight
For the ends of Being and ideal Grace.
I love thee to the level of every day's
Most quiet need, by sun and candlelight.
I love thee freely, as men strive for Right;
I love thee purely, as they turn from Praise.
I love thee with the passion put to use
In my old griefs, and with my childhood's faith.
I love thee with a love I seemed to lose
With my lost saints,—I love thee with the breath,
Smiles, tears, of all my life!—and, if God choose,
I shall but love thee better after death.

ELIZABETH BARRETT BROWNING

18

A LAST CONFESSION

WHAT lively lad most pleasured me
Of all that with me lay?
I answer that I gave my soul
And loved in misery,
But had great pleasure with a lad
That I loved bodily.

Flinging from his arms I laughed
To think his passion such
He fancied that I gave my soul
Did but our bodies touch,
And laughed upon his breast to think
Beast gave beast as much.

I gave what other women gave
That stepped out of their clothes,
But when this soul, its body off,
Naked to naked goes,
He it has found shall find therein
What none other knows.

And give his own and take his own
And rule in his own right;
And though it loved in misery
Close and cling so tight,
There's not a bird of day that dare
Extinguish that delight.

WILLIAM BUTLER YEATS

TO LUCASTA, GOING TO
THE WARS

TELL me not, Sweet, I am unkind,
    That from the nunnery
Of thy chaste breast and quiet mind
    To war and arms I fly.

True, a new mistress now I chase,
    The first foe in the field;
And with a stronger faith embrace
    A sword, a horse, a shield.

Yet this inconstancy is such
    As thou too shalt adore;
I could not love thee, Dear, so much,
    Loved I not Honour more.

RICHARD LOVELACE

LOVE THAT IS FIRST AND LAST

LOVE, that is first and last of all things made,
The light that has the living world for shade,
The spirit that for temporal veil has on
The souls of all men woven in unison,
One fiery raiment with all lives inwrought
And lights of sunny and starry deed and thought,
And always through new act and passion new
Shines the divine same body and beauty through,
The body spiritual of fire and light
That is to worldly noon as noon to night;

Love, that is flesh upon the spirit of man
And spirit within the flesh whence breath began;
Love, that keeps all the choir of lives in chime;
Love, that is blood within the veins of time;
That wrought the whole world without stroke of hand,
Shaping the breadth of sea, the length of land,
And with the pulse and motion of his breath
Through the great heart of the earth strikes life and
    death
The sweet twain chords that made the sweet tune live
Through day and night of things alternative,
Through silence and through sound of stress and strife,
And ebb and flow of dying death and life;
Love, that sounds loud or light in all men's ears,
Whence all men's eyes take fire from sparks of tears,
That binds on all men's feet or chains or wings;
Love, that is root and fruit of terrene things;
Love, that the whole world's waters shall not drown,
The whole world's fiery forces not burn down;
Love, that what time his own hands guard his head
The whole world's wrath and strength shall not strike
    dead;
Love, that if once his own hands make his grave
The whole world's pity and sorrow shall not save;
Love that for very life shall not be sold,
Nor bought nor bound with iron nor with gold;
So strong that heaven, could love bid heaven farewell,
Would turn to fruitless and unflowering hell;
So sweet that hell, to hell could love be given,
Would turn to splendid and sonorous heaven;
Love that is fire within thee and light above,
And lives by grace of nothing but of love;
Through many and lovely thoughts and much desire
Led these twain to the life of tears and fire;
Through many and lovely days and much delight

21

Led these twain to the lifeless life of night.
　Yea, but what then? albeit all this were thus,
And soul smote soul and left it ruinous,
And love led love as eyeless men lead men,
Through chance by chance to deathward—
　Ah, what then?
Hath love not likewise led them further yet,
Out through the years where memories rise and set,
Some large as suns, some moon-like warm and pale,
Some starry-sighted, some through clouds that sail
Seen as red flame through special float of fume,
Each with the blush of its own spectral bloom
On the fair face of its own coloured light,
Distinguishable in all the host of night,
Divisible from all the radiant rest
And separable in splendour? Hath the best
Light of love's all, of all that burn and move,
A better heaven than heaven is? Hath not love
Made for all these their sweet particular air
To shine in, their own beams and names to bear,
Their ways to wander and their wards to keep,
Till story and song and glory and all things sleep?
Hath he not plucked from death of lovers dead
Their musical soft memories, and kept red
The rose of their remembrance in men's eyes,
The sunsets of their stories in his skies,
The blush of their dead blood in lips that speak
Of their dead lives, and in the listener's cheek
That trembles with the kindling pity lit
In gracious hearts for some sweet fever-fit,
A fiery pity enkindled of pure thought
By tales that make their honey out of nought,
The faithless faith that lives without belief
Its light life through, the griefless ghost of grief?
Yea, as warm night refashions the sere blood

In storm-struck petal or in sun-struck bud,
With tender hours and tempering dew to cure
The hunger and thirst of day's distemperature
And ravin of the dry discolouring hours,
Hath he not bid relume their flameless flowers
With summer fire and heat of lamping song,
And bid the short-lived things, long dead, live long,
And thought remake their wan funereal fames,
And the sweet shining signs of women's names
That mark the months out and the weeks anew
He moves in changeless change of seasons through
To fill the days up of his dateless year
Flame from Queen Helen to Queen Guenevere?
For first of all the sphery signs whereby
Love severs light from darkness, and most high,
In the white front of January there glows
The rose-red sign of Helen like a rose:
And gold-eyed as the shore flower shelterless
Whereon the sharp-breathed sea blows bitterness,
A storm-star that the seafarers of love
Strain their wind-wearied eyes for glimpses of,
Shoots keen through February's grey frost and damp
The lamplike star of Hero for a lamp;
The star that Marlowe sang into our skies
With mouth of gold, and morning in his eyes;
And in clear March across the rough blue sea
The signal sapphire of Alcyone
Makes bright the blown brows of the windfoot year;
And shining like a sunbeam-smitten tear
Full ere it fall, the fair next sign in sight
Burns opal-wise with April-coloured light
When air is quick with song and rain and flame,
My birth-month star that in love's heaven hath name
Iseult, a light of blossom and beam and shower,
My singing sign that makes the song-tree flower;

23

Next like a pale and burning pearl beyond
The rose-white sphere of flower-named Rosamond
Signs the sweet head of Maytime; and for June
Flares like an angered and storm-reddening moon
Her signal sphere, whose Carthaginian pyre
Shadowed her traitor's flying sail with fire;
Next, glittering as the wine-bright jacinth-stone,
A star south-risen that first to music shone,
The keen girl-star of golden Juliet bears
Light northward to the month whose forehead wears
Her name for flower upon it, and his trees
Mix their deep English song with Veronese;
And like an awful sovereign chrysolite
Burning, the supreme fire that blinds the night,
The hot gold head of Venus kissed by Mars,
A sun-flower among small sphered flowers of stars,
The light of Cleopatra fills and burns
The hollow of heaven whence ardent August yearns;
And fixed and shining as the sister-shed
Sweet tears for Phaethon disorbed and dead,
The pale bright autumn's amber-coloured sphere,
That through September sees the saddening year
As love sees change through sorrow, hath to name
Francesca's; and the star that watches flame
The embers of the harvest overgone
Is Thisbe's, slain of love in Babylon,
Set in the golden girdle of sweet signs
A blood-bright ruby; last save one light shines
An Eastern wonder of sphery chrysopras,
The star that made men mad, Angelica's;
And latest named and lordliest, with a sound
Of swords and harps in heaven that ring it round,
Last love-light and last love-song of the year's,
Gleams like a glorious emerald Guenevere's.

ALGERNON CHARLES SWINBURNE

MEN LOVED WHOLLY BEYOND WISDOM

MEN loved wholly beyond wisdom
Have the staff without the banner.
Like a fire in a dry thicket,
Rising within women's eyes
Is the love men must return.
Heart, so subtle now, and trembling,
What a marvel to be wise,
To love never in this manner!
To be quiet in the fern
Like a thing gone dead and still,
Listening to the prisoned cricket
Shake its terrible, dissembling
Music in the granite hill.

LOUISE BOGAN

SONG: I FEED A FLAME WITHIN

I FEED a flame within, which so torments me,
That it both pains my heart, and yet contents me:
'Tis such a pleasing smart, and I so love it,
That I had rather die than once remove it.

Yet he for whom I grieve shall never know it;
My tongue does not betray, nor my eyes show it:
Not a sigh, nor a tear, my pain discloses,
But they fall silently, like dew on roses.

Thus to prevent my love from being cruel,
My heart's the sacrifice, as 't is the fuel:
And while I suffer this, to give him quiet,
My faith rewards my love, tho' he deny it.

On his eyes will I gaze, and there delight me;
Where I conceal my love, no frown can fright me:
To be more happy, I dare not aspire;
Nor can I fall more low, mounting no higher.

JOHN DRYDEN

EXPLANATIONS OF LOVE

THERE is a place where love begins and a place where
    love ends.
There is a touch of two hands that foils all dictionaries.
There is a look of eyes fierce as a big Bethlehem open-
    house furnace or a little green-eyed acetylene torch.
There are single careless bywords portentous as the big
    bend in the Mississippi River.
Hands, eyes, bywords—out of these love makes battle-
    grounds and workshops.
There is a pair of shoes love wears and the coming is a
    mystery.
There is a warning love sends and the cost of it is never
    written till long afterward.
There are explanations of love in all languages and not
    one found wiser than this:
There is a place where love begins and a place where
    love ends—and love asks nothing.

CARL SANDBURG

BY FIAT OF ADORATION

THIS is what we really want
Who drink the kingdom of the heart
A toast to the imagination

She is a flowering in a doorway
Eyes cheeks haze of hair
Stepping out of time into here

This is what we really have
Who see the one we adore becoming
The two that she is in the light

Ah God bounces all the waters
From hand to jubilant hand
He cannot contain Himself

But comes over into being
With benediction of painted cloud
The being whom to look at is to become

By fiat of adoration do we reach
The very muscle of miracle
The ease with which beauty is beauty

OSCAR WILLIAMS

27

A MATCH

If love were what the rose is,
  And I were like the leaf,
Our lives would grow together
In sad or singing weather,
Blown fields or flowerful closes,
  Green pleasure or gray grief;
If love were what the rose is,
  And I were like the leaf.

If I were what the words are,
  And love were like the tune,
With double sound and single
Delight our lips would mingle,
With kisses glad as birds are
  That get sweet rain at noon;
If I were what the words are,
  And love were like the tune.

If you were life, my darling,
  And I your love were death,
We'd shine and snow together
Ere March made sweet the weather
With daffodil and starling
  And hours of fruitful breath;
If you were life, my darling,
  And I your love were death.

If you were thrall to sorrow,
  And I were page to joy,
We'd play for lives and seasons
With loving looks and treasons

28

And tears of night and morrow
   And laughs of maid and boy;
If you were thrall to sorrow,
   And I were page to joy.

If you were April's lady,
   And I were lord in May,
We'd throw with leaves for hours
And draw for days with flowers,
Till day like night were shady
   And night were bright like day;
If you were April's lady,
   And I were lord in May.

If you were queen of pleasure,
   And I were king of pain,
We'd hunt down love together,
Pluck out his flying feather,
And teach his feet a measure,
   And find his mouth a rein;
If you were queen of pleasure,
   And I were king of pain.

ALGERNON CHARLES SWINBURNE

MY LOVE IS LIKE TO ICE

My love is like to ice, and I to fire:
How comes it then that this her cold so great
Is not dissolved through my so hot desire,
But harder grows the more I her entreat?
Or how comes it that my exceeding heat
Is not allayed by her heart-frozen cold,
But that I burn much more in boiling sweat,
And feel my flames augmented manifold?
What more miraculous thing may be told,
That fire, which all things melts, should harden ice,
And ice, which is congeal'd with senseless cold,
Should kindle fire by wonderful device?
Such is the power of love in gentle mind,
That it can alter all the course of kind.

EDMUND SPENSER

SPRING NIGHT

THE park is filled with night and fog,
    The veils are drawn about the world,
The drowsy lights along the paths
    Are dim and pearled.

Gold and gleaming the empty streets,
    Gold and gleaming the misty lake,
The mirrored lights like sunken swords,
    Glimmer and shake.

Oh, is it not enough to be
Here with this beauty over me?

My throat should ache with praise, and I
Should kneel in joy beneath the sky.
O beauty, are you not enough?
Why am I crying after love
With youth, a singing voice, and eyes
To take earth's wonder with surprise?

Why have I put off my pride,
Why am I unsatisfied,—
I, for whom the pensive night
Binds her cloudy hair with light,—
I, for whom all beauty burns
Like incense in a million urns?
O beauty, are you not enough?
Why am I crying after love?

SARA TEASDALE

ALL FOR LOVE

O TALK not to me of a name great in story;
The days of our youth are the days of our glory;
And the myrtle and ivy of sweet two-and-twenty
Are worth all your laurels, though ever so plenty.
What are garlands and crowns to the brow that is
    wrinkled?
'Tis but as a dead flower with May-dew besprinkled;
Then away with all such from the head that is hoary—
What care I for the wreaths that can only give glory?
Oh Fame!—if I e'er took delight in thy praises,
'Twas less for the sake of thy high-sounding phrases,
Than to see the bright eyes of the dear one discover
She thought that I was not unworthy to love her.

31

There chiefly I sought thee, there only I found thee!
Her glance was the best of the rays that surround thee;
When it sparkled o'er aught that was bright in my story,
I knew it was love, and I felt it was glory.

GEORGE GORDON, LORD BYRON

IT IS NOT BEAUTY I DEMAND

It is not Beauty I demand,
   A crystal brow, the moon's despair,
Nor the snow's daughter, a white hand,
   Nor mermaid's yellow pride of hair:

Tell me not of your starry eyes,
   Your lips that seem on roses fed,
Your breasts, where Cupid's tumbling lies
   Nor sleeps for kissing of his bed:—

A bloomy pair of vermeil cheeks
   Like Hebe's in her ruddiest hours,
A breath that softer music speaks
   Than summer winds a-wooing flowers,—

These are but gauds: nay, what are lips?
   Coral beneath the ocean-stream,
Whose brink when your adventurer sips
   Full oft he perisheth on them.

And what are cheeks but ensigns oft
   That wave hot youth to fields of blood?
Did Helen's breast, though ne'er so soft,
   Do Greece or Ilium any good?

Eyes can with baleful ardor burn;
   Poison can breathe, that erst perfumed;
There's many a white hand holds an urn
   With lovers' hearts to dust consumed.

For crystal brows—there's naught within;
   They are but empty cells for pride;
He who the Siren's hair would win
   Is mostly strangled in the tide.

Give me, instead of Beauty's bust,
   A tender heart, a loyal mind
Which with temptation I could trust,
   Yet never linked with error find,—

One in whose gentle bosom I
   Could pour my secret heart of woes,
Like the care-burthened honey-fly
   That hides his murmurs in the rose,—

My earthly Comforter! whose love
   So indefeasible might be
That, when my spirit won above,
   Hers could not stay, for sympathy.

GEORGE DARLEY

MENDACITY

TRUTH is love and love is truth,
Either neither in good sooth:
Truth is truth and love is love,
Give us grace to taste thereof;
But if truth offend my sweet,
Then I will have none of it,

33

And if love offend the other,
Farewell truth, I will not bother.

Happy truth when truth accords
With the love in lovers' words!
Harm not truth in any part,
But keep its shadow from love's heart.
Men must love, though lovers' lies
Outpall the stars in florid skies,
And none may keep, and few can merit,
The fond joy that they inherit.

Who with love at his command
Dares give truth a welcome hand?
Believe it, or believe it not,
'Tis a lore most vainly got.
Truth requites no penny-fee,
Niggard's honey feeds no bee;
Ere this trick of truth undo me,
Little love, my love, come to me.

A. E. COPPARD

HER MOOD AROUND ME

HER mood around me is a summer wave
And our room's ceiling is its silk of surface.

Beyond the house, the ledges gaunt with shadow
Forethink a hollower blue crueler at evening.

Along my sleepless thigh her touch is gentle
As the tender underfoot of a small wave.

Wrestling in the arms of currents a headland bell
Is counting the sea today all day, all day.

Her hair is soft before the softer touch
That folds us like a shallowing foam. Sleep, now,

And surf of breath in our dreams fall and lull.
But up what corridors thrums the flood's growl?

BREWSTER GHISELIN

IT IS THAT BANE OF SELF
IN LOVE

IT is that bane of self in love
When all should be of love's self the dove,
That perfect creature's constant balm,
That is, a wholesome ball of calm.

But since we fought, we tore our skins,
Each raving in an ecstasy.
Thus thought love's world we had gone in,
Who had gone but in a storm'd sea.

'Twere to have been equal we hoped.
But hope too much, not love enough,
Made two who on a straw have groped;
Hands, tumid, closed on chaos' stuff.

Nor can we prove that human love
More solid is than thought's empire.
Since of the other each was above,
Under, was only ideas' fire.

Love is but warm simplicity.
It wants no divinity,
That clothes our human life in clothes,
Curled, rolled, woven, lover.

RICHARD EBERHART

35

DEAR LADY, WHEN THOU FROWNEST

Dear lady, when thou frownest,
    And my true love despisest,
And all thy vows disownest
    That sealed my venture wisest;
I think thy pride's displeasure
Neglects a matchless treasure
Exceeding price and measure.

But when again thou smilest,
    And love for love returnest,
And fear with joy beguilest,
    And takest truth in earnest;
Then, though I sheer adore thee,
The sum of my love for thee
Seems poor, scant, and unworthy.

Robert Bridges

IF THIS BE LOVE

If this be love, then let me leap
Into the abstract austerity,
Into the abysm where I peep
Shuddering with temerity,
O the unearthly loyalty,

Till the cold trees silver
Smoothly to a patine touched
And afternoon, like a golden bee,
Pulls, unwinds the spooled eyes;

Hold, hold in body's brace
Her curved shining, thus destroy
The virgin ecstasy of her face,
Contaminate with experience
The ghostly praise and young
Of her full wisdom sung.

And a cone of love around the honey
Comes; but the bee cuts there.

If it could be triumphant
No cruelty could be kinder:
It is sheer world all sunny
And time's out of his dry lair;
So high then is rapture higher,
Being compounded of this pain,
That the icy pinnacles of desire
Melt, and fires of blood congeal,
Till all's the quality of the real.
If this be love! O I remember
Tempest, and abysm gone.

RICHARD EBERHART

AH, HOW SWEET IT IS
TO LOVE

AH, how sweet it is to love,
Ah, how gay is young desire!
And what pleasing pains we prove
When we first approach Love's fire.

Pains of Love be sweeter far
Than all other pleasures are.

Sighs which are from lovers blown,
Do but gently heave the heart;
Ev'n the tears they shed alone
Cure like trickling balm their smart.
Lovers when they lose their breath
Bleed away in easy death.

Love and time with reverence use,
Treat them like a parting friend,
Nor the golden gifts refuse
Which in youth sincere they send;
For each year their price is more,
And they less simple than before.

Love, like spring-tides full and high,
Swells in ev'ry youthful vein;
But each tide does less supply,
Till they quite shrink in again.
If a flow in age appear,
'Tis but rain, and runs not clear.

JOHN DRYDEN

IF THIS BE LOVE

To live in hell, and heaven to behold;
To welcome life, and die a living death;
To sweat with heat, and yet be freezing cold;
To grasp at stars, and lie the earth beneath;
To tread a maze that never shall have end;
To burn in sighs, and starve in daily tears;
To climb a hill, and never to descend;
Giants to kill, and quake at childish fears;
To pine for food, and watch the Hesperian tree;
To thirst for drink, and nectar still to draw;
To live accurst, whom men hold blest to be;
And weep those wrongs which never creature saw;
If this be love, if love in these be founded,
My heart is love, for these in it are grounded.

HENRY CONSTABLE (?)

LOVE'S ALCHEMY

SOME that have deeper digged love's mine than I,
Say, where his centric happiness doth lie.
  I have loved, and got, and told,
But should I love, get, tell, till I were old,
I should not find that hidden mystery.
  Oh! 'tis imposture all;
And as no chemic yet the elixir got,
  But glorifies his pregnant pot
  If by the way to him befall
Some odoriferous thing, or medicinal,
  So lovers dream a rich and long delight,
  But get a winter-seeming summer's night.

39

Our ease, our thrift, our honor, and our day
Shall we for this vain bubble's shadow pay?
    Ends love in this, that my man
Can be as happy as I can, if he can
Endure the short scorn of a bridegroom's play?
    That loving wretch that swears
'Tis not the bodies marry, but the minds,
    Which he in her angelic finds,
    Would swear as justly that he hears,
In that day's rude hoarse minstrelsy, the spheres.
    Hope not for mind in women; at their best
    Sweetness and wit, they are but mummy, possessed.

JOHN DONNE

SONG

    I PRITHEE send me back my heart,
        Since I cannot have thine;
    For if from yours you will not part,
        Why then shouldst thou have mine?

    Yet now I think on't, let it lie;
        To find it were in vain,
    For th' hast a thief in either eye
        Would steal it back again.

    Why should two hearts in one breast lie,
        And yet not lodge together?
    O love, where is thy sympathy,
        If thus our breasts thou sever?

    But love is such a mystery,
        I cannot find it out;

For when I think I'm best resolved,
    I then am most in doubt.

Then farewell care, and farewell woe,
    I will no longer pine;
For I'll believe I have her heart
    As much as she hath mine.

SIR JOHN SUCKLING

LOVE'S EXCHANGE

LOVE, any devil else but you
Would for a given soul give something too.
At court your fellows every day
Give the art of rhyming, huntsmanship, or play,
For them which were their own before;
Only I have nothing, which gave more,
But am, alas! by being lowly, lower.

I ask no dispensation now
To falsify a tear, or sigh, or vow;
I do not sue from thee to draw
A *non obstante* on nature's law;
These are prerogatives, they inhere
In thee and thine; none should forswear
Except that he Love's minion were.

Give me thy weakness, make me blind,
Both ways, as thou and thine, in eyes and mind.
Love, let me never know that this
Is love, or that love childish is;
Let me not know that others know

41

That she knows my pains, lest that so
A tender shame make me mine own new woe.

If thou give nothing, yet thou'rt just,
Because I would not thy first motions trust.
Small towns which stand stiff till great shot
Enforce them, by war's law condition not.
Such in Love's warfare is my case;
I may not article for grace,
Having put Love at last to show this face;

This face, by which he could command
And change the idolatry of any land,
This face, which, whereso'er it comes,
Can call vowed men from cloisters, dead from tombs,
And melt both poles at once, and store
Deserts with cities, and make more
Mines in the earth than quarries were before.

For this, Love is enraged with me,
Yet kills not. If I must example be
To future rebels; if the unborn
Must learn by my being cut up and torn;
Kill, and dissect me, Love; for this
Torture against thine own end is;
Racked carcasses make ill anatomies.

JOHN DONNE

II

I Hereby Swear:

Affirmations of Love

HOUSE SONNET

I HEREBY swear that to uphold your house
I would lay my bones in quick destroying lime
Or turn my flesh to timber for all time;
Cut down my womanhood; lop off the boughs
Of that perpetual ecstasy that grows
From the heart's core; condemn it as a crime
If it be broader than a beam, or climb
Above the stature that your roof allows.
I am not the hearthstone nor the cornerstone
Within this noble fabric you have builded;
Not by my beauty was its cornice gilded;
Not on my courage were its arches thrown:
My lord, adjudge my strength, and set me where
I bear a little more than I can bear.

ELINOR WYLIE

TO CELIA

NOT, Celia, that I juster am,
  Or better than the rest!
For I would change each hour like them,
  Were not my heart at rest.

But I am tied to very thee
  By every thought I have;
Thy face I only care to see,
  Thy heart I only crave.

All that in woman is adored
  In thy dear self I find;
For the whole sex can but afford
  The handsome and the kind.

45

Why then should I seek further store
    And still make love anew?
When change itself can give no more,
    'Tis easy to be true.

SIR CHARLES SEDLEY

THE INDIAN SERENADE

I ARISE from dreams of thee
In the first sweet sleep of night,
When the winds are breathing low,
And the stars are shining bright:
I arise from dreams of thee,
And a spirit in my feet
Hath led me—who knows how?
To thy chamber window, Sweet!

The wandering airs they faint
On the dark, the silent stream—
The Champak odors fail
Like sweet thoughts in a dream;
The nightingale's complaint,
It dies upon her heart;—
As I must on thine,
Oh, belovèd as thou art!

Oh lift me from the grass!
I die! I faint! I fail!
Let thy love in kisses rain
On my lips and eyelids pale.
My cheek is cold and white, alas!
My heart beats loud and fast;—
Oh! press it to thine own again,
Where it will break at last.

PERCY BYSSHE SHELLEY

SILENT NOON

Your hands lie open in the long fresh grass,—
The finger-points look through like rosy blooms:
Your eyes smile peace. The pasture gleams and glooms
'Neath billowing skies that scatter and amass.
All round our nest, far as the eye can pass,
Are golden kingcup-fields with silver edge
Where the cow-parsley skirts the hawthorn-hedge.
'Tis visible silence, still as the hour-glass.
Deep in the sun-searched growths the dragon-fly
Hangs like a blue thread loosened from the sky:—
So this winged hour is dropped to us from above.
Oh! clasp we to our hearts, for deathless dower,
This close-companioned inarticulate hour
When twofold silence was the song of love.

DANTE GABRIEL ROSSETTI

I FOLLOW, LO, THE FOOTING

I follow, lo, the footing
  Still of my lovely cruel,
Proud of herself that she is beauty's jewel.
  And fast away she flieth,
  Love's sweet delight deriding,
In woods and groves sweet Nature's treasure hiding.
  Yet cease I not pursuing,
  But since I thus have sought her,
Will run me out of breath till I have caught her.

BEN JONSON

47

TO A LADY, THAT DESIRED
I WOULD LOVE HER

Now you have freely given me leave to love,
        What will you do?
Shall I your mirth, or passion move
        When I begin to woo?
Will you torment, or scorn, or love me too?

Each petty beauty can disdain, and I,
        'Spite of your hate,
Without your leave can see, and die.
        Dispense a nobler fate!
'Tis easy to destroy: you may create.

Then give me leave to love, and love me too:
        Now with design
To raise, as love's cursed rebels do,
        When puling poets whine,
Fame to their beauty, from their blubbered eyne.

Grief is a puddle, and reflects not clear
        Your beauty's rays;
Joys are pure streams: your eyes appear
        Sullen in sadder lays:
In cheerful numbers they shine bright with praise,

Which shall not mention, to express you fair
        Wounds, flames, and darts,
Storms in your brow, nets in your hair,—
        Suborning all your parts,
Or to betray, or capture captive hearts.

I'll make your eyes like morning suns appear,
        As mild, and fair;
Your brow as crystal smooth, and clear;
        And your dishevelled hair
Shall flow like a calm region of the air.

Rich nature's store (which is the poet's treasure)
        I'll spend to dress
Your beauties, if your mine of pleasure
        In equal thankfulness
You but unlock, so we each other bless.

THOMAS CAREW

SONG

No, no, fair heretic, it needs must be
        But an ill love in me,
        And worse for thee.
For were it in my power,
To love thee now this hour
        More than I did the last:
'Twould then so fall,
        I might not love at all.
Love that can flow, and can admit increase,
Admits as well an ebb, and may grow less.
True love is still the same; the torrid zones,
        And those more frigid ones,
        It must now know.
For love, grown cold or hot,
        Is lust or friendship, not
        The thing we have.
For that's a flame would die,
Held down or up too high:
Then think I love more than I can express,
And would love more, could I but love thee less.

SIR JOHN SUCKLING

TRUTH DOTH TRUTH DESERVE

WHO doth desire that chaste his wife should be,
First be he true, for truth doth truth deserve:
Then such be he as she his worth may see,
And one man still credit with her preserve.
Not toying kind, nor causelessly unkind;
Not stirring thoughts, nor yet denying right;
Not spying faults, nor in plain errors blind;
Never hard hand, nor ever reins too light.
As far from want, as far from vain expense
(The one doth force, the latter doth entice);
Allow good company, but keep from thence
All filthy mouths that glory in their vice.
This done, thou hast no more, but leave the rest
To virtue, fortune, time, and woman's breast.

SIR PHILIP SIDNEY

WHAT ARE WE FIRST

WHAT are we first? First, animals; and next
Intelligences at a leap; on whom
Pale lies the distant shadow of the tomb,
And all that draweth on the tomb for text.
Into which state comes Love, the crowning sun:
Beneath whose light the shadow loses form.
We are the lords of life, and life is warm.
Intelligence and instinct now are one.
But nature says: "My children most they seem
When they least know me: therefore I decree
That they shall suffer." Swift doth young Love flee,
And we stand wakened, shivering from our dream.

Then if we study Nature we are wise,
Thus do the few who live but with the day:
The scientific animals are they.—
Lady, this is my sonnet to your eyes.

GEORGE MEREDITH

LOVE IN TIME'S DESPITE

You who are given to me to Time are given
Before through time I stretched my hand to catch
Yours in the flying race. Oh we were driven
By rivalry of him who has no match.

For that cold conqueror, unfeeling lover,
Who robs your deep heart's treasuries as in play,
Trampling your tender harvests over and over,
Where no door is at ease can find his way.

His light embrace is subtle and keen as thought;
Yet, perfect careful lover, he has no care
For you at all, is naught and leaves you naught.

And we who love and love again can dare
To keep in his despite our summer still,
Which flowered, but shall not wither, at his will.

EDWIN MUIR

51

A MODEST LOVE

THE lowest trees have tops, the ant her gall,
    The fly her spleen, the little sparks their heat;
The slender hairs cast shadows, though but small,
    And bees have stings, although they be not great;
Seas have their source, and so have shallow springs;
And love is love, in beggars as in kings.

Where rivers smoothest run, deep are the fords;
    The dial stirs, yet none perceives it move;
The firmest faith is in the fewest words;
    The turtles cannot sing, and yet they love:
True hearts have eyes and ears, no tongues to speak;
They hear and see, and sigh, and then they break.

                                        SIR EDWARD DYER

GOOD-NIGHT

GOOD-NIGHT? ah! no; the hour is ill
    Which severs those it should unite;
Let us remain together still,
    Then it will be *good* night.

How can I call the lone night good,
    Though thy sweet wishes wing its flight?
Be it not said, thought, understood,
    Then it will be *good* night.

To hearts which near each other move
    From evening close to morning light,
The night *is* good; because, my love,
    They never *say* good-night.

                                    PERCY BYSSHE SHELLEY

52

MY DIET

Now, by my love, the greatest oath that is,
  None loves you half so well as I:
  I do not ask your love for this;
But, for heaven's sake, believe me, or I die.
  No servant e'er but did deserve
His master should believe that he does serve;
And I'll ask no more wages, though I starve.

'Tis no luxurious diet this, and sure
  I shall not by't too lusty prove;
  Yet shall it willingly endure,
If't can but keep together life and love.
  Being your prisoner and your slave,
I do not feasts and banquets look to have,
A little bread and water's all I crave.

On'a sigh of pity I a year can live,
  One tear will keep me twenty at least,
  Fifty a gentle look will give;
An hundred years on one kind word I'll feast:
  A thousand more will added be,
If you an inclination have for me;
And all beyond is vast eternity.

ABRAHAM COWLEY

53

ALL-OVER LOVE

'Tis well, 'tis well with them (say I)
Whose short-lived passions with themselves can die:
    For none can be unhappy, who
    'Midst all his ills a time does know
(Though ne'er so long) when he shall not be so.

What ever parts of me remain,
Those parts will still the love of thee retain;
    For 'twas not only in my heart,
    But like a god by powerful art,
'Twas all in all, and all in every part.

My affection no more perish can
Than the first matter that compounds a man.
    Hereafter if one dust of me
    Mixed with another's substance be,
'Twill leaven that whole lump with love of thee.

Let nature if she please disperse
My atoms over all the universe,
    At the last they easily shall
    Themselves know, and together call;
For thy love, like a mark, is stamped on all.

ABRAHAM COWLEY

THE FIRST DAY

I wish I could remember the first day,
    First hour, first moment of your meeting me,
    If bright or dim the season, it might be
Summer or Winter for aught I can say;

So unrecorded did it slip away,
So blind was I to see and to foresee,
So dull to mark the budding of my tree
That would not blossom yet for many a May.
If only I could recollect it, such
A day of days! I let it come and go
As traceless as a thaw of bygone snow;
It seemed to mean so little, meant so much;
If only now I could recall that touch,
First touch of hand in hand—Did one but know!

CHRISTINA GEORGINA ROSSETTI

CHILD AND MAIDEN

AH, Chloris! could I now but sit
    As unconcern'd as when
Your infant beauty could beget
    No pleasure, nor no pain!
When I the dawn used to admire,
    And praised the coming day,
I little thought the rising fire
    Would take my rest away.

Your charms in harmless childhood lay
    Like metals in a mine;
Age from no face takes more away
    Than youth conceal'd in thine.
But as your charms insensibly
    To their perfection prest,
So love as unperceived did fly,
    And in my bosom rest.

My passion with your beauty grew,
    While Cupid at my heart,
Still as his mother favour'd you,
    Threw a new flaming dart:
Each gloried in their wanton part;
    To make a lover, he
Employ'd the utmost of his art—
    To make a beauty, she.

SIR CHARLES SEDLEY

I FEAR THY KISSES

I FEAR thy kisses, gentle maiden,
    Thou needest not fear mine;
My spirit is too deeply laden
    Ever to burthen thine.

I fear thy mien, thy tones, thy motion,
    Thou needest not fear mine;
Innocent is the heart's devotion
    With which I worship thine.

PERCY BYSSHE SHELLEY

YOU SAY I LOVE NOT

You say I love not, 'cause I do not play
Still with your curls and kiss the time away.
You blame me, too, because I can't devise
Some sport to please those babies in your eyes:

By Love's religion, I must here confess it,
The most I love when I the least express it.
Small griefs find tongues; full casks are ever found
To give, if any, yet but little sound.
Deep waters noiseless are; and this we know,
That chiding streams betray small depths below.
So when Love speechless is she doth express
A depth in love, and that depth bottomless.
Now since my love is tongueless, know me such,
Who speak but little 'cause I love so much.

ROBERT HERRICK

LOVE IS ENOUGH

LOVE is enough: though the World be a-waning
And the woods have no voice but the voice of complain-
ing,
Though the sky be too dark for dim eyes to discover
The gold-cups and daisies fair blooming thereunder,
Though the hills be held shadows, and the sea a dark
wonder
And this day draw a veil over all deeds passed over,
Yet their hands shall not tremble, their feet shall not
falter;
The void shall not weary, the fear shall not alter
These lips and these eyes of the loved and the lover.

WILLIAM MORRIS

MY TRUE LOVE HATH
MY HEART

My true love hath my heart, and I have his,
By just exchange one for the other given:
I hold his dear, and mine he cannot miss,
There never was a better bargain driven:
His heart in me keeps me and him in one,
My heart in him his thoughts and senses guides:
He loves my heart, for once it was his own,
I cherish his because in me it bides:

His heart his wound receivèd from my sight.
My heart was wounded with his wounded heart,
For as from me on him his heart did light,
So still methought in me his heart did smart,
Both equal hurt in this change sought our bliss:
My true love hath my heart, and I have his.

SIR PHILIP SIDNEY

III

Never Told Can Be:

Heights & Depths of Love

NEVER SEEK TO TELL THY LOVE

NEVER seek to tell thy love,
Love that never told can be;
For the gentle wind does move
Silently, invisibly.

I told my love, I told my love,
I told her all my heart;
Trembling, cold, in ghastly fears,
Ah! she doth depart.

Soon as she was gone from me,
A traveller came by,
Silently, invisibly:
He took her with a sigh.

WILLIAM BLAKE

ONE DAY I WROTE HER NAME

ONE day I wrote her name upon the strand,
But came the waves and washed it away:
Again I wrote it with a second hand,
But came the tide and made my pains his prey.
Vain man, said she, that dost in vain essay
A mortal thing so to immortalize,
For I myself shall like to this decay,
And so my name be wiped out likewise.
Not so (quoth I) let baser things devise
To die in dust, but you shall live by fame:

61

My verse your virtues shall eternalize,
And in the heavens write your glorious name.
Whereas when death shall all the world subdue,
Our love shall live, and later life renew.

EDMUND SPENSER

SONG

I CAN'T be talkin' of love, dear,
I can't be talkin' of love.
If there be one thing I can't talk of
That one thing do be love.

But that's not sayin' that I'm not lovin'—
Still water, you know, runs deep,
An' I do be lovin' so deep, dear,
I be lovin' you in my sleep.

But I can't be talkin' of love, dear,
I can't be talkin' of love,
If there be one thing I can't talk of
That one thing do be love.

ESTHER MATHEWS

SHALL I COMPARE THEE?

SHALL I compare thee to a summer's day?
Thou art more lovely and more temperate.
Rough winds do shake the darling buds of May,
And summer's lease hath all too short a date:

Sometimes too hot the eye of heaven shines,
And often is his gold complexion dimmed:
And every fair from fair sometime declines,
By chance, or nature's changing course, untrimmed:
But thy eternal summer shall not fade
Nor lose possession of that fair thou owest;
Nor shall Death brag thou wanderest in his shade
When in eternal lines to time thou growest.
So long as men can breathe or eyes can see
So long lives this, and this gives life to thee.

WILLIAM SHAKESPEARE

ONE WORD IS TOO OFTEN PROFANED

ONE word is too often profaned
    For me to profane it,
One feeling too falsely disdained
    For thee to disdain it;
One hope is too like despair
    For prudence to smother,
And pity from thee more dear
    Than that from another.

I can give not what men call love,
    But wilt thou accept not
The worship the heart lifts above
    And the Heavens reject not,—
The desire of the moth for the star,
    Of the night for the morrow,
The devotion to something afar
    From the sphere of our sorrow?

PERCY BYSSHE SHELLEY

LOOK INTO THY HEART

Loving in truth, and fain in verse my love to show,
That she, dear she, might take some pleasure of my
pain,—
Pleasure might cause her read, reading might make her
know,
Knowledge might pity win, and pity grace obtain,—
I sought fit words to paint the blackest face of woe,
Studying inventions fine, her wits to entertain,
Oft turning others' leaves, to see if thence would flow
Some fresh and fruitful showers upon my sunburnt
brain.
But words came halting forth, wanting Invention's stay;
Invention, Nature's child, fled step-dame Study's blows;
And others' feet still seemed but strangers' in my way.
Thus, great with child to speak, and helpless in my
throes,
Biting my truant pen, beating myself for spite;
"Fool," said my Muse to me, "look in thy heart, and
write."

Sir Philip Sidney

MY LOVE IS STRENGTHEN'D

My love is strengthen'd, though more weak in seeming;
I love not less, though less the show appear:
That love is merchandised whose rich esteeming
The owner's tongue doth publish everywhere.
Our love was new, and then but in the spring,
When I was wont to greet it with my lays;
As Philomel in Summer's front doth sing

And stops her pipe in growth of riper days:
Not that the Summer is less pleasant now
Than when her mournful hymns did hush the night,
But that wild music burthens every bough,
And sweets grown common lose their dear delight.
  Therefore, like her, I sometime hold my tongue,
  Because I would not dull you with my song.

WILLIAM SHAKESPEARE

WHEN IN THE CHRONICLE OF
WASTED TIME

WHEN in the chronicle of wasted time
I see descriptions of the fairest wights,
And beauty making beautiful old rhyme
In praise of ladies dead and lovely knights,
Then, in the blazon of sweet beauty's best,
Of hand, of foot, of lip, of eye, of brow,
I see their antique pen would have expressed
Even such a beauty as you master now
So all their praises are but prophecies
Of this our time, all you prefiguring;
And, for they looked but with divining eyes,
They had not skill enough your worth to sing:
For we, which now behold these present days,
Have eyes to wonder, but lack tongues to praise.

WILLIAM SHAKESPEARE

65

PAST RUINED ILION

PAST ruined Ilion Helen lives,
  Alcestis rises from the shades;
Verse calls them forth; 'tis verse that gives
  Immortal youth to mortal maids.

Soon shall Oblivion's deepening veil
  Hide all the peopled hills you see,
The gay, the proud, while lovers hail
  These many summers you and me.

WALTER SAVAGE LANDOR

MY MISTRESS' EYES ARE NOTHING LIKE THE SUN

MY mistress' eyes are nothing like the sun;
Coral is far more red than her lips' red:
If snow be white, why then her breasts are dun;
If hairs be wires, black wires grow on her head.
I have seen roses damasked, red and white,
But no such roses see I in her cheeks;
And in some perfumes is there more delight
Than in the breath that from my mistress reeks.
I love to hear her speak, yet well I know
That music hath a far more pleasing sound;
I grant I never saw a goddess go;
My mistress, when she walks, treads on the ground:
And yet, by heaven, I think my love as rare
As any she belied with false compare.

WILLIAM SHAKESPEARE

NOT MARBLE, NOR THE GILDED MONUMENTS

Not marble, nor the gilded monuments
Of princes, shall outlive this powerful rhyme;
But you shall shine more bright in these contents
Than unswept stone, besmear'd with sluttish time.
When wasteful war shall statues overturn,
And broils root out the work of masonry,
Nor Mars his sword nor war's quick fire shall burn
The living record of your memory.
'Gainst death and all-oblivious enmity
Shall you pace forth; your praise shall still find room
Even in the eyes of all posterity
That wear this world out to the ending doom.
    So, till the judgment that yourself arise,
    You live in this, and dwell in lovers' eyes.

WILLIAM SHAKESPEARE

"NOT MARBLE, NOR THE GILDED MONUMENTS"

THE praisers of women in their proud and beautiful
    poems
Naming the grave mouth and the hair and the eyes
Boasted those they loved should be forever remembered
These were lies

The words sound but the face in the Istrian sun is for-
    gotten

67

The poet speaks but to her dead ears no more
The sleek throat is gone—and the breast that was
        troubled to listen
Shadow from door

Therefore I will not praise your knees nor your fine
        walking
Telling you men shall remember your name as long
As lips move or breath is spent or the iron of English
Rings from a tongue

I shall say you were young and your arms straight and
        your mouth scarlet
I shall say you will die and none will remember you
Your arms change and none remember the swish of your
        garments
Nor the click of your shoe

Not with my hand's strength not with difficult labor
Springing the obstinate words to the bones of your breast
And the stubborn line to your young stride and the
        breath to your breathing
And the beat to your haste
Shall I prevail on the hearts of unborn men to remember

(What is a dead girl but a shadowy ghost
Or a dead man's voice but a distant and vain affirmation
Like dream words most)

Therefore I will not speak of the undying glory of
        women
I will say you were young and straight and your skin fair
And you stood in the door and the sun was a shadow of
        leaves on your shoulders
And a leaf on your hair

68

I will not speak of the famous beauty of dead women
I will say the shape of a leaf lay once on your hair
Till the world ends and the eyes are out and the mouths
    broken
Look! It is there!

ARCHIBALD MacLEISH

KAROLIN'S SONG

THOUGH I am young, and cannot tell,
  Either what death, or love is well,
Yet I have heard, they both bear darts,
  And both do aim at human hearts:
And then again, I have been told
  Love wounds with heat, as death with cold;
So that I fear, they do but bring
  Extremes to touch, and mean one thing.

As in a ruin, we it call
  One thing to be blown up, or fall
Or to our end, like way may have,
  By a flash of lightning or a wave:
So love's inflamed shaft or brand,
  May kill, as soon as death's cold hand;
Except love's fires the virtue have
  To fright the frost out of the grave.

BEN JONSON

THE LINNET

I HEARD a linnet courting
  His lady in the spring:
His mates were idly sporting,
  Nor stayed to hear him sing
    His song of love.—
I fear my speech distorting
    His tender love.

The phrases of his pleading
  Were full of young delight;
And she that gave him heeding
  Interpreted aright
    His gay, sweet notes,—
So sadly marred in the reading,—
    His tender notes.

And when he ceased, the hearer
  Awaited the refrain,
Till swiftly perching nearer
  He sang his song again,
    His pretty song:—
Would that my verse spake clearer
    His tender song!

Ye happy, airy creatures!
  That in the merry spring
Think not of what misfeatures
  Or cares the year may bring;
    But unto love
Resign your simple natures,
    To tender love.

ROBERT BRIDGES

TO DELIA

UNTO the boundless ocean of thy beauty,
Runs this poor river, charged with streams of zeal:
Returning thee the tribute of my duty,
Which here my love, my youth, my plaints reveal.
Here I unclasp the book of my charged soul,
Where I have cast the accounts of all my care:
Here have I summed my sighs, here I enroll
How they were spent for thee; look what they are:
Look on the dear expenses of my youth,
And see just how I reckon with thine eyes:
Examine well thy beauty with my truth,
And cross my cares ere greater sums arise.
Read it (sweet maid) though it be done but slightly;
Who can show all his love, doth love but lightly.

SAMUEL DANIEL

THE BROKEN HEART

HE is stark mad, who ever says
   That he hath been in love an hour,
Yet not that love so soon decays
   But that it can ten in less space devour;
Who will believe me, if I swear
That I have had the plague a year?
   Who would not laugh at me, if I should say
   I saw a *flask of powder burn a day*?

Ah, what a trifle is a heart
   If once into Love's hands it come!
All other griefs allow a part

71

To other griefs, and ask themselves but some;
They come to us, but us Love draws,
He swallows us, and never chaws:
    By him, as by chained shot, whole ranks do die,
    He is the tyrant Pike, our hearts the Fry.

If 'twere not so, what did become
    Of my heart, when I first saw thee?
I brought a heart into the room,
    But from the room, I carried none with me:
If it had gone to thee, I know
Mine would have taught thine heart to show
    More pity unto me: but Love, alas,
    At one first blow did shiver it as glass.

Yet nothing can to nothing fall,
    Nor any place be empty quite,
Therefore I think my breast hath all
    Those pieces still, though they be not unite;
And now as broken glasses show
A hundred lesser faces, so
    My rags of heart can like, wish, and adore,
    But after one such love, can love no more.

JOHN DONNE

THE LADY'S "YES"

"Yes," I answered you last night;
  "No," this morning, sir, I say:
Colors seen by candle-light
  Will not look the same by day.

When the viols played their best,
  Lamps above, and laughs below,
Love me sounded like a jest,
  Fit for *yes* or fit for *no.*

Call me false or call me free,
  Vow, whatever light may shine,—
No man on your face shall see
  Any grief for change on mine.

Yet the sin is on us both;
  Time to dance is not to woo;
Wooing light makes fickle troth,
  Scorn of *me* recoils on *you.*

Learn to win a lady's faith
  Nobly, as the thing is high,
Bravely, as for life and death,
  With a loyal gravity.

Lead her from the festive boards,
  Point her to the starry skies,
Guard her, by your truthful words,
  Pure from courtship's flatteries.

By your truth she shall be true,
  Ever true, as wives of yore;
And her *yes,* once said to you,
  Shall be Yes for evermore.

ELIZABETH BARRETT BROWNING

SECRET LOVE

I HID my love when young till I
Couldn't hear the buzzing of a fly;
I hid my love to my despite
Till I could not bear to look at light:
I dare not gaze upon her face
But left her memory in each place;
Where e'er I saw a wildflower lie
I kissed and bade my love goodbye.

I met her in the greenest dells
Where dewdrops pearl the wood bluebells.
The lost breeze kissed her bright blue eye,
The bee kissed and went singing by,
A sunbeam found a passage there,—
A gold chain round her neck so fair;
As secret as the wild bee's song
She lay there all the summer long.

I hid my love in field and town
Till e'en the breeze would knock me down,
The bees seemed singing ballads o'er,
The fly's bass turned a lion's roar;
And even silence found a tongue
To haunt me all the summer long;
The riddle nature could not prove
Was nothing else but secret love.

JOHN CLARE

74

THE QUARREL

SUDDENLY, after the quarrel, while we waited,
Disheartened, silent, with downcast looks, nor stirred
Eyelid nor finger, hopeless both, yet hoping
Against all hope to unsay the sundering word:

While all the room's stillness deepened, deepened about
    us,
And each of us crept his thought's way to discover
How, with as little sound as the fall of a leaf,
The shadow had fallen, and lover quarreled with lover;

And while, in the quiet, I marveled—alas, alas—
At your deep beauty, your tragic beauty, torn
As the pale flower is torn by the wanton sparrow—
This beauty, pitied and loved, and now forsworn;

It was then, when the instant darkened to its darkest,—
When faith was lost with hope, and the rain conspired
To strike its gray arpeggios against our heartstrings,—
When love no longer dared, and scarcely desired:

It was then that suddenly, in the neighbor's room,
The music started: that brave quartette of strings
Breaking out of the stillness, as out of our stillness,
Like the indomitable heart of life that sings

When all is lost; and startled from our sorrow,
Tranced from our grief by that diviner grief,
We raised remembering eyes, each looked at other,
Blinded with tears of joy; and another leaf

Fell silently as that first; and in the instant
The shadow had gone, our quarrel became absurd;
And we rose, to the angelic voices of the music,
And I touched your hand, and we kissed, without a word.

CONRAD AIKEN

THE LITTLE TOIL OF LOVE

I HAD no time to hate, because
The grave would hinder me,
And life was not so ample I
Could finish enmity.

Nor had I time to love; but since
Some industry must be,
The little toil of love, I thought,
Was large enough for me.

EMILY DICKINSON

PRAYER TO VENUS

FAIREST of fair, O lady mine, Venus,
Daughter of Jove and spouse of Vulcanus,
Thou gladdener of the Mount of Citheron,
For all the love thou haddest for Adon
Have pity on my tears and bitter smart
And take my humble prayer unto thy heart.
Alas, I have no words with which to tell
The injuries and the torments of Love's hell;
My heart may not its sufferings betray;
I am so perplexed I know not what to say
Save "Mercy, lady bright, that knowest well
My thought, and see'st the injuries I feel,
Consider and have pity on my sore
As truly as I shall forevermore,
Well as i may, thy faithful servant be,
And wage forever war on chastity.
If thou wilt help, I hereby make my vow,
To boast of feats of arms I care not now,
Nor ask, tomorrow, to have victory,
Nor proud renown, nor any vain glory
Of prize of arms, abroad on trumpets blown,
But I would have complete possession
Of Emily, and in thy service die;
Find thou the manner how—I care not, I,
Nor know henceforth, whether it better be
To vanquish them or have them vanquish me,
So that I have my lady in my arms."

GEOFFREY CHAUCER

(Modern English by John Hall Wheelock)

WOMEN

WOMEN have no wilderness in them,
They are provident instead,
Content in the tight hot cell of their hearts
To eat dusty bread.

They do not see cattle cropping red winter grass,
They do not hear
Snow water going down under culverts
Shallow and clear.

They wait, when they should turn to journeys,
They stiffen, when they should bend.
They use against themselves that benevolence
To which no man is friend.

They cannot think of so many crops to a field
Or of clean wood cleft by an ax.
Their love is an eager meaninglessness
Too tense, or too lax.

They hear in every whisper that speaks to them
A shout and a cry.
As like as not, when they take life over their door-sills
They should let it go by.

LOUISE BOGAN

IV

Endearing Young Charms:

Youth, Beauty, Grace

TO HELEN

HELEN, thy beauty is to me
  Like those Nicaean barks of yore,
That gently, o'er a perfumed sea,
  The weary, wayworn wanderer bore
  To his own native shore.

On desperate seas long wont to roam,
  Thy hyacinth hair, thy classic face,
Thy Naiad airs, have brought me home
  To the glory that was Greece
  And the grandeur that was Rome.

Lo! in yon brilliant window-niche
  How statue-like I see thee stand,
The agate lamp within thy hand!
  Ah, Psyche, from the regions which
  Are Holy Land!

EDGAR ALLAN POE

SHE WALKS IN BEAUTY

SHE walks in beauty, like the night
  Of cloudless climes and starry skies;
And all that's best of dark and bright
  Meet in her aspect and her eyes:
Thus mellow'd to that tender light
  Which heaven to gaudy day denies.

81

One shade the more, one ray the less,
    Had half impair'd the nameless grace
Which waves in every raven tress,
    Or softly lightens o'er her face;
Where thoughts serenely sweet express
    How pure, how dear their dwelling-place.

And on that cheek, and o'er that brow,
    So soft, so calm, yet eloquent,
The smiles that win, the tints that glow,
    But tell of days in goodness spent,
A mind at peace with all below,
    A heart whose love is innocent!

GEORGE GORDON, *Lord Byron*

CLEOPATRA

THE barge she sat in, like a burnish'd throne,
Burn'd on the water; the poop was beaten gold,
Purple the sails, and so perfumed, that
The winds were love-sick with them, the oars were
    silver,
Which to the tune of flutes kept stroke, and made
The water which they beat to follow faster,
As amorous of their strokes. For her own person,
It beggar'd all description; she did lie
In her pavilion,—cloth-of-gold of tissue,—
O'er picturing that Venus where we see
The fancy outwork nature; on each side her
Stood pretty-dimpled boys, like smiling Cupids,
With divers-colour'd fans, whose wind did seem
To glow the delicate cheeks which they did cool,
And what they undid did.
82

Her gentlewomen, like the Nereides,
So many mermaids, tended her i' the eyes,
And made their bends adornings; at the helm
A seeming mermaid steers; the silken tackle
Swell with the touches of those flower-soft hands
That yarely frame the office. From the barge
A strange invisible perfume hits the sense
Of the adjacent wharfs. The city cast
Her people out upon her, and Antony,
Enthron'd i' the market-place, did sit alone,
Whistling to the air; which, but for vacancy,
Had gone to gaze on Cleopatra too
And made a gap in nature.

Age cannot wither her, nor custom stale
Her infinite variety; other women cloy
The appetites they feed, but she makes hungry
Where most she satisfies.

WILLIAM SHAKESPEARE

SLEEPING BEAUTY

OH, sight too dearly bought!
She sleeps, and though those eyes
Which lighten Cupid's skies
Be closed, yet such a grace
Environeth that place
That I, through wonder, to grow faint am brought;
Suns, if eclipsed ye have such power divine,
Oh, how can I endure you when ye shine?

WILLIAM DRUMMOND

WAS THIS THE FACE

Was this the face that launched a thousand ships
And burnt the topless towers of Ilium?
Sweet Helen, make me immortal with a kiss.
Her lips suck forth my soul; see where it flies!—
Come, Helen, come, give me my soul again.
Here will I dwell, for Heaven is in these lips,
And all is dross that is not Helena.
I will be Paris, and for love of thee,
Instead of Troy, shall Wertenberg be sacked:
And I will combat with weak Menelaus,
And wear thy colours on my plumèd crest:
Yea, I will wound Achilles in the heel,
And then return to Helen for a kiss.
Oh, thou art fairer than the evening air
Clad in the beauty of a thousand stars;
Brighter art thou than flaming Jupiter
When he appeared to hapless Semele:
More lovely than the monarch of the sky
In wanton Arethusa's azured arms:
And none but thou shalt be my paramour.

CHRISTOPHER MARLOWE

PART OF PLENTY

When she carries food to the table and stoops down
—Doing this out of love—and lays soup with its good
Tickling smell, or fry winking from the fire
And I look up, perhaps from a book I am reading
Or other work: there is an importance of beauty
Which can't be accounted for by there and then,

And attacks me, but not separately from the welcome
Of the food, or the grace of her arms.

When she puts a sheaf of tulips in a jug
And pours in water and presses to one side
The upright stems and leaves that you hear creak,
Or loosens them, or holds them up to show me,
So that I see the tangle of their necks and cups
With the curls of her hair, and the body they are held
Against, and the stalk of the small waist rising
And flowering in the shape of breasts;
Whether in the bringing of the flowers or the food
She offers plenty, and is part of plenty,
And whether I see her stooping, or leaning with the
      flowers,
What she does is ages old, and she is not simply,
No, but lovely in that way.

BERNARD SPENCER

CHERRY-RIPE

CHERRY-RIPE, ripe, ripe, I cry,
Full and fair ones; come and buy!
If so be you ask me where
They do grow, I answer there,
Where my Julia's lips do smile;
There's the land, or cherry-isle,
Those plantations fully show
All the year where cherries grow.

ROBERT HERRICK

MEN CALL YOU FAIR

Men call you fair, and you do credit it,
For that your self ye daily such do see:
But the true fair, that is the gentle wit,
And virtuous mind, is much more praised of me.
For all the rest, how ever fair it be,
Shall turn to nought and loose that glorious hue:
But only that is permanent and free
From frail corruption, that doth flesh ensue.
That is true beauty: that doth argue you
To be divine and born of heavenly seed:
Deriv'd from that fair Spirit, from whom all true
And perfect beauty did at first proceed.
He only fair, and what he fair hath made,
All other fair like flowers untimely fade.

EDMUND SPENSER

ASK ME NO MORE

Ask me no more where Jove bestows,
When June is past, the fading rose;
For in your beauty's orient deep
These flowers, as in their causes, sleep.

Ask me no more whither do stray
The golden atoms of the day,
For, in pure love, heaven did prepare
Those powders to enrich your hair.

Ask me no more whither doth haste
The nightingale when May is past;
For in your sweet dividing throat
She winters, and keeps warm her note.

Ask me no more where those stars light
That downwards fall in dead of night,
For in your eyes they sit, and there
Fixèd become as in their sphere.

Ask me no more if east or west
The phœnix builds her spicy nest;
For unto you at last she flies,
And in your fragrant bosom dies.

THOMAS CAREW

SHE'S BUT A LASSIE YET

MY love she's but a lassie yet,
A lightsome lovely lassie yet;
  It scarce wad do
  To sit an' woo
Down by the stream so glassy yet.

But there's a braw time coming yet,
When we may gang a-roaming yet;
  An' hint wi' glee
  O' joys to be,
When fa's the modest gloaming yet.

She's neither proud nor saucy yet,
She's neither plump nor gaucy yet;
   But just a jinking,
   Bonnie blinking
Hilty-skilty lassie yet.

But O her artless smile's mair sweet
Than hinny or than marmalete;
   An' right or wrang,
   Ere it be lang,
I'll bring her to a parley yet.

JAMES HOGG

FROM FAIREST CREATURES

FROM fairest creatures we desire increase,
That thereby beauty's rose might never die,
But as the riper should by time decease,
His tender heir might bear his memory:
But thou, contracted to thine own bright eyes,
Feed'st thy light's flame with self-substantial fuel,
Making a famine where abundance lies,
Thyself thy foe, to thy sweet self too cruel.
Thou that art now the world's fresh ornament
And only herald to the gaudy spring,
Within thine own bud buriest thy content
And, tender churl, mak'st waste in niggarding.
Pity the world, or else this glutton be,
To eat the world's due, by the grave and thee.

WILLIAM SHAKESPEARE

88

CHERRY-RIPE

THERE is a garden in her face
   Where roses and white lilies blow;
A heavenly paradise is that place,
   Wherein all pleasant fruits do flow:
     There cherries grow which none may buy
     Till "Cherry-ripe" themselves do cry.

Those cherries fairly do enclose
   Of orient pearls a double row,
Which when her lovely laughter shows,
   They look like rose-buds fill'd with snow;
     Yet them nor peer nor prince can buy
     Till "Cherry-ripe" themselves do cry.

Her eyes like angels watch them still;
   Her brows like bended bows do stand,
Threat'ning with piercing frowns to kill
   All that attempt with eye or hand
     Those sacred cherries to come nigh,
     Till "Cherry-ripe" themselves do cry.

THOMAS CAMPION

ALL THIS WORLD'S RICHES

YE tradeful merchants that, with weary toil,
Do seek most precious things to make your gain,
And both the Indias of their treasure spoil,
What needeth you to seek so far in vain?
For lo! my love doth in herself contain

89

All this world's riches that may far be found:
If sapphires, lo! her eyes be sapphires plain;
If rubies, lo! her lips be rubies sound;
If pearls, her teeth be pearls, both pure and round;
If ivory, her forehead ivory ween;
If gold, her locks are finest gold on ground;
If silver, her fair hands are silver sheen:
But that which fairest is but few behold:
Her mind, adorned with virtues manifold.

EDMUND SPENSER

THERE BE NONE OF BEAUTY'S DAUGHTERS

THERE be none of Beauty's daughters
  With a magic like to Thee;
And like music on the waters
  Is thy sweet voice to me:
When, as if its sound were causing
The charmed ocean's pausing
The waves lie still and gleaming,
And the lull'd winds seem dreaming:

And the midnight moon is weaving
  Her bright chain o'er the deep,
Whose breast is gently heaving
  As an infant's asleep:
So the spirit bows before thee
To listen and adore thee;
With a full but soft emotion,
Like the swell of Summer's ocean.

GEORGE GORDON, LORD BYRON

HER LIPS

LADY, when I behold the roses sprouting,
Which clad in damask mantles deck the arbours,
And then behold your lips where sweet love harbours,
My eyes present me with a double doubting:
For, viewing both alike, hardly my mind supposes
Whether the roses be your lips or your lips the roses.

ANONYMOUS

HER HAIR

HER hair the net of golden wire,
Wherein my heart, led by my wandering eyes,
So fast entangled is that in no wise
It can, nor will, again retire;
But rather will in that sweet bondage die
Than break one hair to gain its liberty.

ANONYMOUS

A REAL WOMAN

LET the mad poets say whate'er they please
Of the sweets of Faeries, Peris, Goddesses,
There is not such a treat among them all,
Haunters of cavern, lake, and waterfall,
As a real woman, lineal indeed
From Pyrrha's pebbles or old Adam's seed.

JOHN KEATS

91

THE UNFADING BEAUTY

HE that loves a rosy cheek,
  Or a coral lip admires,
Or from star-like eyes doth seek
  Fuel to maintain his fires:
As old Time makes this decay,
So his flames must waste away.

But a smooth and steadfast mind,
  Gentle thoughts and calm desires,
Hearts with equal love combined,
  Kindle never-dying fires.
Where these are not, I despise
Lovely cheeks or lips or eyes.

THOMAS CAREW

SHE IS NOT FAIR TO OUTWARD VIEW

SHE is not fair to outward view
  As many maidens be;
Her loveliness I never knew
  Until she smiled on me.
O then I saw her eye was bright,
A well of love, a spring of light.

But now her looks are coy and cold,
  To mine they ne'er reply,

And yet I cease not to behold
  The love-light in her eye:
Her very frowns are fairer far
Than smiles of other maidens are.

HARTLEY COLERIDGE

FOR ANNE GREGORY

"NEVER shall a young man,
Thrown into despair
By those great honey-colored
Ramparts at your ear,
Love you for yourself alone
And not your yellow hair."

"But I can get a hair-dye
And set such color there,
Brown, or black, or carrot,
That young men in despair
May love me for myself alone
And not my yellow hair."

"I heard an old religious man
But yesternight declare
That he had found a text to prove
That only God, my dear,
Could love you for yourself alone
And not your yellow hair."

WILLIAM BUTLER YEATS

93

WHITENESS, OR CHASTITY

TELL me, where doth whiteness grow,
Not on beds of Scythian snow;
Nor on alabaster hills;
Nor in Canaan's milky rills;
Nor the dainty living land
Of a young queen breast or hand;
Nor on cygnet's lovely necks;
Nor in lap of virgin wax;
Nor upon the soft and sleek
Pillows of the lilies' cheek;
Nor the precious smiling heirs
Of the morning's pearly tears;
Nor the silver-shaming grace
Of the moon's unclouded face:
No; all these candors
Are but the handsome slanders
Cast on the name of genuine whiteness, which
Doth thee alone, for chastity, enrich.

JOSEPH BEAUMONT

SUMMUM BONUM

ALL the breath and the bloom of the year in the bag
of one bee:
All the wonder and wealth of the mine in the heart
of one gem:
In the core of one pearl all the shade and the shine of
the sea:
Breath and bloom, shade and shine, wonder, wealth,
and how far above them—

Truth, that's brighter than gem,
Trust, that's purer than pearl,—
Brightest truth, purest trust in the universe—all were
    for me
  In the kiss of one girl.

ROBERT BROWNING

THE ART OF EYES

WAS it the work of Nature or of Art,
Which tempered so the feature of her face,
That pride and meekness, mixed by equal part,
Do both appear t' adorn her beauty's grace?
For with mild pleasance, which doth pride displace,
She to her love doth lookers' eyes allure;
And with stern countenance back again doth chase
Their looser looks that stir up lusts impure.
With such strange terms her eyes she doth inure,
That with one look she doth my life dismay,
And with another doth it straight secure:
Her smile me draws; her frown me drives away.
  Thus doth she train and teach me with her looks;
  Such art of eyes I never read in books!

EDMUND SPENSER

95

TO CYNTHIA

(On Concealment of Her Beauty)

Do not conceal thy radiant eyes,
The star-light of serenest skies,
Lest wanting of their heavenly light,
They turn to Chaos' endless night.

Do not conceal those tresses fair,
The silken snares of thy curled hair,
Lest finding neither gold nor ore
The curious silkworm work no more.

Do not conceal those breasts of thine,
More snow-white than the Apennine,
Lest if there be like cold or frost
The lily be for ever lost.

Do not conceal that fragrant scent,
Thy breath, which to all flowers hath lent
Perfumes, lest it being supprest
No spices grow in all the East.

Do not conceal thy heavenly voice,
Which makes the hearts of gods rejoice,
Lest Music hearing no such thing
The nightingale forget to sing.

Do not conceal nor yet eclipse
Thy pearly teeth with coral lips,
Lest that the seas cease to bring forth
Gems which from thee have all their worth.

Do not conceal no beauty-grace,
That's either in thy mind or face,
Lest virtue overcome by vice
Make men believe no Paradise.

SIR FRANCIS KYNASTON

GRATIANA DANCING AND SINGING

See! with what constant motion
Even, and glorious, as the sun,
  Gratiana steers that noble frame.
Soft as her breast, sweet as her voice
That gave each winding law and poise,
  And swifter than the wings of fame.

She beat the happy pavement
By such a star made firmament,
  Which now no more the roof envies;
But swells up high with Atlas even,
Bearing the brighter, nobler heaven,
  And in her, all the deities.

Each step trod out a lover's thought
And the ambitious hopes he brought,
  Chained to her brave feet with such arts;
Such sweet command, and gentle awe,
As when she ceased, we sighing saw
  The floor lay paved with broken hearts.

So did she move; so did she sing
Like to the harmonious spheres that bring
  Unto their rounds their music's aid;
Which she performed such a way
As all the enamoured world will say
  The graces danced and Apollo played.

Richard Lovelace

TO YOU! TO YOU!

Doubt you to whom my Muse these notes intendeth,
Which now my breast, o'ercharged, to music lendeth?
    To you! to you! all song of praise is due;
Only in you my song begins and endeth.

Who hath the eyes which marry state with pleasure?
Who keeps the key of Nature's chiefest treasure?
    To you! to you! all song of praise is due;
Only for you the heaven forgat all measure.

Who hath the lips where wit in fairness reigneth?
Who womankind at once both decks and staineth?
    To you! to you! all song of praise is due;
Only by you Cupid his crown maintaineth.

Who hath the feet, whose step all sweetness planteth?
Who else, for whom Fame worthy trumpets wanteth?
    To you! to you! all song of praise is due;
Only to you her sceptre Venus granteth.

Who hath the breast, whose milk doth passions nourish?
Whose grace is such, that when it chides doth cherish?
    To you! to you! all song of praise is due;
Only through you the tree of life doth flourish.

Who hath the hand, which without stroke subdueth?
Who long-dead beauty with increase reneweth?
    To you! to you! all song of praise is due;
Only at you all envy hopeless rueth.

Who hath the hair, which loosest fastest tieth?
Who makes a man live then glad when he dieth?

To you! to you! all song of praise is due;
Only of you the flatterer never lieth.

Who hath the voice, which soul from senses sunders?
Whose force but yours the bolts of beauty thunders?
   To you! to you! all song of praise is due;
Only with you not miracles are wonders.

Doubt you to whom my Muse these notes intendeth,
Which now my breast, o'ercharged, to music lendeth?
   To you! to you! all song of praise is due;
Only in you my song begins and endeth.

SIR PHILIP SIDNEY

THE COMPLETE LOVER

For her gait, if she be walking;
Be she sitting, I desire her
For her state's sake; and admire her
For her wit if she be talking;
      Gait and state and wit approve her;
      For which all and each I love her.

Be she sullen, I commend her
For a modest. Be she merry,
For a kind one her prefer I.
Briefly, everything doth lend her
      So much grace, and so approve her,
      That for everything I love her.

WILLIAM BROWNE

O RUDDIER THAN THE CHERRY

O RUDDIER than the cherry,
O sweeter than the berry,
   O Nymph more bright
   Than moonshine night,
Like kidlings blithe and merry.
Ripe as the melting cluster,
No lily has such lustre,
   Yet hard to tame
   As raging flame,
And fierce as storms that bluster.

JOHN GAY

HER TRIUMPH

SEE the Chariot at hand here of Love,
   Wherein my Lady rideth!
Each that draws is a swan or a dove,
   And well the car Love guideth.
As she goes, all hearts do duty
     Unto her beauty;
And, enamored, do wish, so they might
     But enjoy such a sight,
That they still were to run by her side,
Through swords, through seas, whither she would ride.

Do but look on her eyes, they do light
   All that Love's world compriseth!

Do but look on her hair, it is bright
  As Love's star when it riseth!
Do but mark, her forehead's smoother
    Than words that soothe her!
And from her arched brows such a grace
    Sheds itself through the face,
As alone there triumphs to the life
All the gain, all the good, of the elements' strife.

Have you seen but a bright lily grow
  Before rude hands have touched it?
Have you marked but the fall o' the snow
  Before the soil hath smutched it?
Have you felt the wool of beaver,
    Or swan's down ever?
Or have smelt o' the bud o' the brierr
    Or the nard in the fire?
Or have tasted the bag o' the bee?
O so white, O so soft, O so sweet is she!

                BEN JONSON

OF PHYLLIS

    IN petticoat of green,
     Her hair about her eyne,
       Phyllis beneath an oak
       Sat milking her fair flock:
Among that sweet-strained moisture, rare delight,
Her hand seemed milk in milk, it was so white.

            WILLIAM DRUMMOND
              101

A WELCOME

Welcome, welcome, do I sing,
Far more welcome than the spring;
He that parteth from you never
Shall enjoy a spring forever.

He that to the voice is near,
  Breaking from your ivory pale,
Need not walk abroad to hear
  The delightful nightingale.

He that looks still on your eyes,
  Though the winter have begun
To benumb our arteries,
  Shall not want the summer's sun.

He that still may see your cheeks,
  Where all rareness still reposes,
Is a fool if e'er he seeks
  Other lilies, other roses.

He to whom your soft lip yields,
  And perceives your breath in kissing,
All the odors of the fields
  Never, never shall be missing.

He that question would anew
  What fair Eden was of old,
Let him rightly study you,
  And a brief of that behold.

Welcome, welcome, then I sing,
Far more welcome than the spring;
He that parteth from you never,
Shall enjoy a spring forever.

WILLIAM BROWNE

102

THE STREAM

(Addressed to a Young Lady)

SWEET stream, that winds through yonder glade,
Apt emblem of a virtuous maid:
Silent and chaste she steals along,
Far from the world's gay busy throng,
With gentle yet prevailing force,
Intent upon her destined course;
Graceful and useful all she does,
Blessing and blest where'er she goes,
Pure-bosomed as that watery glass,
And heaven reflected in her face.

WILLIAM COWPER

TO MISTRESS MARGARET HUSSEY

MERRY Margaret,
As midsummer flower,
Gentil as falcon
Or hawk of the tower;
   With solace and gladness,
Much mirth and no madness,
All good and no badness,
So joyously,
So maidenly,
So womanly
Her demeaning
In every thing,—
Far, far passing

That I can endite
Or suffice to write
Of merry Margaret,
As midsummer flower,
Gentil as falcon
Or hawk of the tower.
  As patient and as still
And as full of good will
As fair Isiphill,
Coliander,
Sweet pomander,
Good Cassaunder;
Steadfast of thought,
Well made, well wrought;
Far may be sought
Erst that ye can find
So courteous, so kind
As merry Margaret,
This midsummer flower,
Gentil as falcon
Or hawk of the tower.

JOHN SKELTON

WHAT GUILE IS THIS?

WHAT guile is this, that those her golden tresses
She doth attire under a net of gold;
And with sly skill so cunningly them dresses,
That which is gold or hair, may scarce be told?
Is it that men's frail eyes, which gaze too bold,
She may entangle in that golden snare;
And being caught may craftily enfold
Their weaker hearts, which are not well aware?

Take heed therefore, mine eyes, how ye do stare
Henceforth too rashly on that guileful net,
In which if ever ye entrapped are,
Out of her bands ye by no means shall get.
Folly it were for any being free,
To covet fetters, though they golden be.

EDMUND SPENSER

THE LOOKING GLASS

WHEN this crystal shall present
Your beauty to your eye,
Think! that lovely face was meant
To dress another by.
For not to make them proud
These glasses are allowed
To those who're fair,
But to compare
The inward beauty with the outward grace,
And make them fair in soul as well as face.

JAMES SHIRLEY

GO NOT, HAPPY DAY

Go not, happy day,
  From the shining fields,
Go not, happy day,
  Till the maiden yields.
Rosy is the West,
  Rosy is the South,
Roses are her cheeks,
  And a rose her mouth.
When the happy *Yes*
  Falters from her lips,
Pass and blush the news
  O'er the blowing ships.
Over blowing seas,
  Over seas at rest,
Pass the happy news,
  Blush it through the West;
Till the red man dance
  By his cedar tree,
And the red man's babe
  Leap, beyond the sea.
Blush from West to East,
  Blush from East to West,
Till the West is East,
  Blush it through the West.
Rosy is the West,
  Rosy is the South,
Roses are her cheeks,
  And a rose her mouth.

ALFRED, LORD TENNYSON

V

A Rosy Wreath:

Tokens of Love

DELIGHT IN DISORDER

A SWEET disorder in the dress
Kindles in clothes a wantonness:
A lawn about the shoulders thrown
Into a fine distraction:
An erring lace, which here and there
Enthrals the crimson stomacher:
A cuff neglectful, and thereby
Ribbands to flow confusedly:
A winning wave, deserving note,
In the tempestuous petticoat:
A careless shoe-string, on whose tie
I see a wild civility:
Do more bewitch me than when art
Is too precise in every part.

ROBERT HERRICK

MADRIGAL

MY Love in her attire doth show her wit,
    It doth so well become her;
For every season she hath dressings fit,
    For Winter, Spring, and Summer.
        No beauty she doth miss
            When all her robes are on:
        But Beauty's self she is
            When all her robes are gone.

ANONYMOUS
109

WHENAS IN SILKS MY JULIA GOES

WHENAS in silks my Julia goes,
Then, then, methinks, how sweetly flows
That liquefaction of her clothes.
Next, when I cast mine eyes and see
The brave vibration each way free,
O how that glittering taketh me!

ROBERT HERRICK

ON A GIRDLE

THAT which her slender waist confined,
Shall now my joyful temples bind;
No monarch but would give his crown,
His arms might do what this has done.

It was my heaven's extremest sphere,
The pale which held that lovely deer,
My joy, my grief, my hope, my love,
Did all within this circle move!

A narrow compass! and yet there
Dwelt all that's good, and all that's fair!
Give me but what this ribband bound,
Take all the rest the sun goes round!

EDMUND WALLER

SONG

STILL to be neat, still to be dressed,
As you were going to a feast,
Still to be powdered, still perfumed,
Lady, it is to be presumed,
Though art's hid causes are not found,
All is not sweet, all is not sound.

Give me a look, give me a face,
That makes simplicity a grace,
Robes loosely flowing, hair as free;
Such sweet neglect more taketh me
Than all the adulteries of art.
They strike mine eye, but not my heart.

BEN JONSON

TO AMARANTHA

That She Should Dishevel Her Hair

AMARANTHA sweet and fair,
Ah, braid no more that shining hair!
As my curious hand or eye
Hovering round thee, let it fly!

Let it fly as unconfined
As its calm ravisher the wind,
Who hath left his darling, th' East,
To wanton o'er that spicy nest.

Every tress must be confest,
But neatly tangled at the best;

111

Like a clue of golden thread
Most excellently ravelléd.

Do not then wind up that light
In ribbands, and o'ercloud in night
Like the sun in's early ray;
But shake your head, and scatter day!

RICHARD LOVELACE

HE JESTS AT SCARS,
THAT NEVER FELT A WOUND

HE jests at scars, that never felt a wound.
But, soft! what light through yonder window breaks?
It is the east, and Juliet is the sun!
Arise, fair sun, and kill the envious moon,
Who is already sick and pale with grief,
That thou her maid art far more fair than she:
Be not her maid, since she is envious;
Her vestal livery is but sick and green,
And none but fools do wear it; cast it off.
It is my lady; O! it is my love:
O! that she knew she were.
She speaks, yet she says nothing: what of that?
Her eye discourses; I will answer it.
I am too bold, 'tis not to me she speaks:
Two of the fairest stars in all the heaven,
Having some business, do entreat her eyes
To twinkle in their spheres till they return.
What if her eyes were there, they in her head?
The brightness of her cheek would shame those stars
As daylight doth a lamp; her eyes in heaven

Would through the airy region stream so bright
That birds would sing and think it were not night.
See! how she leans her cheek upon her hand:
O! that I were a glove upon that hand,
That I might touch that cheek.

WILLIAM SHAKESPEARE

AT NIGHT

HOME, home from the horizon far and clear,
  Hither the soft wings sweep;
Flocks of the memories of the day draw near
  The dovecote doors of sleep.

Oh, which are they that come through sweetest light
  Of all these homing birds?
Which with the straightest and the swiftest flight?
  Your words to me, your words!

ALICE MEYNELL

LOVE IN A LIFE

ROOM after room,
I haunt the house through
We inhabit together.
Heart, fear nothing, for, heart, thou shalt find her—
Next time, herself!—not the trouble behind her
Left in the curtain, the couch's perfume!

113

As she brushed it, the cornice-wreath blossomed anew:
Yon looking-glass gleamed at the wave of her feather.

Yet the day wears,
And door succeeds door;
I try the fresh fortune—
Range the wide house from the wing to the centre.
Still the same chance! she goes out as I enter.
Spend my whole day in the quest,—who cares?
But 'tis twilight, you see,—with such suites to explore,
Such closets to search, such alcoves to importune!

ROBERT BROWNING

PACKET OF LETTERS

IN the shut drawer, even now, they rave and grieve—
To be approached at times with the frightened tear;
Their cold to be drawn away from, as one, at nightfall,
Draws the cloak closer against the cold of the marsh.

There, there, the thugs of the heart did murder.
There, still in murderers' guise, two stand embraced, embalmed.

LOUISE BOGAN

A LOVE FOR PATSY

SEE the little maunderer
Stretch out on the grass!
His heart is burst asunder
The pieces cry Alas.

Upright, fat pink pieces
Of fluffy cloud float overhead.
The little facets of his eyes
Split by salty tears, so tired

Of seeing pieces of the world
Close, and rustling grass,
Caws of an old unpleasant bird
Are sounds that say Alas;

They float like notes in the funny paper,
Round notes with sharp little tails.
Oh I'm blue, the supine moper
Says, I'm trapped in the toils

Of Patsy's black black hair.
Her hair is like the cool dry night
That waves through the window-bar
Where a moody jailbird sits apart

Shuffling his broken heart. I'm sad
As I can be. Her black
Black hair can never be compared
To dull dichotomic

Trees or prickly grass, inflated
Clouds, even a great
One draped on the sun. Over-rated
Senseless things to stare at,

115

One here one there they're strewn,
Impinging pieces left out of
The world. Her eyes are green!
Oh oh, he says, I die of love.

See the weeping little wretch
He rolls in a frenzy!
In all the world no two things match
But the green eyes of Patsy.

JOHN THOMPSON, JR.

KISSING

COME hither Womankind and all their worth,
Give me thy kisses as I call them forth.
Give me the billing-kiss, that of the dove,
  A kiss of love;
The melting-kiss, a kiss that doth consume
  To a perfume;
The extract-kiss, of every sweet a part,
  A kiss of art;
The kiss which ever stirs some new delight,
  A kiss of might;
The twaching smacking kiss, and when you cease
  A kiss of peace;
The music-kiss, crotchet and quaver time,
  The kiss of rhyme;
The kiss of eloquence, which doth belong
  Unto the tongue;
The kiss of all the sciences in one,
  The Kiss alone.
So 'tis enough.

LORD HERBERT of Cherbury

MY PICTURE, LEFT IN SCOTLAND

I now think Love is rather deaf than blind,
  For else it could not be,
        That she
  Whom I adore so much, should so slight me,
And cast my suit behind.
I'm sure my language to her was as sweet,
    And every close did meet
    In sentence of as subtle feet,
    As hath the youngest he
    That sit in shadow of Apollo's tree.

    Oh! but my conscious fears,
      That fly my thoughts between,
    Tell me that she hath seen
    My hundreds of gray hairs
      Told six and forty years,
  Read so much waste as she cannot embrace
  My mountain belly and my rocky face,
And all these, through her eyes, have stopped her ears.

                                        BEN JONSON

SONG

  THE blushing rose and purple flower,
    Let grow too long, are soonest blasted;
  Dainty fruit, though sweet, will sour,
    And rot in ripeness, left untasted.
  Yet here is one more sweet than these;
  The more you taste, the more she'll please.

117

Beauty that's enclosed with ice,
   Is a shadow chaste as rare;
Then how much those sweets entice,
   That have issue full as fair!
Earth cannot yield from all her powers
One equal for dame Venus' bowers.

PHILIP MASSINGER

THE FAIR SINGER

To make a final conquest of all me,
Love did compose so sweet an enemy,
In whom both beauties to my death agree,
Joining themselves in fatal harmony;
That while she with her eyes my heart does bind,
She with her voice might captivate my mind.

I could have fled from one but singly fair;
My disentangled soul itself might save,
Breaking the curléd trammels of her hair.
But how should I avoid to be her slave,
Whose subtle art invisible can wreathe
My fetters of the very air I breathe?

It had been easy fighting in some plain,
Where victory might fight in equal choice,
But all resistance against her is vain,
Who has the advantage of both eyes and voice;
And all my forces needs must be undone,
She having gainéd both the wind and sun.

ANDREW MARVELL

VI

In New Surprise:

World Transformed by Love

HER SWEET VOICE

You that think Love can convey
    No other way,
But through the eyes, into the heart
    His fatal dart,
Close up those casements and but hear
      This siren sing,
      And on the wing
Of her sweet voice it shall appear
That Love can enter at the ear.

Open, unveil your eyes, behold
    The curious mould
Where that voice dwells, and as we know
    When the cocks crow
      We freely may
      Gaze on the day,
So may you, when the musick's done,
Awake and see the rising sun.

THOMAS CAREW

LOVE IN THE VALLEY

UNDER yonder beech-tree single on the greensward,
   Couched with her arms behind her golden head,
Knees and tresses folded to slip and ripple idly,
   Lies my young love sleeping in the shade.
Had I the heart to slide an arm beneath her,
   Press her parting lips as her waist I gather slow,

121

Waking in amazement she could not but embrace me:
  Then would she hold me and never let me go?

Shy as the squirrel and wayward as the swallow,
  Swift as the swallow along the river's light
Circleting the surface to meet his mirror'd winglets,
  Fleeter she seems in her stay than in her flight.
Shy as the squirrel that leaps among the pine-tops,
  Wayward as the swallow overhead at set of sun,
She whom I love is hard to catch and conquer,
  Hard, but O the glory of the winning were she won!

Happy happy time, when the white star hovers
  Low over dim fields fresh with bloomy dew,
Near the face of dawn, that draws athwart the darkness,
  Threading it with colour, like yewberries the yew.
Thicker crowd the shades as the grave East deepens
  Glowing, and with crimson a long cloud swells,
Maiden still the morn is; and strange she is, and secret;
  Strange her eyes; her cheeks are cold as cold sea-
    shells.

Hither she comes; she comes to me; she lingers,
  Deepens her brown eyebrows, while in new surprise
High rise the lashes in wonder of a stranger;
  Yet am I the light and living of her eyes.
Something friends have told her fills her heart to brim-
    ming,
  Nets her in her blushes, and wounds her, and tames.—
Sure of her haven, O like a dove alighting,
  Arms up, she dropp'd: our souls were in our names.

GEORGE MEREDITH

SONG

Nay but you, who do not love her,
　Is she not pure gold, my mistress?
Holds earth aught—speak truth—above her?
　Aught like this tress, see, and this tress,
And this last fairest tress of all,
So fair, see, ere I let it fall?

Because, you spend your lives in praising;
　To praise, you search the wide world over:
Then why not witness, calmly gazing,
　If earth holds aught—speak truth—above her?
Above this tress, and this, I touch
But cannot praise, I love so much!

ROBERT BROWNING

ONE CARELESS LOOK

One gloomy eve I roam'd about
　Neath Oxey's hazel bowers,
While timid hares were darting out,
　To crop the dewy flowers;
And soothing was the scene to me,
　Right pleasèd was my soul,
My breast was calm as summer's sea
　When waves forget to roll.

But short was Even's placid smile,
　My startled soul to charm,

123

When Nelly lightly skipt the stile,
  With milk-pail on her arm:
One careless look on me she flung,
  As bright as parting day;
And like a hawk from covert sprung,
  It pounced my peace away.

JOHN CLARE

COME NIGHT, COME ROMEO

COME night; come, Romeo; come, thou day in night;
For thou wilt lie upon the wings of night
Whiter than new snow on a raven's back.—
Come, gentle night,—come, loving, black-brow'd night,
Give me my Romeo; and, when he shall die,
Take him and cut him out in little stars,
And he will make the face of heaven so fine,
That all the world will be in love with night,
And pay no worship to the garish sun.—
O, I have bought the mansion of a love,
But not possest it; and, though I am sold,
Not yet enjoy'd: so tedious is this day,
As is the night before some festival
To an impatient child that hath new robes
And may not wear them.

WILLIAM SHAKESPEARE

124

THE SUN RISING

Busy old fool, unruly Sun,
　　Why dost thou thus,
Through windows, and through curtains, call on us?
Must to thy motions lovers' seasons run?
　　Saucy pedantic wretch, go chide
　　Late school-boys and sour prentices,
　Go tell court-huntsmen that the king will ride,
　Call country ants to harvest offices;
Love, all alike, no season knows nor clime,
Nor hours, days, months, which are the rags of time.

　　Thy beams so reverend and strong
　　Why shouldst thou think?
I could eclipse and cloud them with a wink,
But that I would not lose her sight so long.
　　If her eyes have not blinded thine,
　　Look, and to-morrow late tell me,
　Whether both th' Indias of spice and mine
　Be where thou left'st them, or lie here with me.
Ask for those kings whom thou saw'st yesterday,
And thou shalt hear, "All here in one bed lay."

　　She's all states, and all princes I;
　　Nothing else is;
Princes do but play us; compared to this,
All honor's mimic, all wealth alchemy.
　　Thou, Sun, art half as happy as we,
　　In that the world's contracted thus;
　Thine age asks ease, and since thy duties be
　To warm the world, that's done in warming us.
Shine here to us, and thou art everywhere;
This bed thy center is, these walls thy sphere.

JOHN DONNE

HE IS MINE

E'EN like two little bank-dividing brooks,
　　That wash the pebbles with their wanton streams,
And having ranged and search'd a thousand nooks,
　　Meet both at length in silver-breasted Thames,
　　　　Where in a greater current they conjoin:
So I my best-belovèd's am; so he is mine.

E'en so we met; and after long pursuit,
　　E'en so we joined; we both became entire;
No need for either to renew a suit.
　　For I was flax and he was flames of fire:
　　　　Our firm-united souls did more than twine;
So I my best-belovèd's am; so he is mine.

If all those glittering monarchs that command
　　The servile quarters of this earthly ball,
Should tender, in exchange, their shares of land,
　　I would not change my fortunes for them all,
　　　　Their wealth is but a counter to my coin:
The world's but theirs; but my belovèd's mine.

FRANCIS QUARLES

TO ALTHEA, FROM PRISON

WHEN Love with unconfinèd wings
　　Hovers within my gates,
And my divine Althea brings
　　To whisper at the grates;

When I lie tangled in her hair
   And fettered to her eye,
The birds that wanton in the air
   Know no such liberty.

When flowing cups run swiftly round
   With no allaying Thames,
Our careless heads with roses bound,
   Our hearts with loyal flames;
When thirsty grief in wine we steep,
   When healths and draughts go free,
Fishes that tipple in the deep
   Know no such liberty.

When, like committed linnets, I
   With shriller throat shall sing
The sweetness, mercy, majesty,
   And glories of my king;
When I shall voice aloud how good
   He is, how great should be,
Enlarged winds, that curl the flood,
   Know no such liberty.

Stone walls do not a prison make,
   Nor iron bars a cage;
Minds innocent and quiet take
   That for an hermitage;
If I have freedom in my love,
   And in my soul am free,
Angels alone, that soar above,
   Enjoy such liberty.

RICHARD LOVELACE

127

SPRING AIR

In blows the loitering air of spring,
Scarcely a-blow, a-blow, a lively gas.
It makes the secret life-cells ring
And quicken, while the blood-waves pass.
Floss nothingness, we feel it cling,
Resile,—silent as space, unseen as glass
Unlustred, softer than the weakest thing.
Such air can enter nostrils, sudden as light
The eye, fair words the ear, or flight
The nerve-knot, or your unexpected love
My startled heart. Down from above,
Or from the south, or flowered west,
Or from the oceaned east, or here
Blown first by spring, this air possessed
By spring is Ah! so lithe this year.
The curtain flies before this wonder.
Talk fast. Speak swift before the heart's asunder.

And for this guile . . . no cold-ice gates?
Nothing to hold it quietly down, a-down,
The while the senses sleep? Full spates
Of air enter this room in town.
Such air draws creatures to their mates
And, wild, peels off the winter's brown
From tree; ruffles the bird and motivates
The northern winging to the utmost nest;
Breaks out the bud's first scent and, lest
Two living things escape and keep hearts steady,
Beguiles us at this window; heady
And rich, murmurs; touches like flesh
Of loving fingers, timorous but sure.
Intoxicant is this mild, fresh

Warm breath of spring, all mad and pure.
Is this my hand in yours? Am I
So close? Wait till the insinuant wind's gone by. . .

GENE DERWOOD

THE GOOD MORROW

I WONDER by my troth, what thou and I
Did, till we loved? Were we not weaned till then,
But sucked on country pleasures, childishly?
Or snorted we in the seven sleepers' den?
'Twas so; but this, all pleasures fancies be.
If ever any beauty I did see,
Which I desired, and got, 'twas but a dream of thee.

And now good morrow to our waking souls,
Which watch not one another out of fear;
For love all love of other sights controls,
And makes one little room an everywhere.
Let sea-discoverers to new worlds have gone,
Let maps to other, worlds on worlds have shown;
Let us possess one world, each hath one, and is one.

My face in thine eye, thine in mine appears,
And true plain hearts do in the faces rest;
Where can we find two better hemispheres
Without sharp north, without declining west?
Whatever dies was not mixed equally;
If our two loves be one, or thou and I
Love so alike that none do slacken, none can die.

JOHN DONNE

129

SONG

THE lark now leaves his watery nest,
  And climbing shakes his dewy wings.
He takes this window for the East,
  And to implore your light he sings—
Awake, awake; the morn will never rise
Till she can dress her beauty at your eyes.

The merchant bows unto the seaman's star,
  The plowman from the sun his season takes;
But still the lover wonders what they are
  Who look for day before his mistress wakes.
Awake, awake! break through your veils of lawn!
Then draw your curtains, and begin the dawn!

WILLIAM DAVENANT

FAIR IS MY LOVE

FAIR is my Love, when her fair golden hairs
With the loose wind ye waving chance to mark;
Fair, when the rose in her red cheeks appears;
Or in her eyes the fire of love does spark.
Fair, when her breast, like a rich laden bark,
With precious merchandise she forth doth lay;
Fair, when that cloud of pride, which oft doth dark
Her goodly light, with smiles she drives away,
But fairest she, when so she doth display
The gate with pearls and rubies richly dight
Through which her words so wise do make their way
To bear the message of her gentle spright.
The rest be works of Nature's wonderment;
But this the work of heart's astonishment.

EDMUND SPENSER

THE MOWER'S SONG

My mind was once the true survey
Of all these meadows fresh and gay;
And in the greenness of the grass
Did see its hopes as in a glass;
When Juliana came, and she
What I do to the grass, does to my thoughts and me.

But these, while I with sorrow pine,
Grew more luxuriant still and fine;
That not one blade of grass you spied,
But had a flower on either side;
When Juliana came, and she
What I do to the grass, does to my thoughts and me.

Unthankful meadows, could you so
A fellowship so true forego,
And in your gaudy may-games meet,
While I lay trodden under feet?
When Juliana came, and she
What I do to the grass, does to my thoughts and me.

But what you in compassion ought,
Shall now by my revenge be wrought:
And flowers, and grass, and I and all,
Will in one common ruin fall.
For Juliana comes, and she
What I do to the grass, does to my thoughts and me.

And thus, ye meadows, which have been
Companions of my thoughts more green,
Shall now the heraldry become
With which I shall adorn my tomb;
For Juliana comes, and she
What I do to the grass, does to my thoughts and me.

ANDREW MARVELL

131

DIVINELY SUPERFLUOUS BEAUTY

THE storm-dances of gulls, the barking game of seals,
Over and under the ocean . . .
Divinely superfluous beauty
Rules the games, presides over destinies, makes trees
    grow
And hills tower, waves fall.
The incredible beauty of joy
Stars with fire the joining of lips, O let our loves too
Be joined, there is not a maiden
Burns and thirsts for love
More than my blood for you, by the shore of seals while
    the wings
Weave like a web in the air
Divinely superfluous beauty.

ROBINSON JEFFERS

THE MIRAGE

I LIVED a life without love, and saw the being
I loved on every branch; then that bare tree
Stood up with all its branches up, a great harp
Growing straight out of the ground, and there I saw
A squadron of bright birds clothing the bare limbs;
The music notes sat on the harp; it was all love.

This was the heart inside the starved body;
Love grew images like cactus, and planted roses
On the walls of the mirage, and the garden grew
Shining with perfume and the senses dwindled to dew,
132

IN NEW SURPRISE: *World Transformed by Love*

The century was rolled into one formation aloft,
A cloud, like St. Veronica's handkerchief of love.

There I saw the face of the one without whom
I lived, two soft jewels implanted in her face,
Her hair pouring around her face without sound,
And her love for me sprang on her skin like dew,
Pearl-grey as the flower of the brain she lay
Quivering on the soft cushion of the great day.

I heard a roar of buildings at my conscience,
I looked up and saw a wall of windows glowing,
And there my love leaned out of each window,
There she leaned out multiplied like heaven
In that vast wall of lights, every light her face,
Suns of a thousand mornings ranging on one day.

And all the machines were running, and yes, great
Was the sound of their running downward and down
Into the blind chutes of their rooted feet,
And all of the windows quivered with my many loves,
Like apples they fell off, at one windfall, all,
And I awoke on the starved pavements of no love.

OSCAR WILLIAMS

SONG TO A FAIR YOUNG LADY

Going Out of the Town in the Spring

Ask not the cause why sullen spring
  So long delays her flowers to bear,
Why warbling birds forget to sing,
  And winter storms invert the year.
Chloris is gone, and fate provides
To make it spring where she resides.

Chloris is gone, the cruel fair;
  She cast not back a pitying eye,
But left her lover in despair,
  To sigh, to languish, and to die.
Ah, how can those fair eyes endure
To give the wounds they will not cure!

Great god of love, why hast thou made
  A face that can all hearts command,
That all religions can invade,
  And change the laws of every land?
Where thou hadst placed such power before,
Thou shouldst have made her mercy more.

When Chloris to the temple comes,
  Adoring crowds before her fall;
She can restore the dead from tombs,
  And every life but mine recall.
I only am by love designed
To be the victim for mankind.

JOHN DRYDEN

THE CANONIZATION

For God's sake hold your tongue, and let me love;
  Or chide my palsy, or my gout;
  My five gray hairs, or ruined fortune flout;
With wealth your state, your mind with arts improve;
    Take you a course, get you a place,
    Observe his Honor, or his Grace;
Or the king's real, or his stamped face
  Contemplate; what you will, approve,
  So you will let me love.

Alas! alas! who's injured by my love?
  What merchant's ships have my sighs drowned?
  Who says my tears have overflowed his ground?
When did my colds a forward spring remove?
    When did the heats which my veins fill
    Add one more to the plaguy bill?
Soldiers find wars, and lawyers find out still
  Litigious men, which quarrels move
  Though she and I do love.

Call's what you will, we are made such by love;
  Call her one, me another fly,
  We're tapers too, and at our own cost die,
And we in us find the eagle and the dove.
    The phoenix riddle hath more wit
    By us; we two being one, are it;
So, to one neutral thing both sexes fit.
  We die and rise the same, and prove
  Mysterious by this love.

We can die by it, if not live by love,
  And if unfit for tomb or hearse

Our legend be, it will be fit for verse;
And if no piece of chronicle we prove,
    We'll build in sonnets pretty rooms;
    As well a well-wrought urn becomes
The greatest ashes, as half-acre tombs,
    And by these hymns all shall approve
    Us canonized for love;

And thus invoke us, "You whom reverend love
    Made one another's hermitage;
    You, to whom love was peace, that now is rage;
Who did the whole world's soul contract, and drove
    Into the glasses of your eyes;
    So made such mirrors, and such spies,
That they did all to you epitomize—
    Countries, towns, courts beg from above
    A pattern of your love."

JOHN DONNE

JENNY KISS'D ME

JENNY kiss'd me when we met,
    Jumping from the chair she sat in;
Time, you thief, who love to get
    Sweets into your list, put that in!
Say I'm weary, say I'm sad,
    Say that health and wealth have miss'd me,
Say I'm growing old, but add,
        Jenny kiss'd me.

LEIGH HUNT

DOVER BEACH

THE sea is calm to-night,
The tide is full, the moon lies fair
Upon the straits;—on the French coast the light
Gleams and is gone; the cliffs of England stand,
Glimmering and vast, out in the tranquil bay.
Come to the window, sweet is the night-air!
Only, from the long line of spray
Where the sea meets the moon-blanched land,
Listen! you hear the grating roar
Of pebbles which the waves draw back, and fling,
At their return, up the high strand,
Begin, and cease, and then again begin,
With tremulous cadence slow, and bring
The eternal note of sadness in.

Sophocles long ago
Heard it on the Ægean, and it brought
Into his mind the turbid ebb and flow
Of human misery; we
Find also in the sound a thought,
Hearing it by this distant northern sea.

The sea of faith
Was once, too, at the full, and round earth's shore
Lay like the folds of a bright girdle furled.
But now I only hear
Its melancholy, long, withdrawing roar,
Retreating, to the breath
Of the night-wind, down the vast edges drear
And naked shingles of the world.

Ah, love, let us be true
To one another! for the world, which seems

To lie before us like a land of dreams,
So various, so beautiful, so new,
Hath really neither joy, nor love, nor light,
Nor certitude, nor peace, nor help for pain;
And we are here as on a darkling plain
Swept with confused alarms of struggle and flight,
Where ignorant armies clash by night.

MATTHEW ARNOLD

WHEN, IN DISGRACE WITH FORTUNE AND MEN'S EYES

WHEN, in disgrace with fortune and men's eyes,
I all alone beweep my outcast state
And trouble deaf heaven with my bootless cries
And look upon myself and curse my fate,
Wishing me like to one more rich in hope,
Featured like him, like him with friends possessed,
Desiring this man's art and that man's scope,
With what I most enjoy contented least;
Yet in these thoughts myself almost despising,
Haply I think on thee, and then my state,
Like to the lark at break of day arising
From sullen earth, sings hymns at heaven's gate;
For thy sweet love remembered such wealth brings
That then I scorn to change my state with kings.

WILLIAM SHAKESPEARE

138

UPON PHYLLIS WALKING IN A MORNING BEFORE SUN-RISING

THE sluggish morn as yet undrest,
My Phyllis brake from out her east;
As if she'd made a match to run
With Venus, usher to the sun.
The trees like yeomen of her guard,
Serving more for pomp than ward,
Rank't on each side with loyal duty,
Weave branches to enclose her beauty.
The plants whose luxury was lopt,
Or age with crutches underpropt;
Whose wooden carcasses are grown
To be but coffins of their own;
Revive, and at her general dole
Each receives his ancient soul;
The winged choristers began
To chirp their matins: and the fan
Of whistling winds like organs play'd,
Until their voluntaries made
The wakened earth in odours rise
To be her morning sacrifice.
The flowers, call'd out of their beds,
Start, and raise up their drowsy heads;
And he that for their colour seeks,
May find it vaulting in her cheeks,
Where roses mix: no civil war
Between her York and Lancaster.
The marigold whose courtier's face
Echoes the sun, and doth unlace
Her at his rise, at his full stop
Packs and shuts up her gaudy shop,

Mistakes her cue, and doth display:
Thus Phyllis antedates the day.
   These miracles had cramp't the sun,
Who thinking that his kingdom's won,
Powders with light his frizzled locks,
To see what saint his lustre mocks.
The trembling leaves through which he play'd,
Dappling the walk with light and shade,
Like lattice-windows, give the spy
Room but to peep with half an eye;
Lest her full orb his sight should dim,
And bid us all good-night in him,
Till she would spend a gentle ray
To force us a new fashion'd day.
But what religious palsy's this
Which makes the boughs divest their bliss?
And that they may her footsteps straw,
Drop their leaves with shivering awe?
Phyllis perceives, and (lest her stay
Should wed October unto May;
And as her beauty caus'd a Spring,
Devotion might an Autumn bring)
Withdrew her beams, yet made no night,
But left the sun her curate-light.

JOHN CLEVELAND

WATCHING YOU WALK

WATCHING you walk slowly across a stage,
Suddenly I am become aware of all the past;
Of all the tragic maids and queens of every age,
Of Joan, whose love the flames could not arrest.

Of those to whom always love was the first duty,
Who saw behind the crooked world the ugly and weak,
Whose kindliness was no gesture; no condescending pity
Could rule their actions; those whom Time broke,

But whom he could not totally destroy.
Hearing the truth you give to these dead words,
Whose writer feared the life they might enjoy,
I can recall the mating orchestra of birds

Behind your voice, as lying by the lake,
You read me Owen, and I, too deeply moved,
Watched the swans for a moment before I spoke
The trivialities, unable to tell you how I loved.

Watching your fingers curl about a painted death,
I am suddenly glad that it is April, that you are queen
Of all the sordid marches of my bruised heart,
That, loving you, the poplars never seemed so green.

Glad of my lonely walk beside the sunken river,
Thinking of you while seeing the tufts of ash,
The chestnut candles and unreal magnolia's wax flower;
Glad that, in loving you, the whole world lives afresh.

RUTHVEN TODD

141

FIAMETTA

FIAMETTA walks under the quincebuds
  In a gown the color of flowers;
Her small breasts shine through the silken stuff
  Like raindrops after showers.
The green hem of her dress is silk, but duller
Than her eye's green color.

Her shadow restores the grass's green—
  Where the sun had gilded it;
The air has given her copper hair
  The sanguine that was requisite.
Whatever her flaws, my lady
Has no fault in her young body.

She leans with her long slender arms
  To pull down morning upon her—
Fragrance of quince, white light and falling cloud.
  The day shall have lacked due honor
Until I shall have rightly praised
Her standing thus with slight arms upraised.

JOHN PEALE BISHOP

TWO LOOK AT TWO

LOVE and forgetting might have carried them
A little further up the mountain side
With night so near, but not much further up.
They must have halted soon in any case
142

With thoughts of the path back, how rough it was
With rock and washout, and unsafe in darkness;
When they were halted by a tumbled wall
With barbed-wire binding. They stood facing **this,**
Spending what onward impulse they still had
In one last look the way they must not go,
On up the failing path, where, if a stone
Or earthslide moved at night, it moved itself;
No footstep moved it. "This is all," they sighed,
"Good-night to woods." But not so; there was more.
A doe from round a spruce stood looking at them
Across the wall, as near the wall as they.
She saw them in their field, they her in hers.
The difficulty of seeing what stood still,
Like some up-ended boulder split in two,
Was in her clouded eyes: they saw no fear there.
She seemed to think that two thus they were safe.
Then, as if they were something that, though strange,
She could not trouble her mind with too long,
She sighed and passed unscared along the wall.
"*This,* then, is all. What more is there to ask?"
But no, not yet. A snort to bid them wait.
A buck from round the spruce stood looking at them
Across the wall as near the wall as they.
This was an antlered buck of lusty nostril,
Not the same doe come back into her place.
He viewed them quizzically with jerks of head,
As if to ask, "Why don't you make some motion?
Or give some sign of life? Because you can't.
I doubt if you're as living as you look."
Thus till he had them almost feeling dared
To stretch a proffering hand—and a spell-breaking.
Then he too passed unscared along the wall.
Two had seen two, whichever side you spoke from.
"This *must* be all." It was all. Still they stood,

143

A great wave from it going over them,
As if the earth in one unlooked-for favor
Had made them certain earth returned their love.

ROBERT FROST

THE FLOWER

THE sun was gold over the water and the voices golden,
  Air was all summer in one hour, and none
Among us at the foot of the old wall with vine laden
  But loved each other and would not be gone,

Nor let this life in the hot sun cool to evening,
  Or care, or cross our shadows, or speak much.
Fragrant and still and slow, the garden murmured
  And we flowered with it like gold blossom to touch

That no one would gather all and carry away, silence
  In no motion whirling us all together like light,

And the light going, and the sweetness more, and only
    You there that would be shining in the night,

You only that always of that garden would be summer,
    And day was nothing, the names of faces, the hour
Nothing that was not you, not the water or voices,
    Nor the air the sun warmed to open the flower.

I crossed the garden, going a little away from them all,
    To take for you, to take then the moment, take you
And the green gold summering garden forever and ever
    And the water, and shadows where sun came through.

But bringing it back, great in my hands and heavy
    With itself and time, thinking no one saw under the
      tree
This flower for you, I looked up, and there in sunlight
    You were running, running, with a flower for me.

JOHN HOLMES

VERSES COPIED FROM THE WINDOW OF AN OBSCURE LODGING-HOUSE

STRANGER! whoe'er thou art, whose restless mind,
Like me within these walls is cribbed, confined;
Learn how each want that heaves our mutual sigh
A woman's soft solicitudes supply.
From her white breast retreat all rude alarms,
Or fly the magic circle of her arms;

145

While souls exchanged alternate grace acquire,
And passions catch from passion's glorious fire:
What though to deck this roof no arts combine,
Such forms as rival every fair but mine;
No nodding plumes, our humble couch above,
Proclaim each triumph of unbounded love;
No silver lamp with sculptured Cupids gay,
O'er yielding beauty pours its midnight ray;
Yet Fanny's charms could Time's slow flight beguile,
Soothe every care, and make each dungeon smile:
In her, what kings, what saints have wished, is given.
Her heart is empire, and her love is heaven.

ANONYMOUS

VII

Love Will Find Out the Way:

Courtship

LOVE WILL FIND OUT THE WAY

OVER the mountains
    And over the waves,
Under the fountains
    And under the graves;
Under floods that are deepest,
    Which Neptune obey,
Over rocks that are steepest,
    Love will find out the way.

When there is no place
    For the glow-worm to lie,
When there is no space
    For receipt of a fly;
When the midge dares not venture
    Lest herself fast she lay,
If Love come, he will enter
    And will find out the way.

You may esteem him
    A child for his might;
Or you may deem him
    A coward for his flight;
But if she whom Love doth honour
    Be conceal'd from the day—
Set a thousand guards upon her,
    Love will find out the way.

Some think to lose him
    By having him confined;
And some do suppose him,
    Poor heart! to be blind;

149

But if ne'er so close ye wall him,
  Do the best that ye may,
Blind Love, if so ye call him,
  He will find out his way.

You may train the eagle
  To stoop to your fist;
Or you may inveigle
  The Phœnix of the east;
The lioness, you may move her
  To give over her prey;
But you'll ne'er stop a lover—
  He will find out the way.

If the earth it should part him,
  He would gallop it o'er;
If the seas should o'erthwart him,
  He would swim to the shore;
Should his Love become a swallow,
  Through the air to stray,
Love will lend wings to follow,
  And will find out the way.

There is no striving
  To cross his intent;
There is no contriving
  His plots to prevent;
But if once the message greet him
  That his True Love doth stay,
If Death should come and meet him,
  Love will find out the way!

ANONYMOUS

LAVENDER'S BLUE

LAVENDER'S blue, dilly, dilly, lavender's green,
   When I'm a King, dilly, dilly, you shall be Queen;
Who told you so, dilly, dilly, who told you so?
   'Twas mine own heart, dilly, dilly, that told me so.

Call up your men, dilly, dilly, set them to work,
   Some with a rake, dilly, dilly, some with a fork;
Some to make hay, dilly, dilly, some to thresh corn,
   While you and I, dilly, dilly, keep ourselves warm.

If it should hap, dilly, dilly, if it should chance,
   We shall be gay, dilly, dilly, we shall both dance;
Lavender's blue, dilly, dilly, lavender's green,
   When I'm a King, dilly, dilly, you shall be Queen.

ANONYMOUS

COMIN' THRO' THE RYE

GIN a body meet a body
   Comin' thro' the rye,
Gin a body kiss a body,
   Need a body cry?
Every lassie has her laddie—
   Ne'er a ane hae I;
Yet a' the lads they smile at me
   When comin' thro' the rye.
Amang the train there is a swain
   I dearly lo'e mysel';
But whaur his hame, or what his name,
   I dinna care to tell.

151

Gin a body meet a body
Comin' frae the town,
Gin a body greet a body,
Need a body frown?
Every lassie has her laddie—
Ne'er a ane hae I;
Yet a' the lads they smile at me
When comin' thro' the rye.
Amang the train there is a swain
I dearly lo'e mysel';
But whaur his hame, or what his name,
I dinna care to tell.

ROBERT BURNS

THE LOOK

STREPHON kissed me in the spring,
Robin in the fall,
But Colin only looked at me
And never kissed at all.

Strephon's kiss was lost in jest,
Robin's lost in play,
But the kiss in Colin's eyes
Haunts me night and day.

SARA TEASDALE

TO CHLOE, WHO WISHED HERSELF YOUNG ENOUGH FOR ME

CHLOE, why wish you that your years
　　Would backward run, till they meet mine,
That perfect likeness which endears
　　Things unto things might us combine?
Our ages so in date agree
That twins do differ more than we.

There are two births; the one when light
　　First strikes the new awakened sense;
The other when two souls unite;
　　And we must count our life from thence.
When you loved me and I loved you,
The both of us were born anew.

Love then to us did new souls give,
　　And in those souls did plant new powers;
Since when another life we live,
　　The breath we breathe is his, not ours;
Love makes those young whom age doth chill,
And whom he finds young, keeps young still.

Love, like that angel that shall call
　　Our bodies from the silent grave,
Unto one age doth raise us all,
　　None too much, none too little have.
Nay, that the difference may be none,
He makes two not alike, but one.

WILLIAM CARTWRIGHT

153

RECUERDO

WE were very tired, we were very merry—
We had gone back and forth all night on the ferry.
It was bare and bright, and smelled like a stable—
But we looked into a fire, we leaned across a table,
We lay on a hill-top underneath the moon;
And the whistles kept blowing, and the dawn came soon.

We were very tired, we were very merry—
We had gone back and forth all night on the ferry;
And you ate an apple, and I ate a pear,
From a dozen of each we had bought somewhere;
And the sky went wan, and the wind came cold,
And the sun rose dripping, a bucketful of gold.

We were very tired, we were very merry—
We had gone back and forth all night on the ferry.
We hailed, "Good-morrow, mother!" to a shawl-covered
    head,
And bought a morning paper, which neither of us read;
And she wept, "God bless you!" for the apples and pears,
And we gave her all our money but our subway fares.

EDNA ST. VINCENT MILLAY

LOVE BADE ME WELCOME

LOVE bade me welcome; yet my soul drew back,
    Guilty of dust and sin.
But quick-eyed Love, observing me grow slack
    From my first entrance in,

154

Drew nearer to me, sweetly questioning
      If I lacked any thing.

"A guest," I answered, "worthy to be here":
      Love said, "You shall be he."
"I the unkind, ungrateful? Ah my dear!
      I cannot look on thee."
Love took my hand, and smiling did reply,
      "Who made the eyes but I?"

"Truth, Lord, but I have marred them: let my shame
      Go where it doth deserve."
"And know you not," says Love, "who bore the blame?"
      "My dear, than I will serve."
"You must sit down," says Love, "and taste my meat."
      So I did sit and eat.

GEORGE HERBERT

THE DANCE

> ROBIN is a lovely lad,
> No lass a smoother ever had.
> Tommy hath a look as bright
> As is the rosy morning light.
> Tib is dark and brown of hue,
> But like her color firm and true.
> Jinny hath a lip to kiss
> Wherein a spring of nectar is.
> Simkin well his mirth can place
> And words to win a woman's grace.
> Sib is all in all to me,
> There is no queen of love but she.
> Let us in a lover's round
> Circle all this happy ground.

155

Softly, softly trip and go,
The light foot fairies jet it so.
Forward then and back again,
Here and there and everywhere,
Winding to and winding fro,
Skipping high and louting low.
And like lovers hand in hand
March around and make a stand.

GEORGE MASON AND JOHN EARSDEN

NO, NO, POOR SUFFERING HEART

No, no, poor suffering heart, no change endeavor,
Choose to sustain the smart, rather than leave her;
My ravished eyes behold such charms about her,
I can die with her, but not live without her.
One tender sigh of hers to see me languish,
Will more than pay the price of my past anguish:
Beware, O cruel fair, how you smile on me,
'Twas a kind look of yours that has undone me.

Love has in store for me one happy minute,
And she will end my pain who did begin it;
Then no day void of bliss, or pleasure leaving,
Ages shall die away without perceiving:
Cupid shall guard the door the more to please us,
And keep out time and death, when they would seize us:
Time and delight shall depart, and say in flying,
Love has found out a way to live by dying.

JOHN DRYDEN

SONG

My dear mistress has a heart
   Soft as those kind looks she gave me,
When with love's resistless art,
   And her eyes, she did enslave me.
But her constancy's so weak,
   She's so wild and apt to wander,
That my jealous heart would break
   Should we live one day asunder.

Melting joys about her move,
   Killing pleasures, wounding blisses;
She can dress her eyes in love,
   And her lips can arm with kisses.
Angels listen when she speaks;
   She's my delight, all mankind's wonder;
But my jealous heart would break
   Should we live one day asunder.

                    JOHN WILMOT, *Earl of Rochester*

THE ENCHANTMENT

I DID but look and love awhile,
   'Twas but for one half-hour;
Then to resist I had no will,
   And now I have no power.

To sigh and wish is all my ease;
   Sighs which do heat impart
Enough to melt the coldest ice
   Yet cannot warm your heart.

157

O would your pity give my heart
   One corner of your breast,
'Twould learn of yours the winning art
   And quickly steal the rest.

THOMAS OTWAY

I WILL NOT LET THEE GO

I WILL not let thee go.
Ends all our month-long love in this?
   Can it be summed up so,
   Quit in a single kiss?
I will not let thee go.

I will not let thee go.
If thy words' breath could scare thy deeds,
   As the soft south can blow
   And toss the feathered seeds,
Then might I let thee go.

I will not let thee go.
Had not the great sun seen, I might;
   Or were he reckoned slow
   To bring the false to light,
Then might I let thee go.

I will not let thee go.
The stars that crowd the summer skies
   Have watched us so below
   With all their million eyes,
I dare not let thee go.

I will not let thee go.
Have we not chid the changeful moon,

Now rising late, and now
Because she set too soon,
And shall I let thee go?

I will not let thee go.
Have not the young flowers been content,
Plucked ere their buds could blow,
To seal our sacrament?
I cannot let thee go.

I will not let thee go.
I hold thee by too many bands:
Thou sayest farewell, and lo!
I have thee by the hands,
And will not let thee go.

ROBERT BRIDGES

THAT WOMEN ARE BUT MEN'S SHADOWS

FOLLOW a shadow, it still flies you;
  Seem to fly, it will pursue;
So court a mistress, she denies you;
  Let her alone, she will court you.
Say, are not women truly then
  Styled but the shadows of us men?

At morn and even shades are longest;
  At noon they are or short or none;
So men at weakest, they are strongest,
  But grant us perfect, they're not known.
Say, are not women truly then
  Styled but the shadows of us men?

BEN JONSON

THE LOVERS

THEY looked up to the sky, whose floating glow
    Spread like a rosy ocean, vast and bright;
They gazed upon the glittering sea below,
    Whence the broad moon rose circling into sight;
They heard the wave's splash, and the wind so low.
    And saw each other's dark eyes darting light
Into each other—and, beholding this,
Their lips drew near, and clung into a kiss;

A long, long kiss, a kiss of youth, and love,
    And beauty, all concentrating like rays
Into one focus, kindled from above;
    Such kisses as belong to early days,
Where heart, and soul, and sense, in concert move,
    And the blood's lava, and the pulse a blaze,
Each kiss a heart-quake—for a kiss's strength,
I think, it must be reckoned by its length.

By length I mean duration; theirs endured
    Heaven knows how long—no doubt they never
        reckoned;
And if they had, they could not have secured
    The sum of their sensations to a second:
They had not spoken; but they felt allured,
    As if their souls and lips each other beckoned,
Which, being joined, like swarming bees they clung—
Their hearts the flowers from whence the honey sprung.

GEORGE GORDON, LORD BYRON

160

CLAIMING A SECOND KISS
BY DESERT

CHARIS, guess, and do not miss,
Since I drew a morning kiss
From your lips, and sucked an air
Thence, as sweet as you are fair,
What my Muse and I have done;
    Whether we have lost or won,
If by us the odds were laid,
That the bride, allowed a maid,
Looked not half so fresh and fair,
With the advantage of her hair,
And her jewels to the view
Of the assembly, as did you!
    Or that did you sit or walk,
You were more the eye and talk
Of the court, today, than all
Else that glistered in Whitehall;
So as those that had your sight
Wished the bride were changed tonight,
And did think such rites were due
To no other Grace but you!
    Or, if you did move tonight
In the dances, with what spite
Of your peers you were beheld,
That at every motion swelled
So to see a lady tread
As might all the Graces lead,
And was worthy, being so seen,
To be envied of the queen.
    Or if you would yet have stayed,
Whether any would upbraid
To himself his loss of time;

161

Or have charged his sight of crime,
To have left all sight for you.
Guess of these which is the true;
And if such a verse as this
May not claim another kiss.

BEN JONSON

LOVE ME LITTLE, LOVE
ME LONG

LOVE me little, love me long,
Is the burden of my song.
Love that is too hot and strong
    Burneth soon to waste.
Still, I would not have thee cold,
Not too backward, nor too bold;
Love that lasteth till 'tis old
    Fadeth not in haste.
        Love me little, love me long,
        Is the burden of my song.

If thou lovest me too much,
It will not prove as true as touch;
Love me little, more than such,
    For I fear the end.
I am with little well content,
And a little from thee sent
Is enough, with true intent

162

To be steadfast friend.
  Love me little, love me long, etc.

Say thou lov'st me while thou live;
I to thee my love will give,
Never dreaming to deceive
  Whiles that life endures.
Nay, and after death, in sooth,
I to thee will keep my truth,
As now, when in my May of youth;
  This my love assures.
    Love me little, love me long, etc.

Constant love is moderate ever,
And it will through life persever;
Give me that, with true endeavor
  I will it restore.
A suit of durance let it be
For all weathers—that for me,
For the land or for the sea,
  Lasting evermore.
    Love me little, love me long, etc.

Winter's cold, or summer's heat,
Autumn's tempests, on it beat,
It can never know defeat,
  Never can rebel.
Such the love that I would gain,
Such the love, I tell thee plain,
Thou must give, or woo in vain;
  So to thee, farewell!
    Love me little, love me long,
      Is the burden of my song.

ANONYMOUS

ESCAPE ME?—NEVER

Escape me?
Never—
Beloved!
While I am I, and you are you,
   So long as the world contains us both,
   Me the loving and you the loth,
While the one eludes, must the other pursue.
My life is a fault at last, I fear:
   It seems too much like a fate; indeed
   Though I do my best I shall scarce succeed.
But what if I fail of my purpose here?
It is but to keep the nerves at strain,
   To dry one's eyes and laugh at a fall,
And, baffled, get up and begin again—
   So the chase takes up one's life, that's all.
While, look but once from your farthest bound
   At me so deep in the dust and dark,
No sooner the old hope drops to ground
   Than a new one, straight to the self-same mark,
   I shape me—
   Ever
   Removed!

ROBERT BROWNING

WHISTLE AN' I'LL COME TO YE, MY LAD

O whistle an' I'll come to ye, my lad,
O whistle and I'll come to ye, my lad,
Tho' father an' mother an' a' should gae mad,
O whistle an' I'll come to ye, my lad.

164

But warily tent when ye come to court me,
And come nae unless the back-yett be a-jee;
Syne up the back-stile, and let naebody see,
And come as ye were na comin to me,
And come as ye were na comin to me.
   O whistle an' I'll come, etc.

At kirk, or at market, whene'er ye meet me,
Gang by me as tho' that ye car'd not a flie;
But steal me a blink o' your bonie black e'e,
Yet look as ye were na lookin to me,
Yet look as ye were na lookin to me.
   O whistle an' I'll come, etc.

Aye vow and protest that ye care na for me,
And whiles ye may lightly my beauty a-wee;
But court na anither, tho' jokin ye be,
For fear that she wile your fancy frae me,
For fear that she wile your fancy frae me.
   O whistle an' I'll come, etc.

         ROBERT BURNS

A DEVOUT LOVER

I HAVE a mistress, for perfections rare
In every eye, but in my thoughts most fair.
Like tapers on the altar shine her eyes;
Her breath is the perfume of sacrifice;
And whereso'er my fancy would begin,
Still her perfection lets religion in.
We sit and talk, and kiss away the hours
As chastely as the morning dews kiss flowers:
I touch her, like my beads, with devout care,
And come unto my courtship as my prayer.
        THOMAS RANDOLPH

165

CASTARA

LIKE the violet, which alone
　　Prospers in some happy shade,
My Castara lives unknown,
　　To no looser eye betrayed:
　　　　For she's to herself untrue
　　　　Who delights i' the public view

Such is her beauty as no arts
　　Have enriched with borrowed grace.
Her high birth no pride imparts,
　　For she blushes in her place.
　　　　Folly boasts a glorious blood;
　　　　She is noblest, being good.

Cautious, she knew never yet
　　What a wanton courtship meant;
Nor speaks loud to boast her wit,
　　In her silence, eloquent.
　　　　Of herself survey she takes,
　　　　But 'tween men no difference makes.

She obeys with speedy will
　　Her grave parents' wise commands;
And so innocent, that ill
　　She nor acts, nor understands.
　　　　Women's feet run still astray
　　　　If to ill they know the way.

She sails by that rock, the court,
　　Where oft virtue splits her mast;
And retiredness thinks the port
　　Where her fame may anchor cast.
　　　　Virtue safely cannot sit
　　　　Where vice is enthroned for wit.

She holds that day's pleasure best
  Where sin waits not on delight;
Without mask, or ball, or feast,
  Sweetly spends a winter's night.
        O'er that darkness whence is thrust
        Prayer and sleep, oft governs lust.

She her throne makes reason climb,
  While wild passions captive lie;
And, each article of time,
  Her pure thoughts to heaven fly;
        All her vows religious be,
        And she vows her love to me.

                                    WILLIAM HABINGTON

TAKE HOME THIS HEART

TAKE home this travelled heart. It has been lost.
It has been wandering in the world alone,
Inland and seaward, hill, and cape, and coast,
Seeking a home and altar of its own.

I looked at leaves; at clouds; at sunlit stone;
In fire at its imaginary view.
The weathervane said where the wind had gone.
The waves had much to say, and nothing new.

I rubbed the colors of the world away.
Nothing was left but form, and that was strange,
Not human, for I saw it would not die,
But last forever, and forever change.

                                                        167

I listened north and west for natural words,
But nothing spoke by day or sang by night,
Nothing, from leafy earth or heaven starred,
Like human wrath and wisdom and delight.

The streets are false and foreign where we go.
The hills mean nothing you and I can guess.
The new year wheels the colored seasons through,
Not to reward us, or to bruise, or bless,

But as antiphony to all our thought,
Inevitable and universal voice,
Whether we grieve or laugh, or love or not,
Or murder or beget, and thus rejoice.

I went toward sunlight, where the wisest go,
And saw such life contending with such death,
I cut the hateful paradox in two—
Then in the sudden cold I caught my breath,

And learned the truth. I seized the severed ends.
With fingers numb, I tied the precious knot.
Mortality lay certain in my hands,
The simple answer so profoundly sought.

Let all our thought be of each other now,
Gentle as time is not; and be so plain,
So patient in our love, that each will know
His fear of mortal loneliness is vain.

Take home my heart, and take it into yours,
And light the waiting fire, and close the doors,
And let me in the firelight touch your face,
And tell you love has led me to this place.

JOHN HOLMES

APPRENTICED

He sings:

COME out and hear the waters shoot, the owlet hoot, the
   owlet hoot;

Yon crescent moon, a golden boat, hangs dim behind
   the tree, O!

The dropping thorn makes white the grass, O sweetest
   lass, and sweetest lass;

Come out and smell the ricks of hay adown the croft
   with me, O!

She answers:

My granny nods before her wheel, and drops her reel,
   and drops her reel;

My father with his crony talks as gay as gay can be, O!

But all the milk is yet to skim, ere wax light dim, ere
   wax light dim;

How can I step adown the croft, my 'prentice lad, with
   thee, O?

He replies:

And must ye bide? yet waiting's long, and love is strong,
   and love is strong;

And O, had I but served the time that takes so long to
   flee, O!

And thou, my lass, by morning light wast all in white,
   wast all in white,

And parson stood within the rails, a-marrying me and
   thee, O!

JEAN INGELOW

TO HIS COY LOVE

I PRAY thee leave, love me no more,
  Call home the heart you gave me,
I but in vain that saint adore,
  That can, but will not save me.
These poor half kisses kill me quite;
  Was ever man thus served?
Amidst an ocean of delight
  For pleasure to be starved.

Show me no more those snowy breasts
  With azure riverets branchéd,
Where, whilst mine eyes with plenty feasts,
  Yet is my thirst not stanchéd.
O Tantalus, thy pains ne'er tell,
  By me thou are prevented,
'Tis nothing to be plagued in hell,
  But thus in heaven tormented.

Clip me no more in those dear arms,
  Nor thy life's comfort call me;
O, these are but too pow'rful charms,
  And do but more enthral me.
But see, how patient I am grown,
  In all this coil about thee;
Come, nice thing, let my heart alone,
  I cannot live without thee.

MICHAEL DRAYTON

VIII

Gather Ye Rosebuds:

Make Haste, Sweet Love

MAKE HASTE, SWEET LOVE

FRESH spring, the herald of love's mighty king,
In whose coat armour richly are display'd
All sorts of flowers the which on earth do spring
In goodly colours gloriously array'd.
Go to my love, where she is careless lay'd,
Yet in her winter's bower not well awake:
Tell her the joyous time will not be stay'd
Unless she do him by the forelock take.
Bid her therefore herself soon ready make,
To wait on love amongst his lovely crew:
Where every one that misseth then her make,
Shall be by him punish'd with penance due.
Make haste therefore, sweet love, whilst it is prime,
For none can call again the passèd time.

EDMUND SPENSER

SWEET-AND-TWENTY

O MISTRESS mine, where are you roaming?
O, stay and hear! your true love's coming,
    That can sing both high and low:
Trip no further, pretty sweeting;
Journeys end in lovers meeting,
    Every wise man's son doth know.

What is love? 'tis not hereafter;
Present mirth hath present laughter;
    What's to come is still unsure:
In delay there lies no plenty;
Then come kiss me, sweet-and-twenty!
    Youth's a stuff will not endure.

WILLIAM SHAKESPEARE

173

TO HIS COY MISTRESS

HAD we but world enough, and time,
This coyness, Lady, were no crime.
We would sit down, and think which way
To walk and pass our long love's day.
Thou by the Indian Ganges' side
Shouldst rubies find: I by the tide
Of Humber would complain. I would
Love you ten years before the Flood;
And you should, if you please, refuse
Till the conversion of the Jews.
My vegetable love should grow
Vaster than empires, and more slow:
An hundred years should go to praise
Thine eyes and on thy forehead gaze;
Two hundred to adore each breast,
But thirty thousand to the rest;
An age at least to every part,
And the last age should show your heart.
For, Lady, you deserve this state;
Nor would I love at lower rate.

But at my back I always hear
Time's wingèd chariot hurrying near;
And yonder all before us lie
Deserts of vast eternity
Thy beauty shall no more be found,
Nor, in thy marble vault, shall sound
My echoing song: then worms shall try
That long preserv'd virginity,
And your quaint honour turn to dust,
And into ashes all my lust.
The grave's a fine and private place,

But none I think do there embrace.
Now therefore, while the youthful hue
Sits on thy skin like morning dew,
And while thy willing soul transpires
At every pore with instant fires,
Now let us sport us while we may,
And now, like amorous birds of prey,
Rather at once our time devour
Than languish in his slow-chapt power.
Let us roll all our strength and all
Our sweetness up into one ball,
And tear our pleasures with rough strife
Thorough the iron gates of life.
Thus, though we cannot make our sun
Stand still, yet we will make him run.

ANDREW MARVELL

TO THE VIRGINS,
TO MAKE MUCH OF TIME

GATHER ye rosebuds while ye may,
    Old Time is still a-flying:
And this same flower that smiles to-day
    To-morrow will be dying.

The glorious lamp of heaven, the sun,
    The higher he's a-getting,
The sooner will his race be run,
    And nearer he's to setting.

That age is best which is the first,
    When youth and blood are warmer;

175

But being spent, the worse, and worst
    Times still succeed the former.

Then be not coy, but use your time,
    And while ye may, go marry:
For having lost but once your prime,
    You may for ever tarry.

ROBERT HERRICK

THE GARDEN OF LOVE

I WENT to the Garden of Love,
And saw what I never had seen:
A Chapel was built in the midst,
Where I used to play on the green.

And the gates of this chapel were shut,
And "Thou shalt not" writ over the door;
So I turned to the Garden of Love,
That so many sweet flowers bore;

And I saw it was fillèd with graves,
And tombstones where flowers should be;
And priests in black gowns were walking their rounds,
And binding with briars my joys and desires.

WILLIAM BLAKE

BLUE GIRLS

TWIRLING your blue skirts, travelling the sward
Under the towers of your seminary,
Go listen to your teachers old and contrary
Without believing a word.

Tie the white fillets then about your hair
And think no more of what will come to pass
Than bluebirds that go walking on the grass
And chattering on the air.

Practice your beauty, blue girls, before it fail;
And I will cry with my loud lips and publish
Beauty which all our power shall never establish,
It is so frail.

For I could tell you a story which is true;
I know a lady with a terrible tongue,
Blear eyes fallen from blue,
All her perfections tarnished—yet it is not long
Since she was lovelier than any of you.

JOHN CROWE RANSOM

BID ADIEU TO MAIDENHOOD

BID adieu, adieu, adieu,
  Bid adieu to girlish days,
Happy love is come to woo
  Thee and woo thy girlish ways—
The zone that doth become thee fair,
The snood upon thy yellow hair,

When thou has heard his name upon
    The bugles of the cherubim
Begin thou softly to unzone
    Thy girlish bosom unto him
And softly to undo the snood
That is the sign of maidenhood.

JAMES JOYCE

IT WAS A LOVER AND HIS LASS

IT was a lover and his lass,
    With a hey, and a ho, and a hey nonino,
That oe'r the green corn-field did pass
    In the spring time, the only pretty ring time,
When birds do sing, hey ding a ding, ding;
Sweet lovers love the spring.

Between the acres of the rye,
    With a hey, and a ho, and a hey nonino,
These pretty country folks would lie,
    In the spring time, the only pretty ring time,
When birds do sing, hey ding a ding, ding;
Sweet lovers love the spring.

This carol they began that hour,
    With a hey, and a ho, and a hey nonino,
How that a life was but a flower
    In the spring time, the only pretty ring time,
When birds do sing, hey ding a ding, ding;
Sweet lovers love the spring.

And therefore take the present time.
    With a hey, and a ho, and a hey nonino,
For love is crownèd with the prime

In the spring time, the only pretty ring time,
When birds do sing, hey ding a ding, ding;
Sweet lovers love the spring.

WILLIAM SHAKESPEARE

LOVE'S PHILOSOPHY

THE fountains mingle with the river
And the rivers with the ocean,
The winds of heaven mix for ever
With a sweet emotion;
Nothing in the world is single,
All things by a law divine
In one another's being mingle—
Why not I with thine?

See the mountains kiss high heaven,
And the waves clasp one another;
No sister-flower would be forgiven
If it disdain'd its brother:
And the sunlight clasps the earth,
And the moon beams kiss the sea—
What are all these kissings worth,
If thou kiss not me?

PERCY BYSSHE SHELLEY

TO DIANEME

GIVE me one kiss,
And no more;
If so be, this
Makes you poor;

To enrich you,
I'll restore
For that one, two
Thousand score.

ROBERT HERRICK

179

TO DIANEME, AGAIN

Sweet, be not proud of those two eyes,
Which, star-like, sparkle in their skies;
Nor be you proud that you can see
All hearts your captives, yours yet free;
Be you not proud of that rich hair,
Which wantons with the love-sick air;
Whenas that ruby which you wear,
Sunk from the tip of your soft ear,
Will last to be a precious stone
When all your world of beauty's gone.

Robert Herrick

COME INTO THE GARDEN, MAUD

Come into the garden, Maud,
   For the black bat, night, has flown,
Come into the garden, Maud,
   I am here at the gate alone;
And the woodbine spices are wafted abroad,
   And the musk of the rose is blown.

For a breeze of morning moves,
   And the planet of love is on high,
Beginning to faint in the light that she loves
   On a bed of daffodil sky,
To faint in the light of the sun she loves,
   To faint in his light, and to die.

All night have the roses heard
   The flute, violin, bassoon;

All night has the casement jessamine stirred
    To the dancers dancing in tune;
Till a silence fell with the waking bird,
    And a hush with the setting moon.

I said to the lily, "There is but one,
    With whom she has heart to be gay.
When will the dancers leave her alone?
    She is weary of dance and play."
Now half to the setting moon are gone,
    And half to the rising day;
Low on the sand and loud on the stone
    The last wheel echoes away.

I said to the rose, "The brief night goes
    In babble and revel and wine.
O young lord-lover, what sighs are those,
    For one that will never be thine?
But mine, but mine," so I sware to the rose,
    "Forever and ever, mine."

And the soul of the rose went into my blood,
    As the music clashed in the Hall;
And long by the garden lake I stood,
    For I heard your rivulet fall
From the lake to the meadow and on to the
      wood,
    Our wood, that is dearer than all;

From the meadow your walks have left so sweet
    That whenever a March-wind sighs
He sets the jewel-print of your feet
    In violets blue as your eyes,
To the woody hollows in which we meet
    And the valleys of Paradise.

The slender acacia would not shake
    One long milk-bloom on the tree;
The white lake-blossom fell into the lake
    As the pimpernel dozed on the lea;
But the rose was awake all night for your sake,
    Knowing your promise to me;
The lilies and roses were all awake,
    They sighed for the dawn and thee.

Queen rose of the rosebud garden of girls,
    Come hither, the dances are done,
In gloss of satin and glimmer of pearls,
    Queen lily and rose in one;
Shine out, little head, sunning over with curls,
    To the flowers, and be their sun.

There has fallen a splendid tear
    From the passion-flower at the gate.
She is coming, my dove, my dear;
    She is coming, my life, my fate.
The red rose cries, "She is near, she is near;"
    And the white rose weeps, "She is late;"
The larkspur listens, "I hear, I hear;"
    And the lily whispers, "I wait."

She is coming, my own, my sweet;
    Were it ever so airy a tread,
My heart would hear her and beat,
    Were it earth in an earthy bed;
My dust would hear her and beat,
    Had I lain for a century dead,
Would start and tremble under her feet,
    And blossom in purple and red.

ALFRED, LORD TENNYSON

TO A LADY, ASKING HIM HOW LONG HE WOULD LOVE HER

It is not, Celia, in our power
To say how long our love will last;
It may be we within this hour
May lose those joys we now do taste;
The blessed, that immortal be,
From change in love are only free.

Then, since we mortal lovers are,
Ask not how long our love will last;
But while it does, let us take care
Each minute be with pleasure passed:
Were it not madness to deny
To live because we're sure to die?

SIR GEORGE ETHEREGE

PLEASURES, BEAUTY, YOUTH ATTEND YE

Pleasures, beauty, youth attend ye,
  Whilst the Spring of nature lasteth;
Love and melting thoughts befriend ye,
  Use the time ere Winter hasteth.
    Active blood and free delight
    Place and privacy invite.
  Do, do! be kind as fair,
  Lose not opportunity for air.

183

She is cruel that denies it,
    Bounty best appears in granting,
Stealth of sport as soon supplies it,
    Whilst the dues of love are wanting.
        Here's the sweet exchange of bliss
        When each whisper proves a kiss.
In the game are felt no pains,
For in all the loser gains.

                                        JOHN FORD

ADVICE TO A GIRL

NEVER love unless you can
Bear with all the faults of man!
Men sometimes will jealous be,
Though but little cause they see,
And hang the head as discontent,
And speak what straight they will repent

Men that but one saint adore,
Make a show of love to more;
Beauty must be scorned in none,
Though but truly served in one:
For what is courtship but disguise?
True hearts may have dissembling eyes.

Men, when their affairs require,
Must a while themselves retire;
Sometimes hunt, and sometimes hawk,
And not ever sit and talk—
If these and such-like you can bear,
Then like, and love, and never fear!

                                        THOMAS CAMPION

A SONG

FAIR, sweet and young, receive a prize
Reserved for your victorious eyes:
From crowds, whom at your feet you see,
O pity, and distinguish me;
    As I from thousand beauties more
Distinguish you, and only you adore.

    Your face for conquest was designed,
Your every motion charms my mind;
Angels, when you your silence break,
Forget their hymns to hear you speak;
    But when at once they hear and view,
Are loath to mount, and long to stay with you.

    No graces can your form improve
But all are lost, unless you love;
While that sweet passion you disdain,
Your veil and beauty are in vain.
    In pity then prevent my fate,
For after dying all reprieve's too late.

JOHN DRYDEN

PERSUASIONS TO LOVE

For that lovely face will fail,
Beauty's sweet, but beauty's frail;
'Tis sooner past, 'tis sooner done
Than summer's rain or winter's sun,
Most fleeting when it is most dear;
'Tis gone, while we but say 'tis here.
These curious locks so aptly twined,
Whose every hair a soul doth bind,
Will change their auburn hue and grow
White and cold as winter's snow.

That eye which now is Cupid's nest
Will prove his grave, and all the rest
Will follow; in the cheek, chin, nose,
Nor lily shall be found nor rose;
And what will then become of all
Those whom now you servants call?
Like swallows, when your summer's done
They'll fly and seek some warmer sun.

For when the storms of time have moved
Waves on that cheek that was beloved,
When a fair lady's face is pined
And yellow spread where red once shined,
When beauty, youth and all sweets leave her,
Love may return, but lovers never.

Oh, love me then, and now begin it,
Let us not lose this present minute.

THOMAS CAREW

O DO NOT PRIZE THY BEAUTY

Do not, O do not prize thy beauty at too high a rate,
Love to be loved whilst thou art lovely, lest thou love
       too late;
    Frowns print wrinkles in thy brows,
      At which spiteful age doth smile;
    Women in their froward vows
      Glorying to beguile.

Wert thou the only world's admired thou canst love
      but one,
And many have before been loved, thou art not loved
      alone:
    Couldst thou speak with heavenly grace,
      Sappho might with thee compare;
    Blush the roses in thy face,
      Rosamond was as fair.

Pride is the canker that consumeth beauty in her prime,
They that delight in long debating feel the curse of time:
    All things with the time do change,
      That will not the time obey;
    Some even to themselves seem strange
      Thorough their own delay.

ANONYMOUS

LOVE AND LIFE

ALL my past life is mine no more,
   The flying hours are gone;
Like transitory dreams given o'er,
Whose images are kept in store
   By memory alone.

The time that is to come is not;
   How can it then be mine?
The present moment's all my lot,
And that as fast as it is got,
   Phyllis, is only thine.

Then talk not of inconstancy,
   False hearts and broken vows;
If I by miracle can be
This live-long minute true to thee,
   'Tis all that Heaven allows.

JOHN WILMOT, *Earl of Rochester*

IX

All the Pleasures Prove:

Erotic, Sensuous

Western wind, when will thou blow,
  The small rain down can rain?
Christ, if my love were in my arms
  And I in my bed again!

ANONYMOUS

THE PASSIONATE SHEPHERD
TO HIS LOVE

Come live with me and be my Love,
And we will all the pleasures prove
That hills and valleys, dales and fields,
Or woods or steepy mountain yields.

And we will sit upon the rocks,
And see the shepherds feed their flocks
By shallow rivers, to whose falls
Melodious birds sing madrigals.

And I will make thee beds of roses
And a thousand fragrant posies;
A cap of flowers, and a kirtle
Embroidered all with leaves of myrtle.

A gown made of the finest wool
Which from our pretty lambs we pull;
Fair-lined slippers for the cold,
With buckles of the purest gold.

A belt of straw and ivy-buds
With coral clasps and amber studs;
And if these pleasures may thee move,
Come live with me and be my Love.

Christopher Marlowe

THE NYMPH'S REPLY TO THE SHEPHERD

If all the world and love were young,
And truth in every shepherd's tongue,
These pretty pleasures might me move,
To live with thee and be thy love.

Time drives the flocks from field to fold,
When rivers rage, and rocks grow cold;
And Philomel becometh dumb;
The rest complain of cares to come.

The flowers do fade, and wanton fields
To wayward winter reckoning yields;
A honey tongue, a heart of gall,
Is fancy's spring, but sorrow's fall.

Thy gowns, thy shoes, thy bed of roses,
Thy cap, thy kirtle, and thy posies,
Soon break, soon wither, soon forgotten;
In folly ripe, in reason rotten.

Thy belt of straw and ivy buds,
Thy coral clasps and amber studs,
All these in me no means can move,
To come to thee and be thy love.

But could youth last, and love still breed,
Had joys no date, nor age no need,
Then these delights my mind might move
To live with thee and be thy love.

SIR WALTER RALEIGH

THE BAIT

COME live with me, and be my love,
And we will some new pleasures prove
Of golden sands, and crystal brooks,
With silken lines, and silver hooks.

There will the river whispering run
Warm'd by thine eyes, more than the Sun.
And there the enamor'd fish will stay,
Begging themselves they may betray.

When thou wilt swim in that live bath,
Each fish, which every channel hath,
Will amorously to thee swim,
Gladder to catch thee, than thou him.

If thou, to be so seen, be loath,
By Sun, or Moon, thou darknest both,
And if my self have leave to see,
I need not their light, having thee.

Let others freeze with angling reeds,
And cut their legs, with shells and weeds,
Or treacherously poor fish beset,
With strangling snare, or windowy net:

Let coarse bold hands, from slimy nest
The bedded fish in banks out-wrest,
Or curious traitors, sleevesilk flies
Bewitch poor fishes' wandering eyes.

For thee, thou needst no such deceit,
For thou thy self art thine own bait;
That fish, that is not catch'd thereby,
Alas, is wiser far than I.

JOHN DONNE

TO PHYLLIS, TO LOVE AND LIVE WITH HIM

LIVE, live with me, and thou shalt see
The pleasures I'll prepare for thee;
What sweets the country can afford
Shall bless thy bed and bless thy board.
The soft, sweet moss shall be thy bed
With crawling woodbine over-spread;
By which the silver-shedding streams
Shall gently melt thee into dreams.
Thy clothing, next, shall be a gown
Made of the fleece's purest down.
The tongues of kids shall be thy meat,
Their milk thy drink; and thou shalt eat
The paste of filberts for thy bread
With cream of cowslips butteréd;
Thy feasting-tables shall be hills
With daisies spread and daffodils,
Where thou shalt sit, and red-breast by,
For meat, shall give thee melody.
I'll give thee chains and carcanets
Of primroses and violets.
A bag and bottle thou shalt have,
That richly wrought, and this as brave;
So that as either shall express
The wearer's no mean shepherdess.
At shearing-times, and yearly wakes,
When Themilis his pastime makes,
There thou shalt be; and be the wit,
Nay, more, the feast, and grace of it.
On holidays, when virgins meet
To dance the heyes with nimble feet,
Thou shalt come forth, and then appear

The queen of roses for that year;
And having danced, 'bove all the best,
Carry the garland from the rest.
In wicker baskets maids shall bring
To thee, my dearest shepherdling,
The blushing apple, bashful pear,
The shame-faced plum, all simpering there.
Walk in the groves, and thou shalt find
The name of Phyllis in the rind
Of every straight and smooth-skin tree;
Where kissing that, I'll twice kiss thee.
To thee a sheep-hook I will send,
Be-pranked with ribands to this end,
This, this alluring hook might be
Less for to catch a sheep than me.
Thou shalt have possets, wassails fine,
Not made of ale, but spicéd wine,
To make thy maids and self free mirth,
All sitting near the glittering hearth.
Thou shalt have ribands, roses, rings,
Gloves, garters, stockings, shoes and strings
Of winning colours, that shall move
Others to lust, but me to love.
These, nay, and more, thine own shall be
If thou wilt love, and live with me.

ROBERT HERRICK

LIGHTNING

I FELT the lurch and halt of her heart
   Next my breast, where my own heart was beating;
And I laughed to feel it plunge and bound,
And strange in my blood-swept ears was the sound

195

Of the words I kept repeating,
Repeating with tightened arms, and the hot blood's
    blind-fold art.

Her breath flew warm against my neck,
    Warm as a flame in the close night air;
And the sense of her clinging flesh was sweet
Where her arms and my neck's blood-surge could meet.
    Holding her thus, did I care
That the black night hid her from me, blotted out every
    speck?

I leaned me forward to find her lips,
    And claim her utterly in a kiss,
When the lightning flew across her face,
And I saw her for the flaring space
    Of a second, afraid of the clips
Of my arms, inert with dread, wilted in fear of my kiss.

A moment, like a wavering spark,
    Her face lay there before my breast,
Pale love lost in a snow of fear,
And guarded by a glittering tear,
    And lips apart with dumb cries;
A moment, and she was taken again in the merciful dark.

I heard the thunder, and felt the rain,
    And my arms fell loose, and I was dumb.
Almost I hated her, she was so good,
Hated myself, and the place, and my blood,
    Which burned with rage, as I bade her come
Home, away home, ere the lightning floated forth again.

D. H. LAWRENCE

DAYBREAK

At dawn she lay with her profile at that angle
Which, sleeping, seems the stone face of an angel;
Her hair a harp the hand of a breeze follows
To play, against the white cloud of the pillows.
Then in flush of rose she woke, and her eyes were open
Swimming with blue through the rose of dawn.
From her dew of lips, the drop of one word
Fell, from a dawn of fountains, when she murmured
"Darling" upon my heart the song of the first bird.
"My dream glides in my dream" she said, "come true.
I waken from you to my dream of you."
O then my waking dream dared assume
The audacity of her sleep. Our dreams
Flowed into each other's arms, like dreams.

STEPHEN SPENDER

WHERE BE YOU GOING, YOU DEVON MAID

Where be you going, you Devon maid?
  And what have ye there in the basket?
Ye tight little fairy, just fresh from the dairy,
  Will ye give me some cream if I ask it?

I love your hills and I love your dales,
  And I love your flocks a-bleating;
But oh, on the heather to lie together,
  With both our hearts a-beating!

197

I'll put your basket all safe in a nook;
  Your shawl I'll hang on a willow;
And we will sigh in the daisy's eye,
  And kiss on a grass-green pillow.

JOHN KEATS

VIXI PUELLIS NUPER IDONEUS...

THEY flee from me that sometime did me seek,
  With naked foot stalking within my chamber:
Once have I see them gentle, tame, and meek,
  That now are wild, and do not once remember
  That sometime they have put themselves in danger
To take bread at my hand; and now they range,
Busily seeking in continual change.

Thanked be fortune, it hath been otherwise
  Twenty times better; but once especial—
In thin array: after a pleasant guise,
  When her loose gown did from her shoulders fall,
  And she me caught in her arms long and small,
And therewithal so sweetly did me kiss,
And softly said, 'Dear heart, how like you this?'

It was no dream; for I lay broad awaking:
  But all is turn'd now, through my gentleness,
Into a bitter fashion of forsaking;
  And I have leave to go of her goodness;
  And she also to use new-fangleness.
But since that I unkindly so am servèd,
'How like you this?'—what hath she now deservèd?

SIR THOMAS WYATT

THE EXPENSE OF SPIRIT IN A WASTE OF SHAME

THE expense of spirit in a waste of shame
Is lust in action; and till action, lust
Is perjured, murderous, bloody, full of blame,
Savage, extreme, rude, cruel, not to trust,
Enjoyed no sooner but despisèd straight;
Past reason hunted, and no sooner had
Past reason hated, as a swallowed bait
On purpose laid to make the taker mad;
Mad in pursuit and in possession so;
Had, having, and in quest to have, extreme;
A bliss in proof, and proved, a very woe;
Before, a joy proposed; behind, a dream.
All this the world well knows; yet none knows well
To shun the heaven that leads men to this hell.

WILLIAM SHAKESPEARE

AND LOVE HUNG STILL

AND love hung still as crystal over the bed
    And filled the corners of the enormous room;
The boom of dawn that left her sleeping, showing
    The flowers mirrored in the mahogany table.

O my love, if only I were able
    To protract this hour of quiet after passion,
Not ration happiness but keep this door for ever
    Closed on the world, its own world closed within it.

But dawn's waves trouble with the bubbling minute,
  The names of books come clear upon their shelves,
The reason delves for duty and you will wake
  With a start and go on living on your own.

The first train passes and the windows groan,
  Voices will hector and your voice become
A drum in tune with theirs, which all last night
  Like sap that fingered through a hungry tree
Asserted our one night's identity.

LOUIS MACNEICE

WHAT IS YOUR SUBSTANCE?

WHAT is your substance, whereof are you made,
That millions of strange shadows on you tend?
Since every one hath, every one, one shade,
And you, but one, can every shadow lend.
Describe Adonis, and the counterfeit
Is poorly imitated after you;
On Helen's cheek all art of beauty set,
And you in Grecian tires are painted new:

Speak of the spring and plenty of the year,
The one doth shadow of your beauty show,
The other as your bounty doth appear;
And you in every blessèd shape we know.
In all external grace you have some part,
But you like none, none you, for constant heart.

WILLIAM SHAKESPEARE

AN IMMORALITY

SING we for love and idleness,
Naught else is worth the having.

Though I have been in many a land,
There is naught else in living.

And I would rather have my sweet,
Though rose-leaves die of grieving,

Than do high deeds in Hungary
To pass all men's believing.

EZRA POUND

MY LOVE

MY love
thy hair is one kingdom
   the king whereof is darkness
thy forehead is flight of flowers

thy head is a quick forest
   filled with sleeping birds
thy breasts are swarms of white bees
   upon the bough of thy body
thy body to me is April
in whose armpits is the approach of spring

thy thighs are white horses yoked to a chariot of kings
they are the striking of a good minstrel
between them always is a pleasant song

201

my love
thy head is a casket
  of the cool jewel of thy mind
the hair of thy head is one warrior
  innocent of defeat
thy hair upon thy shoulders is an army
  with victory and with trumpets

thy legs are the trees of dreaming
whose fruit is the very eatage of forgetfulness

thy lips are satraps in scarlet
  in whose kiss is the combinings of kings
thy wrists
are holy
  which are the keepers of the keys of thy blood
thy feet upon thy ankles are flowers in vases of silver

in thy beauty is the dilemma of flutes

    thy eyes are the betrayal
of bells comprehended through incense

E. E. CUMMINGS

THE LUMBERYARD

WE watched our love burn with the lumberyard,
Bats in their wheeling showed our crazed sense,
We stood in fields where weeds with chiggers scrambled,
And stood the heat flush in our face, immense.

Softly the crowd acclaimed the devastation,
And we, we smiled to see the embers twist,
Tottering towers and poles with flashing wires.
We shifted feet when shifting structures kissed.

Up in the sky the stars were red sparks shuttling,
Planes with a scouter's appetite hung by.
And at our backs the Negro huts were lit
With yellow mist, a ghostly gayety.

Sound above all: the cracking and the crocked,
As bones that, whetted by the warmer flames,
Edged into death, until the crimson glow
Vanquished the knotted amber boards, the names.

All banished, all decided, all cast in;
Far back beyond, the trees made silver white
By steaming flames, rose as cold piles of cloud
To cool this mirror of the blazing night.

And we beheld, we watched, as drunk as all,
And gladdened when the bursting peaked and sprung,
Rejoiced to see the threat of fire win,
And sang to see the worthy timbers wrung.

We watched our love burn with the lumberyard,
Magnificent the sight, the sin, the shame,
The vice profusely lavished; wheeled the bats
Silent as we, but crazed, crazed as the flame.

RUTH HERSCHBERGER

203

THE SYRIAN LOVER IN EXILE REMEMBERS THEE, LIGHT OF MY LAND

Rose and amber was the sunset on the river,
Red-rose the hills about Bingariz.
High upon their brows, the black tree-branches
Spread wide across the turquoise sky.
I saw the parrots fly—
A cloud of rising green from the long green grasses,
A mist of gold and green winging fast
Into the gray shadow-silence of the tamarisks.
Pearl-white and wild was the flood below the ford.
I ran down the long hot road to thy door;
Thy door shone—a white flower in the dusk lingering to
  close.
I cast my cloak and climbed to thee,
To thee, Makhir Subatu!

.   .   .   .

Naked she stood and glistening like the stars over her—
Her hair trailed about her like clouds about the moon—
Naked as the soul seeking love,
As the soul that waits for death.
White with benediction, pendulous, unfolding from the
  dark
As the crystal sky of morning, she waited,
And leaned her light above the earth of my desire.
Like a world that spins from the hand of Infinity,
Up from the night I leaped—
To thee, Makhir Subatu!

.   .   .   .

Pearl-bright and wild, a flood without a ford,
The River of Love flowed on.
Her eyes were gleaming sails in a storm,
204

Dipping, swooning, beckoning.
The dawn came and trampled over her;
Gay-arched and wide, the sanctuary of light descended.
It was the altar where I lay;
And I lifted my face at last, praying.
I saw the first glow fall about her,
Like the marble pillars coming forth from the shadow.
I raised my hands, thanking the gods
That in love I had grown so tall
I could touch the two lamps in heaven,
The sun and moon hanging in the low heaven beneath
     her face.
How great through love had I grown
To breathe my flame into the two lamps of heaven!

O eyes of the eagle and the dove,
Eyes red-starred and white-starred,
Eyes that have too much seen, too much confessed,
Close, close, beneath my kisses!
Tell me no more, demand me no more—it is day.
I see the gold-green rain of parrot-wings
Sparkling athwart the gray and rose-gold morning.
I go from thy closed door down the long lone road
To the ricefields beyond the river,
Beyond the river that has a ford.

.   .   .   .

I came to thee with hope, with desire. I have them no
     longer.
Sleep, sleep; I am locked in thee.

.   .   .   .

Thus the exile lover remembers thee, Makhir Subatu!

AJAN SYRIAN

THE MILLER'S DAUGHTER

It is the miller's daughter,
　　And she is grown so dear, so dear,
That I would be the jewel
　　That trembles at her ear:
For hid in ringlets day and night,
I'd touch her neck so warm and white.

And I would be the girdle
　　About her dainty, dainty waist,
And her heart would beat against me,
　　In sorrow and in rest:
And I should know if it beat right,
I'd clasp it round so close and tight.

And I would be the necklace,
　　And all day long to fall and rise
Upon her balmy bosom
　　With her laughter or her sighs:
And I would lie so light, so light,
I scarce should be unclasped at night.

　　　　　　　ALFRED, LORD TENNYSON

RUTH

She stood breast-high amid the corn,
Clasp'd by the golden light of morn,
Like the sweetheart of the sun,
Who many a glowing kiss had won.

On her cheek an autumn flush,
Deeply ripen'd;—such a blush

In the midst of brown was born,
Like red poppies grown with corn.

Round her eyes her tresses fell;
Which were blackest none could tell,
But long lashes veil'd a light
That had else been all too bright.

And her hat with shady brim,
Made her tressy forehead dim;—
Thus she stood amid the stooks,
Praising God with sweetest looks:—

Sure, I said, Heaven did not mean
Where I reap thou shouldst but glean;
Lay thy sheaf adown, and come,
Share my harvest and my home.

THOMAS HOOD

THE FIRE OF LOVE

THE fire of love in youthful blood,
Like what is kindled in brushwood,
        But for a moment burns;
Yet in that moment makes a mighty noise;
It crackles, and to vapor turns,
        And soon itself destroys.

But when crept into aged veins
It slowly burns, and then long remains,
        And with a silent heat,
Like fire in logs, it glows and warms 'em long;
And though the flame be not so great,
        Yet is the heat as strong.

CHARLES SACKVILLE, *Earl of Dorset*

THE NIGHT PIECE, TO JULIA

HER eyes the glow-worm lend thee,
The shooting stars attend thee;
    And the elves also,
    Whose little eyes glow
Like the sparks of fire, befriend thee.

No will-o'-th'-wisp mis-light thee,
Nor snake, or slow-worm bite thee;
    But on, on thy way
    Not making a stay,
Since ghost there's none to affright thee.

Let not the dark thee cumber;
What though the moon does slumber?
    The stars of the night
    Will lend thee their light,
Like tapers clear without number.

Then, Julia, let me woo thee,
Thus, thus to come unto me;
    And when I shall meet
    Thy silv'ry feet,
My soul I'll pour into thee.

ROBERT HERRICK

TO JUDITH ASLEEP

MY dear, darkened in sleep, turned from the moon
That riots on curtain-stir with every breeze
Leaping in moths of light across your back . . .
Far off, then soft and sudden as petals shower

Down from wired roses—silently, all at once—
You turn, abandoned and naked, all let down
In ferny streams of sleep and petaled thighs
Rippling into my flesh's buzzing garden.

Far and familiar your body's myth-map lights,
Traveled by moon and dapple. Sagas were curved
Like scimitars to your hips. The raiders' ships
All sailed to your one port. And watchfires burned
Your image on the hills. Sweetly you drown
Male centuries in your chiaroscuro tide
Of breast and breath. All all my memory's shores
You frighten perfectly, washed familiar and far.

Ritual wars have climbed your shadowed flank
Where bravos dreaming of fair women tore
Rock out of rock to have your cities down
In loot of hearths and trophies of desire.
And desert monks have fought your image back
In a hysteria of mad skeletons.
Bravo and monk (the heads and tails of love)
I stand, a spinning coin of wish and dread,

Counting our life, our chairs, our books and walls,
Our clock whose radium eye and insect voice
Owns all our light and shade, and your white shell
Spiraled in moonlight on the bed's white beach;
Thinking, I might press you to my ear
And all your coils fall out in sounds of surf
Washing away our chairs, our books and walls,
Our bed and wish, our ticking light and dark.

Child, child, and making legend of my wish
Fastened alive into your naked sprawl—
Stir once to stop my fear and miser's panic

That time shall have you last and legendry
Undress to old bones from its moon brocade.
Yet sleep and keep our prime of time alive
Before that death of legend. My dear of all

Saga and century, sleep in familiar-far.
Time still must tick *this is, I am, we are.*

JOHN CIARDI

A STOLEN KISS

Now gentle sleep hath closèd up those eyes
Which, waking, kept my boldest thoughts in awe;
And free access unto that sweet lip lies,
From whence I long the rosy breath to draw.
Methinks no wrong it were if I should steal
From those two melting rubies one poor kiss;
None sees the theft that would the theft reveal,
Nor rob I her of aught what she can miss:
Nay, should I twenty kisses take away,
There would be little sign I had done so.
Why, then, should I this robbery delay?
Oh, she may wake, and therewith angry grow!
Well, if she do, I'll back restore that one,
And twenty hundred thousand more for loan.

GEORGE WITHER

LOVE POEM

O GOLDEN FLEECE she is where she lies tonight
Trammelled in her sheets like midsummer on a bed,
Kisses like moths flitter over her bright
Mouth, and, as she turns her head,
I feel all space move close to give her right.

Where her hand, like a bird on the branch of her arm,
Droops its wings over the bedside as she sleeps,
There the air perpetually remains warm
Since, nested, her hand rested there. And she keeps
Under her green thumb life like a growing poem.

My nine-tiered tigress in the cage of sex
I feed with meat that you tear from my side
To crown your nine months with the paradox:
The love that kisses with a homicide
In robes of generation resurrects.

The bride who rides the hymeneal waterfall
Spawning all possibles in her pools of surplus,
Whom the train rapes going into a tunnel,
The imperial multiplicator nothing can nonplus:
My mother Nature is the origin of it all.

At Pharaoh's Feast and in the family cupboard,
Gay corpse, bright skeleton, and the fly in amber,
She sits with her laws like antlers from her forehead
Enmeshing everyone, with flowers and thunder
Adorning the head that destiny never worried.

GEORGE BARKER

LIGHT BREAKS WHERE NO
SUN SHINES

LIGHT breaks where no sun shines;
Where no sea runs, the waters of the heart
Push in their tides;
And, broken ghost with glowworms in their heads,
The things of light
File through the flesh where no flesh decks the bones.

A candle in the thighs
Warms youth and seed and burns the seeds of age;
Where no seed stirs,
The fruit of man unwrinkles in the stars,
Bright as a fig;
Where no wax is, the candle shows its hairs.

Dawn breaks behind the eyes;
From poles of skull and toe the windy blood
Slides like a sea;
Nor fenced, nor staked, the gushers of the sky
Spout to the rod
Divining in a smile the oil of tears.

Night in the sockets rounds,
Like some pitch moon, the limit of the globes;
Day lights the bone;
Where no cold is, the skinning gales unpin
The winter's robes;
The film of spring is hanging from the lids.

Light breaks on secret lots,
On tips of thought where thoughts smell in the rain;

When logics die,
The secret of the soil grows through the eye,
And blood jumps in the sun;
Above the waste allotments the dawn halts.

DYLAN THOMAS

SONG

Kiss me, sweet. The wary lover
Can your favors keep and cover,
When the common courting jay
All your bounties will betray.
Kiss again; no creature comes.
Kiss, and score up wealthy sums
On my lips thus hardly sund'rëd
While you breathe. First give a hundred.
Then a thousand, then another
Hundred, then unto the other
Add a thousand, and so more;
Till you equal with the store
All the grass that Rumney yields,
Or the sands in Chelsea fields,
Or the drops in silver Thames,
Or the stars that gild his streams
In the silent summer-nights,
When youths ply their stolen delights;
That the curious may not know
How to tell 'em as they flow,
And the envious, when they find
What their number is, be pined.

BEN JONSON

213

UPON THE NIPPLES OF JULIA'S BREAST

HAVE ye beheld (with much delight)
A red rose peeping through a white?
Or else a cherry (double grac'd)
Within a lily? Centre plac'd?
Or ever mark'd the pretty beam,
A strawberry shows half drown'd in cream?
Or seen rich rubies blushing through
A pure smooth pearl, and orient too?
So like to this, nay all the rest,
Is each neat niplet of her breast.

ROBERT HERRICK

AS YOU CAME FROM THE HOLY LAND

As you came from the holy land
  Of Walsinghame,
Met you not with my true love
  By the way as you came?

How shall I know your true love,
  That have met many a one,
As I went to the holy land,
  That have come, that have gone?

She is neither white nor brown,
  But as the heavens fair;
There is none hath a form so divine
  In the earth or the air.

Such a one did I meet, good sir,
  Such an angelic face,

Who like a queen, like a nymph, did appear,
  By her gait, by her grace.

She hath left me here all alone,
  All alone, as unknown,
Who sometime did me lead with herself,
  And me loved as her own.

What's the cause that she leaves you alone,
  And a new way doth take,
Who loved you once as her own,
  And her joy did you make?

I have loved her all my youth,
  But now old, as you see;
Love likes not the falling fruit
  From the withered tree.

Know that Love is a careless child,
  And forgets promise past;
He is blind, he is deaf when he list,
  And in faith never fast.

His desire is a dureless content,
  And a trustless joy;
He is won with a world of despair,
  And is lost with a toy.

Of womenkind such indeed is the love,
  Or the word love abuséd,
Under which many childish desires
  And conceits are excuséd.

But true love is a durable fire,
  In the mind ever burning,
Never sick, never old, never dead,
  From itself never turning.

ANONYMOUS

SONG

Why, lovely charmer, tell me why,
So very kind, so very shy?
Why does that cold forbidding air
Give damps of sorrow and despair?
Or why that smile my soul subdue,
And kindle up my flames anew?

In vain you strive with all your art,
By turns to freeze and fire my heart:
When I behold a face so fair,
So sweet a look, so soft an air,
My ravished soul is charmed all o'er,
I cannot love thee less nor more.

SIR RICHARD STEELE

SO SWEET LOVE SEEMED

So sweet love seemed that April morn,
When first we kissed beside the thorn,
So strangely sweet, it was not strange
We thought that love could never change.

But I can tell—let truth be told—
That love will change in growing old;
Though day by day is naught to see,
So delicate his motions be.

And in the end 'twill come to pass
Quite to forget what once he was,
Nor even in fancy to recall
The pleasure that was all in all.

216

His little spring, that sweet we found,
So deep in summer floods is drowned,
I wonder, bathed in joy complete,
How love so young could be so sweet.

ROBERT BRIDGES

JANE RETREAT

JANE RETREAT falls stark asleep
In her large brown-headed shoulders.

The rest of her starts
Like fish half alive
Under the fumbling dark.

Where will the fire be found
To pilot the dark on Jane half awake?

O Jane Retreat
With your fish in my arms
Tugging through half the night

If only someone would crawl through my veins
To tear out your shoulders and head!

EDWIN HONIG

I WILL ENJOY THEE NOW

I WILL enjoy thee now, my Celia, come,
And fly with me to Love's Elysium.
The giant, Honour, that keeps cowards out
Is but a masquer, and the servile rout
Of baser subjects only bend in vain
To the vast idol; whilst the nobler train
Of valiant lovers daily sail between
The huge Colossus' legs, and pass unseen
Unto the blissful shore. Be bold and wise,
And we shall enter; the grim Swiss denies
Only to tame fools a passage, that not know
He is but form and only frights in show
The duller eyes that look from far; draw near
And thou shalt scorn what we were wont to fear.
We shall see how the stalking pageant goes
With borrow'd legs, a heavy load to those
That made and bear him; not, as we once thought,
The seed of gods, but a weak model wrought
By greedy men, that seek to enclose the common,
And within private arms empale free woman.

Come, then, and mounted on the wings of Love
We'll cut the flitting air and soar above
The monster's head, and in the noblest seats
Of those blest shades quench and renew our heats.
There shall the queens of love and innocence,
Beauty and Nature, banish all offence
From our close ivy-twines; there I'll behold
Thy baréd snow and thy unbraided gold;
There my enfranchised hand on every side
Shall o'er thy naked polish'd ivory slide.
No curtain there, though of transparent lawn,

218

Shall be before thy virgin-treasure drawn;
But the rich mine, to the enquiring eye
Exposed, shall ready still for mintage lie,
And we will coin young Cupids. There a bed
Of roses and fresh myrtles shall be spread,
Under the cooler shades of cypress groves;
Our pillows of the down of Venus' doves,
Whereon our panting limbs we'll gently lay,
In the faint respites of our active play;
That so our slumbers may in dreams have leisure
To tell the nimble fancy our past pleasure,
And so our souls, that cannot be embraced,
Shall the embraces of our bodies taste.
Meanwhile the bubbling stream shall court the shore,
Th' enamour'd chirping wood-choir shall adore
In varied tunes the deity of love;
The gentle blasts of western winds shall move
The trembling leaves, and through their close boughs
    breathe
Still music, whilst we rest ourselves beneath
Their dancing shade; till a soft murmur, sent
From souls entranced in amorous languishment,
Rouse us, and shoot into our veins fresh fire,
Till we in their sweet ecstasy expire.

Then, as the empty bee that lately bore
Into the common treasure all her store,
Flies 'bout the painted field with nimble wing,
Deflow'ring the fresh virgins of the spring,
So will I rifle all the sweets that dwell
In my delicious paradise, and swell
My bag with honey, drawn forth by the power
Of fervent kisses from each spicy flower.
I'll seize the rose-buds in their perfumed bed,
The violet knots, like curious mazes spread

219

O'er all the garden, taste the ripen'd cherry,
The warm firm apple, tipp'd with coral berry;
Then will I visit with a wand'ring kiss
The vales of lilies and the bower of bliss;
And where the beauteous region doth divide
Into two milky ways, my lips shall slide
Down those smooth alleys, wearing as they go
A track for lovers on the printed snow;
Thence climbing o'er the swelling Apennine,
Retire into thy grove of eglantine,
Where I will all those ravish'd sweets distill
Through Love's alembic, and with chemic skill
From the mix'd mass one sovereign balm derive,
Then bring that great elixir to thy hive.

THOMAS CAREW

WHENAS THE NIGHTINGALE
CHANTED HER VESPERS

WHENAS the nightingale chanted her vespers,
And the wild forester couched on the ground,
Venus invited me in the evening whispers
Unto a fragrant field with roses crowned;
    Where she before had sent
    My wishes' complement,
    Unto my heart's content
  Played with me on the green;
    Never Mark Anthony
    Dallied more wantonly
    With the fair Egyptian Queen.

First on her cherry cheeks I mine eyes feasted,
Thence fear of surfeiting made me retire;

Next on her warmer lips, which when I tasted
My duller spirits made active as fire;
    Then we began to dart,
    Each at another's heart,
    Arrows that knew no smart;
  Sweet lips and smiles between.
      Never Mark Anthony
      Dallied more wantonly
      With the fair Egyptian Queen.

Wanting a glass to plait her amber tresses,
Which like a bracelet rich decked mine arm,
Gaudier than Juno wears when as she graces
Jove with embraces more stately than warm;
    Then did she peep in mine
    Eyes' humour crystalline,
    I in her eyes was seen,
  As if we one had been.
      Never Mark Anthony
      Dallied more wantonly
      With the fair Egyptian Queen.

Mystical grammar of amorous glances;
Feeling of pulses, the physic of love,
Rhetorical courtings and musical dances,
Numbering of kisses arithmetic prove.
    Eyes like astronomy,
    Straight-limbed geometry:
    In her heart's ingeny
  Our wits are sharp and keen.
      Never Mark Anthony
      Dallied more wantonly
      With the fair Egyptian Queen.

JOHN CLEVELAND

SONG

Why canst thou not, as others do,
　　Look on me with unwounding eyes?
And yet look sweet, but yet not so;
　　Smile, but not in killing wise;
Arm not thy graces to confound;
Only look, but do not wound.

Why should mine eyes see more in you
　　Than they can see in all the rest?
For I can others' beauties view
　　And not find my heart opprest.
O be as others are to me,
Or let me be more to thee.

ANONYMOUS

X

Falling Star:

Doubt, Infidelity, Hurt

WHY SO PALE AND WAN

WHY so pale and wan, fond lover?
  Prithee why so pale?
Will, when looking well can't move her,
  Looking ill prevail?
  Prithee why so pale?

Why so dull and mute, young sinner?
  Prithee why so mute?
Will, when speaking well can't win her,
  Saying nothing do't?
  Prithee why so mute?

Quit, quit, for shame; this will not move,
  This cannot take her;
If of herself she will not love,
  Nothing can make her:
  The devil take her!

SIR JOHN SUCKLING

SONG

FALSE though she be to me and love,
  I'll ne'er pursue revenge;
For still the charmer I approve,
  Though I deplore her change.

In hours of bliss we oft have met;
  They could not always last;
And though the present I regret,
  I'm grateful for the past.

WILLIAM CONGREVE

THE LOVER'S RESOLUTION

SHALL I, wasting in despair,
Die because a woman's fair?
Or make pale my cheeks with care
'Cause another's rosy are?
Be she fairer than the day,
Or the flowery meads in May,
    If she think not well of me,
    What care I how fair she be?

Should my heart be grieved or pined
'Cause I see a woman kind?
Or a well-disposéd nature
Joined with a lovely feature?
Be she meeker, kinder than
Turtle-dove, or pelican,
    If she be not so to me,
    What care I how kind she be?

Shall a woman's virtues move
Me to perish for her love?
Or her well-deservings known,
Make me quite forget mine own?
Be she with that goodness blessed
Which may merit name of Best,
    If she be not such to me,
    What care I how good she be?

GEORGE WITHER

GO AND CATCH A FALLING STAR

Go and catch a falling star,
  Get with child a mandrake root,
Tell me where all past years are,
  Or who cleft the devil's foot,
Teach me to hear mermaids singing,
Or to keep off envy's stinging,
      And find
      What wind
Serves to advance an honest mind.

If thou beest born to strange sights,
  Things invisible to see,
Ride ten thousand days and nights,
  Till age snow white hairs on thee,
Thou, when thou return'st, wilt tell me
All strange wonders that befell thee,
      And swear
      No where
Lives a woman true, and fair.

If thou find'st one, let me know,
  Such a pilgrimage were sweet;
Yet do not, I would not go,
  Though at next door we might meet;
Though she were true when you met her,
And till last you write your letter,
      Yet she
      Will be
False, ere I come, to two or three.

JOHN DONNE

THE DREAM

DEAR love, for nothing less than thee
Would I have broke this happy dream;
        It was a theme
For reason, much too strong for fantasy.
Therefore thou waked'st me wisely; yet
My dream thou brok'st not, but continued'st it.
Thou art so true that thoughts of thee suffice
To make dreams truths and fables histories;
Enter these arms, for since thou thought'st it best
Not to dream all my dream, let's act the rest.
As lightning, or a taper's light,
Thine eyes, and not thy noise, waked me;
        Yet I thought thee—
For thou lov'st truth—an angel, at first sight;
But when I saw thou saw'st my heart,
And knew'st my thoughts beyond an angel's art,
When thou knew'st what I dreamt, when thou knew'st
    when
Excess of joy would wake me, and cam'st then,
I must confess it could not choose but be
Profane to think thee anything but thee.
Coming and staying show'd thee thee,
But rising makes me doubt that now
        Thou art not thou.
That Love is weak where Fear's as strong as he;
'Tis not all spirit pure and brave
If mixture it of Fear, Shame, Honor have.
Perchance as torches, which must ready be,
Men light and put out, so thou deal'st with me.
Thou cam'st to kindle, go'st to come; then I
Will dream that hope again, but else would die.

JOHN DONNE

LOVE'S DEITY

I LONG to talk with some old lover's ghost,
  Who died before the god of love was born:
I cannot think that he, who then loved most,
  Sunk so low, as to love one which did scorn.
But since this god produced a destiny,
And that vice-nature, custom, lets it be;
  I must love her, that loves not me.

Sure, they which made him god, meant not so much,
  Nor he in his young godhead practised it;
But when an even flame two hearts did touch,
  His office was indulgently to fit
Actives to passives. Correspondency
Only his subject was; it cannot be
  Love, till I love her, that loves me.

But every modern god will now extend
  His vast prerogative, as far as Jove.
To rage, to lust, to write to, to commend,
  All is the purlieu of the god of love.
Oh were we wakened by this tyranny
To ungod this child again, it could not be
  I should love her, who loves not me.

Rebel and atheist too, why murmur I,
  As though I felt the worst that love could do?
Love might make me leave loving, or might try
  A deeper plague, to make her love me too,
Which, since she loves before, I am loath to see;
Falsehood is worse than hate; and that must be,
  If she whom I love, should love me.

JOHN DONNE
229

NON SUM QUALIS ERAM BONAE
SUB REGNO CYNARAE

LAST night, ah, yesternight, betwixt her lips and mine
There fell thy shadow, Cynara! thy breath was shed
Upon my soul between the kisses and the wine;
And I was desolate and sick of an old passion,
    Yea, I was desolate and bow'd my head:
I have been faithful to thee, Cynara! in my fashion.

All night upon mine heart I felt her warm heart beat,
Night-long within mine arms in love and sleep she lay;
Surely the kisses of her bought red mouth were sweet;
But I was desolate and sick of an old passion,
    When I awoke and found the dawn was gray:
I have been faithful to thee, Cynara! in my fashion

I have forgot much, Cynara! gone with the wind,
Flung roses, roses, riotously with the throng,
Dancing, to put thy pale lost lilies out of mind;
But I was desolate and sick of an old passion,
    Yea, all the time, because the dance was long:
I have been faithful to thee, Cynara! in my fashion.

I cried for madder music and for stronger wine,
But when the feast is finish'd and the lamps expire,
Then falls thy shadow, Cynara! the night is thine;
And I am desolate and sick of an old passion,
    Yea, hungry for the lips of my desire:
I have been faithful to thee, Cynara! in my fashion.

ERNEST DOWSON

FALSE LOVE

YE flowery banks o' bonnie Doon,
　　How can ye blume sae fair!
How can ye chaunt, ye little birds,
　　And I sae fu' o' care!

Thou'll break my heart, thou bonnie bird,
　　That sings upon the bough;
Thou minds me o' the happy days
　　When my fause luve was true.

Thou'll break my heart, thou bonnie bird,
　　That sings beside thy mate;
For sae I sat, and sae I sang,
　　And wistna o' my fate.

Aft hae I roved by bonnie Doon,
　　To see the woodbine twine;
And ilka bird sang o' its luve,
　　And sae did I o' mine.

Wi' lightsome heart I pu'd a rose
　　Upon a morn in June;
And sae I flourish'd on the morn,
　　And sae was pu'd o' noon.

Wi' lightsome heart I pu'd a rose
　　Upon its thorny tree;
But my fause luver staw my rose,
　　And left the thorn wi' me.

ROBERT BURNS

231

LETTER TO NEW YORK

In your next letter I wish you'd say
Where you are going and what you are doing:
How are the plays, and after the plays,
What other pleasures you're pursuing.

Taking cabs in the middle of the night,
Driving as if to save your soul
Where the road goes round and round the park
And the meter glares like a moral owl.

And the trees look so queer and green
Standing alone in big black caves,
And suddenly you're in a different place
Where everything seems to happen in waves.

And most of the jokes you just can't catch,
Like dirty words rubbed off a slate,
And the songs are loud but somewhat dim
And it gets so terribly late.

And coming out of the brownstone houses
To the gray sidewalk, the watered street,
One side of the buildings rise with the sun
Like a glistening field of wheat.

Wheat, not oats, dear. I'm afraid
If it's wheat, it's none of your sowing.
Nevertheless I'd like to know
What you are doing and where you are going.

1940   ELIZABETH BISHOP

THE HILL

BREATHLESS, we flung us on the windy hill,
Laughed in the sun, and kissed the lovely grass.
You said, "Through glory and ecstasy we pass;
Wind, sun, and earth remain, the birds sing still,
When we are old, are old. . . ." "And when we die
All's over that is ours; and life burns on
Through other lovers, other lips," said I,
"Heart of my heart, our heaven is now, is won!"
"We are Earth's best, that learnt her lesson here.
Life is our cry. We have kept the faith!" we said;
"We shall go down with unreluctant tread
Rose-crowned into the darkness! . . ." Proud we were,
And laughed, that had such brave true things to say.
And then you suddenly cried, and turned away.

RUPERT BROOKE

SONG

How sweet I roam'd from field to field
And tasted all the summer's pride,
Till I the Prince of Love beheld
Who in the sunny beams did glide!

He show'd me lilies for my hair,
And blushing roses for my brow;
He led me through his gardens fair
Where all his golden pleasures grow.

With sweet May dews my wings were wet,
And Phoebus fir'd my vocal rage;

233

He caught me in his silken net,
And shut me in his golden cage.

He loves to sit and hear me sing,
Then, laughing, sports and plays with me;
Then stretches out my golden wing,
And mocks my loss of liberty.

WILLIAM BLAKE

WHEN I WAS ONE-AND-TWENTY

WHEN I was one-and-twenty
I heard a wise man say,
'Give crowns and pounds and guineas
But not your heart away;
Give pearls away and rubies
But keep your fancy free.'
But I was one-and-twenty,
No use to talk to me.

When I was one-and-twenty
I heard him say again,
'The heart out of the bosom
Was never given in vain;
'Tis paid with sighs a plenty
And sold for endless rue.'
And I am two-and-twenty,
And oh, 'tis true, 'tis true.

A. E. HOUSMAN

THE DOUBLE SHAME

You must live through the time when everything hurts
When the space of the ripe, loaded afternoon
Expands to a landscape of white heat frozen
And trees are weighed down with hearts of stone
And green stares back where you stare alone,
And the walking eyes throw flinty comments
And the words which carry most knives are the blind
Phrases searching to be kind.

Solid and usual objects are ghosts
The furniture carries great cargoes of memory,
The staircase has corners which remember
As fire blows most red in gusty embers,
And each empty dress cuts out an image
In fur and evening and summer and gold
Of her who was different in each.

Pull down the blind and lie on the bed
And clasp the hour in the glass of one room
Against your mouth like a crystal of doom
Take up the book and look at the letters
Hieroglyphs on sand and as meaningless—
Here birds crossed once and cries were uttered
In a mist where sight and sound are blurred.

For the story of those who made mistakes
Of one whose happiness pierced like a star
Eludes and evades between sentences
And the letters break into eyes which read
What the blood is now writing in your head
As though the characters sought for some clue
To their being so perfectly living and dead
In your story, worse than theirs, but true.

Set in the mind of their poet, they compare
Their tragic bliss with your trivial despair
And they have fingers which accuse
You of the double way of shame.
At first you did not love enough
And afterwards you loved too much
And you lacked the confidence to choose
And you have only yourself to blame.

STEPHEN SPENDER

THE CONSTANT LOVER

OUT upon it, I have loved
   Three whole days together!
And am like to love three more,
   If it prove fair weather.

Time shall moult away his wings,
   Ere he shall discover
In the whole wide world again
   Such a constant lover.

But the spite on 't is, no praise
   Is due at all to me:
Love with me had made no stays,
   Had it any been but she.

Had it any been but she,
   And that very face,
There had been at least ere this
   A dozen dozen in her place.

SIR JOHN SUCKLING

236

GIVE ALL TO LOVE

Give all to love;
Obey thy heart;
Friends, kindred, days,
Estate, good-fame,
Plans, credit and the
    Muse,—
Nothing refuse.

'Tis a brave master;
Let it have scope:
Follow it utterly,
Hope beyond hope:
High and more high
It dives into noon,
With wing unspent,
Untold intent;
But it is a god,
Knows its own path
And the outlets of the
    sky.

It was never for the
    mean;
It requireth courage
    stout.
Souls above doubt,
Valor unbending,
It will reward,—
They shall return
More than they were,
And ever ascending.

Leave all for love;
Yet, hear me, yet,

One word more thy heart
    behoved,
One pulse more of firm en-
    deavor,—
Keep thee today,
Tomorrow, forever,
Free as an Arab
Of thy beloved.

Cling with life to the maid;
But when the surprise,
First vague shadow of sur-
    mise
Flits across her bosom
    young
Of a joy apart from thee,
Free be she, fancy-free;
Nor thou detain her ves-
    ture's hem,
Nor the palest rose she flung
From her summer diadem.

Though thou loved her as
    thyself,
As a self of purer clay,
Though her parting dims
    the day,
Stealing grace from all
    alive:
Heartily know,
When half-gods go,
The gods arrive.

RALPH WALDO EMERSON

SONG

Fair Iris I love, and hourly I die,
But not for a lip, nor a languishing eye:
She's fickle and false, and there we agree,
For I am as false and as fickle as she.
We neither believe what either can say;
And, neither believing, we neither betray.
'Tis civil to swear, and say things of course;
We mean not the taking for better or worse.
When present, we love; when absent, agree:
I think not of Iris, nor Iris of me.
The legend of love no couple can find,
So easy to part, or so equally join'd.

John Dryden

WITH HOW SAD STEPS, O MOON

With how sad steps, O Moon, thou climb'st the skies!
How silently, and with how wan a face!
What, may it be that even in heavenly place
That busy archer his sharp arrows tries?
Sure, if that long-with-love-acquainted eyes
Can judge of love, thou feel'st a lover's case,
I read it in thy looks; thy languished grace,
To me, that feel the like, thy state descries.
Then, even of fellowship, O Moon, tell me,
Is constant love deemed there but want of wit?
Are beauties there as proud as here they be?
Do they above love to be loved, and yet
Those lovers scorn whom that love doth possess?
Do they call virtue there ungratefulness?

Sir Philip Sidney

BEING YOUR SLAVE, WHAT
SHOULD I DO BUT TEND

BEING your slave, what should I do but tend
Upon the hours and times of your desire?
I have no precious time at all to spend,
Nor services to do, till you require.
Nor dare I chide the world-without-end hour
Whilst I, my sovereign, watch the clock for you,
Nor think the bitterness of absence sour
When you have bid your servant once adieu;
Nor dare I question with my jealous thought
Where you may be, or your affairs suppose,
But, like a sad slave, stay and think of nought
Save, where you are, how happy you make those.
So true a fool is love that in your will,
Though you do anything, he thinks no ill.

WILLIAM SHAKESPEARE

HER FAIR INFLAMING EYES

HER fair inflaming eyes,
    Chief authors of my cares,
I prayed in humblest wise
    With grace to view my tears:
They beheld me broad awake,
But, alas, no ruth would take.

Then down my prayers made way
    To those most comely parts,
That make her fly or stay

239

As they affect deserts:
But her angry feet, thus moved
Fled with all the parts I loved!

Yet fled they not so fast
    As her enragèd mind:
Still did I after haste,
    Still was I left behind;
Till I found 'twas to no end
With a Spirit to contend.

THOMAS CAMPION

MOTHER, I CANNOT MIND
MY WHEEL

MOTHER, I cannot mind my wheel;
    My fingers ache, my lips are dry:
O, if you felt the pain I feel!
    But O, who ever felt as I?

No longer could I doubt him true—
    All other men may use deceit;
He always said my eyes were blue,
    And often swore my lips were sweet.

WALTER SAVAGE LANDOR

WOMAN'S CONSTANCY

Now thou hast loved me one whole day,
To-morrow when thou leav'st, what wilt thou say?
Wilt thou then antedate some new-made vow?
    Or say that now
We are not just those persons which we were?
Or, that oaths made in reverential fear
Of love, and his wrath, any may forswear?
Or, as true deaths true marriages untie,
So lovers' contracts, images of those,
Bind but till sleep, death's image, them unloose?
    Or your own end to justify,
For having purposed change and falsehood, you
Can have no way but falsehood to be true?
Vain lunatic, against these scapes I could
    Dispute and conquer, if I would;
    Which I abstain to do,
For by to-morrow, I may think so too.

JOHN DONNE

MARK HOW THE BASHFUL
MORN

MARK how the bashful morn, in vain,
Courts the amorous marigold
With sighing blasts and weeping rain;
Yet she refuses to unfold.
But when the planet of the day
Approacheth, with his powerful ray,
   Then she spreads, then she receives
His warmer beams into her virgin leaves.

241

So shalt thou thrive in love, fond boy!
If thy tears and sighs discover
Thy grief, thou never shalt enjoy
The just reward of a bold lover.
But when with moving accents thou
Shalt constant faith and service vow,
    Thy Celia shall receive those charms
With open ears, and with unfolded arms.

THOMAS CAREW

THE RESOLVE

TELL me not of a face that's fair,
    Nor lip and cheek that's red,
Nor of the tresses of her hair,
    Nor curls in order laid,
Nor of a rare seraphic voice
    That like an angel sings;
Though if I were to take my choice
    I would have all these things:
But if thou wilt have me love,
    And it must be a she,
The only argument can move
    Is that she will love me.

The glories of your ladies be
    But metaphors of things,
And but resemble what we see
    Each common object brings.
Roses out-red their lips and cheeks,
    Lilies their whiteness stain;
What fool is he that shadows seeks
    And may the substance gain:

Then if thou'lt have me love a lass,
    Let it be one that's kind:
Else I'm a servant to the glass
    That's with Canary lined.

ALEXANDER BROME

SONG

YE happy swains, whose hearts are free
    From love's imperial chain,
Take warning and be taught by me,
    T' avoid th' enchanting pain.
Fatal the wolves to trembling flocks,
    Fierce winds to blossoms prove,
To careless seamen hidden rocks,
    To human quiet love.

Fly the fair sex, if bliss you prize;
    The snake's beneath the flower:
Whoever gazed on beauteous eyes
    That tasted quiet more?
How faithless is the lover's joy!
    How constant is their care,
The kind with falsehood to destroy,
    The cruel with despair!

SIR GEORGE ETHEREGE

243

OH! DEAR, WHAT CAN THE MATTER BE?

Oh! dear, what can the matter be?
  Dear! dear! What can the matter be?
Oh! dear, what can the matter be?
  Johnny's so long at the fair.

He promised he'd buy me a beautiful fairing,
A gay bit of lace that the lassies are wearing,
He promis'd he'd bring me a bunch of blue ribbons
To tie up my bonny brown hair.

Oh! dear, what can the matter be?
  Dear! dear! What can the matter be?
Oh! dear, what can the matter be?
  Johnny's so long at the fair.

He promis'd he'd buy me a basket of posies,
A garland of lilies, a wreath of red roses,
A little straw hat to set off the blue ribbons
That tie up my bonny brown hair.

ANONYMOUS

A WOMAN'S QUESTIONS

Before I trust my fate to thee,
  Or place my hand in thine,
Before I let thy future give
  Colour and form to mine,
Before I peril all for thee, question thy soul to-night for
  me.

244

I break all slighter bonds, nor feel
    A shadow of regret:
Is there one link within the past
    That holds thy spirit yet?
Or is thy faith as clear and free as that which I can
    pledge to thee?

Does there within thy dimmest dreams
    A possible future shine,
Wherein thy life could henceforth breathe,
    Untouched, unshared by mine?
If so, at any pain or cost, O, tell me before all is lost.

Look deeper still. If thou canst feel,
    Within thy inmost soul,
That thou has kept a portion back,
    While I have staked the whole,
Let no false pity spare the blow, but in true mercy tell
    me so.

Is there within thy heart a need
    That mine cannot fulfil?
One chord that any other hand
    Could better wake or still?
Speak now—lest at some future day my whole life wither
    and decay.

Nay, answer not,—I dare not hear,
    The words would come too late;
Yet I would spare thee all remorse,
    So, comfort thee, my Fate,—
Whatever on my heart may fall—remember, I would risk
    it all!

ADELAIDE ANNE PROCTER
245

SONG

You wrong me, Strephon, when you say,
    I'm jealous or severe,
Did I not see you kiss and play
    With all you came a-near?
Say, did I ever chide for this,
    Or cast one jealous eye
On the bold nymphs, that snatch'd my bliss
    While I stood wishing by.

Yet though I never disapproved
    This modish liberty,
I thought in them you only loved
    Change and variety:
I vainly thought my charms so strong,
    And you so much my slave,
No nymph had power to do me wrong,
    Or break the chains I gave.

But when you seriously address
    With all your winning charms,
Unto a servile shepherdess,
    I'll throw you from my arms:
I'd rather choose you should make love
    To every face you see,
Than Mopsa's dull admirer prove,
    And let her rival me.

'EPHELIA'

246

NEUTRAL TONES

WE stood by a pond that winter day,
And the sun was white, as though chidden of God,
And a few leaves lay on the starving sod;
  —They had fallen from an ash, and were gray.

Your eyes on me were as eyes that rove
Over tedious riddles solved years ago;
And some words played between us to and fro
    On which lost the more by our love.

The smile on your mouth was the deadest thing
Alive enough to have strength to die;
And a grin of bitterness swept thereby
    Like an ominous bird a-wing. . . .

Since then, keen lessons that love deceives,
And wrings with wrong, have shaped to me
Your face, and the God-curst sun, and a tree,
    And a pond edged with grayish leaves.

THOMAS HARDY

ON THE MARRIAGE

Of a Beauteous Young Gentlewoman with an Ancient Man

FONDLY, too curious Nature, to adorn
Aurora with the blushes of the morn:
Why do her rosy lips breathe gums and spice
Unto the East, and sweet to Paradise?
Why do her eyes open the day? her hand
And voice entrance the panther, and command
Incenséd winds; her breasts, the tents of love,
Smooth as the godded swan or Venus' dove,
Soft as the balmy dew whose every touch
Is pregnant—but why those rich spoils, when such
Wonder and perfection must be led
A bridal captive unto Tithon's bed?
Aged and deforméd Tithon! Must thy twine
Circle and blast at once what care and time
Had made for wonder? Must pure beauty have
No other foil but ruin and a grave?
So have I seen the pride of Nature's store,
The orient pearl, chained to the sooty Moor;
So hath the diamond's bright ray been set
In night and wedded to the negro jet.
See, see, how thick those showers of pearl do fall
To weep her ransom or her funeral;
Whose every treasured drop congealed might bring
Freedom and ransom to a fettered king;
While tyrant Wealth stands by, and laughs to see
How he can wed love and antipathy.
Hymen, thy pine burns with adulterate fire.
Thou and thy quivered boy did once conspire
To mingle equal flames, and then no shine
Of gold, but beauty dressed the Paphian shrine.
Roses and lilies kissed; the amorous vine
Did with the fair and straight-limbed elm entwine.

FRANCIS BEAUMONT

INCONSTANCY REPROVED

I DO confess thou'rt smooth and fair,
　And I might have gone near to love thee,
Had I not found the slightest pray'r
　That lips could speak, had pow'r to move thee;
　　　But I can let thee now alone,
　　　As worthy to be loved by none.

I do confess thou'rt sweet; yet find
　Thee such an unthrift of thy sweets,
Thy favors are but like the wind,
　Which kisseth everything it meets:
　　　And since thou canst love more than one,
　　　Thou'rt worthy to be kiss'd by none.

The morning rose that untouch'd stands,
　Arm'd with her briars, how sweet she smells!
But pluck'd, and strain'd through ruder hands,
　Her sweets no longer with her dwells;
　　　But scent and beauty both are gone,
　　　And leaves fall from her, one by one.

Such fate, ere long, will thee betide,
　When thou hast handled been awhile,
Like fair flow'rs to be thrown aside;
　And thou shalt sigh, when I shall smile
　　　To see thy love to every one
　　　Hath brought thee to be lov'd by none.

SIR ROBERT AYTON

I LOVED THEE ONCE

I LOVED thee once, I'll love no more,
   Thine be the grief as is the blame;
Thou art not what thou wast before,
   What reason I should be the same?
     He that can love unloved again,
     Hath better store of love than brain:
   God sends me love my debts to pay,
   While unthrifts fool their love away.

Nothing could have my love o'erthrown,
   If thou hadst still continued mine;
Yea, if thou hadst remained thy own,
   I might perchance have yet been thine.
     But thou thy freedom didst recall,
     That if thou might elsewhere inthrall;
   And then how could I but disdain
   A captive's captive to remain?

When new desires had conquered thee,
   And changed the object of thy will,
It had been lethargy in me,
   Not constancy, to love thee still.
     Yea, it had been a sin to go
     And prostitute affection so,
   Since we are taught no prayers to say
   To such as must to others pray.

Yet do thou glory in thy choice,
   Thy choice of his good fortune boast;
I'll neither grieve nor yet rejoice,
   To see him gain what I have lost;
     The height of my disdain shall be,

> To laugh at him, to blush for thee;
> To love thee still, but go no more
> A begging to a beggar's door.

SIR ROBERT AYTON

TO CYNTHIA WEEPING AND
NOT SPEAKING

WHY are those hours, which Heaven in pity lent
To longing love, in fruitless sorrow spent?
Why sighs my Fair? Why does that bosom move
With any passion stirred, but rising love?
Can discontent find place within that breast,
On whose soft pillows ev'n despair might rest?
Divide thy woes, and give me my sad part.
I am no stranger to an aching heart;
Too well I know the force of inward grief,
And well can bear it, to give you relief:
All love's severest pangs I can endure;
I can bear pain, tho' hopeless of a cure.
I know what 'tis to weep, and sigh, and pray,
To wake all night, yet dread the breaking day;
I know what 'tis to wish, and hope, and all in vain,
And meet, for humble love, unkind disdain.
Anger, and hate, I have been forced to bear,
Nay jealousy—and I have felt despair.
These pains, for you, I have been forced to prove,
For cruel you, when I began to love,
'Till warm compassion took at length my part,
And melted to my wish your yielding heart.
O the dear hour, in which you did resign!
When round my neck your willing arms did twine,
And, in a kiss, you said your heart was mine.

251

Thro' each returning year, may that hour be
Distinguished in the rounds of all eternity;
Gay be the sun, that hour, in all his light,
Let him collect the day, to be more bright,
Shine all, that hour, and let the rest be night.
And shall I all this heaven of bliss receive
From you, yet not lament to see you grieve!
Shall I, who nourished in my breast desire,
When your cold scorn, and frowns forbid the fire,
Now, when a mutual flame you have revealed,
And the dear union of our souls is sealed,
When all my joys complete in you I find,
Shall I not share the sorrows of your mind?
O tell me, tell me all—whence does arise
This flood of tears? whence are these frequent sighs?
Why does that lovely head, like a fair flower
Oppressed with drops of a hard-falling shower,
Bend with its weight of grief, and seem to grow
Downward to earth, and kiss the root of woe?
Lean on my breast, and let me fold thee fast,
Locked in these arms, think all thy sorrows past;
Or, what remain, think lighter made by me;
So I should think, were I so held by thee . . .
Join to my cheek thy cold and dewy face,
And let pale grief to glowing love give place.
O speak—for woe in silence most appears;
Speak, ere my fancy magnify my fears.
Is there a cause which words cannot express?
Can I not bear a part, or make it less?
I know not what to think,—am I in fault
I have not to my knowledge erred in thought,
Nor wandered from my love, nor would I be
Lord of the world to live deprived of thee.
You weep afresh, and at that word you start!
Am I to be deprived then?—must we part!

FALLING STAR: *Doubt, Infidelity, Hurt*

Curse on that word so ready to be spoke,
For through my lips, unmeant by me, it broke.
Oh no, we must not, will not, cannot part,
And my tongue talks unprompted by my heart.
Yet speak, for my distraction grows apace,
And racking fears, and restless doubts increase;
And fears and doubts to jealousy will turn,
The hottest hell, in which a heart can burn.

WILLIAM CONGREVE

KIND ARE HER ANSWERS

KIND are her answers,
But her performance keeps no day;
Breaks time, as dancers
From their own music when they stray.
All her free favours
And smooth words wing my hopes in vain.
O did ever voice so sweet but only feign?
Can true love yield such delay,
Converting joy to pain?

Lost is our freedom,
When we submit to women so:
Why do we need them
When, in their best they work our woe?
There is no wisdom
Can alter ends, by Fate prefixt.
O why is the good of man with evil mixt?
Never were days yet called two,
But one night went betwixt.

THOMAS CAMPION

253

THE BROOK OF THE HEART

HAVE you got a brook in your little heart,
Where bashful flowers blow,
And blushing birds go down to drink,
And shadows tremble so?

And nobody knows, so still it flows,
That any brook is there;
And yet your little draught of life
Is daily drunken there.

Then look out for the little brook in March,
When the rivers overflow,
And the snows come hurrying from the hills,
And the bridges often go.

And later, in August it may be,
When the meadows parching lie,
Beware, lest this little brook of life
Some burning noon go dry!

EMILY DICKINSON

IF WOMEN WOULD BE FAIR

IF women would be fair and yet not fond,
Or that their love were firm, not fickle, still,
I would not marvel that they make men bond,

By service long to purchase their good will.
  But when I see how frail these creatures are,
  I muse that men forget themselves so far.

To mark the choice they make and how they change,
How oft from Phoebus they do fly to Pan,
Unsettled still, like haggards wild they range,
These gentle birds that fly from man to man;
  Who would not scorn, and shake them from the fist,
  And let them fly, fair fools, which way they list?

Yet for disport we fawn and flatter both,
To pass the time when nothing else can please;
And train them to our lure with subtle oath
Till weary of their wiles, ourselves we ease;
  And then we say, when we their fancy try,
  To play with fools, oh, what a fool was I!

EDWARD DE VERE, *Earl of Oxford*

YOU'RE NOT ALONE

You're not alone when you are still alone;
O God, from you that I could private be!
Since you one were, I never since was one,
Since you in me, my self since out of me,
Transported from my self into your being,
Though either distant, present yet to either;
Senseless with too much joy, each other seeing,
And only absent when we are together.

Give me *my* self, and take *your* self again!
Devise some means but how I may forsake you!
So much is mine that doth with you remain,
That taking what is mine, with me I take you.
You do bewitch me . . . O that I could fly
From my self you, or from your own self I!

MICHAEL DRAYTON

XI

Bitter Chill:

Ballads: Sorrow, Revenge

THE EVE OF ST. AGNES

St. Agnes' Eve—Ah, bitter chill it was!
The owl, for all his feathers, was a-cold;
The hare limped trembling through the frozen grass,
And silent was the flock in woolly fold:
Numb were the Beadsman's fingers, while he told
His rosary, and while his frosted breath,
Like pious incense from a censer old,
Seemed taking flight for heaven, without a death,
Past the sweet Virgin's picture, while his prayer he saith.

His prayer he saith, this patient, holy man;
Then takes his lamp, and riseth from his knees,
And back returneth, meager, barefoot, wan,
Along the chapel aisle by slow degrees:
The sculptured dead, on each side, seem to freeze,
Emprisoned in black, purgatorial rails:
Knights, ladies, praying in dumb orat'ries,
He passeth by; and his weak spirit fails
To think how they may ache in icy hoods and mails.

Northward he turneth through a little door,
And scarce three steps, ere Music's golden tongue
Flattered to tears this aged man and poor;
But no—already had his deathbell rung;
The joys of all his life were said and sung:
His was harsh penance on St. Agnes' Eve:
Another way he went, and soon among
Rough ashes sat he for his soul's reprieve,
And all night kept awake, for sinners' sake to grieve.

That ancient Beadsman heard the prelude soft;
And so it chanced, for many a door was wide,

From hurry to and fro. Soon, up aloft,
The silver, snarling trumpets 'gan to chide:
The level chambers, ready with their pride,
Were glowing to receive a thousand guests:
The carved angels, ever eager-eyed,
Stared where upon their heads the cornice rests,
With hair blown back, and wings put cross-wise on their
    breasts.

At length burst in the argent revelry,
With plume, tiara, and all rich array,
Numerous as shadows haunting fairily
The brain, new stuffed, in youth, with triumphs gay
Of old romance. These let us wish away,
And turn, sole-thoughted, to one Lady there,
Whose heart had brooded, all that wintry day,
On love, and winged St. Agnes' saintly care,
As she had heard old dames full many times declare.

They told her how, upon St. Agnes' Eve,
Young virgins might have visions of delight,
And soft adorings from their loves receive
Upon the honeyed middle of the night
If ceremonies due they did aright;
As, supperless to bed they must retire,
And couch supine their beauties, lily white;
Nor look behind, nor sideways, but require
Of Heaven with upward eyes for all that they desire.

Full of this whim was thoughtful Madeline:
The music, yearning like a God in pain,
She scarcely heard: her maiden eyes divine,
Fixed on the floor, saw many a sweeping train
Pass by—she heeded not at all: in vain
Came many a tiptoe, amorous cavalier,

And back retired, not cooled by high disdain;
But she saw not: her heart was otherwhere:
She sighed for Agnes' dreams, the sweetest of the year.

She danced along with vague, regardless eyes,
Anxious her lips, her breathing quick and short:
The hallowed hour was near at hand: she sighs
Amid the timbrels, and the thronged resort
Of whisperers in anger, or in sport;
'Mid looks of love, defiance, hate, and scorn,
Hoodwinked with faery fancy; all amort,
Save to St. Agnes and her lambs unshorn,
And all the bliss to be before to-morrow morn.

So, purposing each moment to retire,
She lingered still. Meantime, across the moors,
Had come young Porphyro, with heart on fire
For Madeline. Beside the portal doors,
Buttressed from moonlight, stands he, and implores
All saints to give him sight of Madeline,
But for one moment in the tedious hours,
That he might gaze and worship all unseen;
Perchance speak, kneel, touch, kiss—in sooth such things
    have been.

He ventures in: let no buzzed whisper tell:
All eyes be muffled, or a hundred swords
Will storm his heart, Love's fev'rous citadel:
For him, those chambers held barbarian hordes,
Hyena foemen, and hot-blooded lords,
Whose very dogs would execrations howl
Against his lineage: not one breast affords
Him any mercy, in that mansion foul,
Save one old beldame, weak in body and in soul.

261

Ah, happy chance! the aged creature came,
Shuffling along with ivory-headed wand,
To where he stood, hid from the torch's flame,
Behind a broad hall pillar, far beyond
The sound of merriment and chorus bland.
He startled her: but soon she knew his face,
And grasped his fingers in her palsied hand,
Saying, "Mercy, Porphyro! hie thee from this place;
They are all here tonight, the whole blood-thirsty race!

"Get hence! get hence! there's dwarfish Hildebrand:
He had a fever late, and in the fit
He cursed thee and thine, both house and land:
Then there's that old Lord Maurice, not a whit
More tame for his gray hairs—Alas me! flit!
Flit like a ghost away."—"Ah, Gossip dear,
We're safe enough; here in this arm-chair sit,
And tell me how—" "Good saints! not here, not here!
Follow me, child, or else these stones will be thy bier."

He followed through a lowly archéd way,
Brushing the cobwebs with his lofty plume;
And as she muttered "Well-a—well-a-day!"
He found him in a little moonlight room,
Pale, latticed, chill, and silent as a tomb.
"Now tell me where is Madeline," said he,
"O tell me, Angela, by the holy loom
Which none but secret sisterhood may see,
When they St. Agnes' wool are weaving piously."

"St. Agnes! Ah! it is St. Agnes' Eve—
Yet men will murder upon holy days.
Thou must hold water in a witch's sieve,
And be liege-lord of all the Elves and Fays
To venture so: it fills me with amaze

To see thee, Porphyro!—St. Agnes' Eve!
God's help! my lady fair the conjurer plays
This very night: good angels her deceive!
But let me laugh awhile,—I've mickle time to grieve."

Feebly she laugheth in the languid moon,
While Porphyro upon her face doth look,
Like puzzled urchin on an agéd crone
Who keepeth close a wondrous riddle-book,
As spectacled she sits in chimney nook.
But soon his eyes grew brilliant, when she told
His lady's purpose; and he scarce could brook
Tears, at the thought of those enchantments cold,
And Madeline asleep in lap of legends old.

Sudden a thought came like a full-blown rose,
Flushing his brow, and in his pained heart
Made purple riot: then doth he propose
A stratagem, that makes the beldame start:
"A cruel man and impious thou art!
Sweet lady, let her pray, and sleep and dream
Alone with her good angels, far apart
From wicked men like thee. Go, go! I deem
Thou canst not surely be the same that thou didst seem."

"I will not harm her, by all saints I swear!"
Quoth Porphyro: "O may I ne'er find grace
When my weak voice shall whisper its last prayer,
If one of her soft ringlets I displace,
Or look with ruffian passion in her face.
Good Angela, believe me, by these tears;
Or I will, even in a moment's space,
Awake, with horrid shout, my foemen's ears,
And beard them, though they be more fanged than
    wolves and bears."

"Ah! why wilt thou affright a feeble soul?
A poor, weak, palsy-stricken churchyard thing,
Whose passing-bell may ere the midnight toll;
Whose prayers for thee, each morn and evening,
Were never missed." Thus plaining, doth she bring
A gentler speech from burning Porphyro;
So woful, and of such deep sorrowing,
That Angela gives promise she will do
Whatever he shall wish, betide her weal or woe.

Which was, to lead him, in close secrecy,
Even to Madeline's chamber, and there hide
Him in a closet, of such privacy
That he might see her beauty unespied,
And win perhaps that night a peerless bride,
While legioned fairies paced the coverlet,
And pale enchantment held her sleepy-eyed.
Never on such a night have lovers met,
Since Merlin paid his Demon all the monstrous debt.

"It shall be as thou wishest," said the Dame:
"All cates and dainties shall be stored there
Quickly on this feast-night: by the tambour frame
Her own lute thou wilt see: no time to spare,
For I am slow and feeble, and scarce dare
On such a catering trust my dizzy head.
Wait here, my child, with patience; kneel in prayer
The while: Ah! thou must needs the lady wed,
Or may I never leave my grave among the dead."

So saying, she hobbled off with busy fear.
The lover's endless minutes slowly passed;
The dame returned, and whispered in his ear
To follow her; with aged eyes aghast
From fright of dim espial. Safe at last,

Through many a dusky gallery, they gain
The maiden's chamber, silken, hushed, and chaste;
Where Porphyro took covert, pleased amain.
His poor guide hurried back with agues in her brain.

Her falt'ring hand upon the balustrade
Old Angela was feeling for the stair,
When Madeline, St. Agnes' charmèd maid,
Rose, like a missioned spirit, unaware:
With silver taper's light, and pious care,
She turned, and down the aged gossip led
To a safe level matting. Now prepare,
Young Porphyro, for gazing on that bed;
She comes, she comes again, like ring-dove frayed and
    fled.

Out went the taper as she hurried in;
Its little smoke, in pallid moonshine, died:
She closed the door, she panted, all akin
To spirits of the air, and visions wide:
No uttered syllable, or, woe betide!
But to her heart, her heart was voluble,
Paining with eloquence her balmy side;
As though a tongueless nightingale should swell
Her throat in vain, and die, heart-stifled, in her dell.

A casement high and triple-arched there was,
All garlanded with carven imageries,
Of fruits, and flowers, and bunches of knot-grass,
And diamonded with panes of quaint device,
Innumerable of stains and splendid dyes,
As are the tiger-moth's deep-damasked wings;
And in the midst, 'mong thousand heraldries,
And twilight saints, and dim emblazonings,
A shielded scutcheon blushed with blood of queens and
    kings.

Full on this casement shone the wintry moon,
And threw warm gules on Madeline's fair breast,
As down she knelt for Heaven's grace and boon;
Rose bloom fell on her hands, together prest,
And on her silver cross soft amethyst,
And on her hair a glory, like a saint:
She seemed a splendid angel, newly drest,
Save wings, for heaven:—Porphyro grew faint:
She knelt, so pure a thing, so free from mortal taint.

Anon his heart revives: her vespers done,
Of all its wreathed pearls her hair she frees;
Unclasps her warmed jewels one by one;
Loosens her fragrant bodice; by degrees
Her rich attire creeps rustling to her knees:
Half-hidden, like a mermaid in sea-weed,
Pensive awhile she dreams awake, and sees,
In fancy, fair St. Agnes in her bed,
But dares not look behind, or all the charm is fled.

Soon, trembling in her soft and chilly nest,
In sort of wakeful swoon, perplexed she lay,
Until the poppied warmth of sleep oppressed
Her soothed limbs, and soul fatigued away;
Flown, like a thought, until the morrow-day;
Blissfully havened both from joy and pain;
Clasped like a missal where swart Paynims pray;
Blinded alike from sunshine and from rain,
As though a rose should shut, and be a bud again.

Stolen to this paradise, and so entranced,
Porphyro gazed upon her empty dress,
And listened to her breathing, if it chanced
To wake into a slumberous tenderness;
Which when he heard, that minute did he bless,

And breathed himself: then from the closet crept,
Noiseless as fear in a wide wilderness,
And over the hushed carpet, silent, stept,
And 'tween the curtains peeped, where, lo!—how fast
    she slept.

Then by the bed-side, where the faded moon
Made a dim, silver twilight, soft he set
A table, and, half anguished, threw thereon
A cloth of woven crimson, gold, and jet:—
O for some drowsy Morphean amulet!
The boisterous, midnight, festive clarion,
The kettle-drum, and far-heard clarinet,
Affray his ears, though but in dying tone:—
The hall-door shuts again, and all the noise is gone.

And still she slept an azure-lidded sleep,
In blanched linen, smooth, and lavendered,
While he from forth the closet brought a heap
Of candied apple, quince, and plum, and gourd;
With jellies soother than the creamy curd,
And lucent syrops, tinct with cinnamon;
Manna and dates, in argosy transferred
From Fez; and spiced dainties, every one,
From silken Samarcand to cedared Lebanon.

These delicates he heaped with glowing hand
On golden dishes and in baskets bright
Of wreathed silver: sumptuous they stand
In the retired quiet of the night,
Filling the chilly room with perfume light.—
"And now, my love, my seraph fair, awake!
Thou art my heaven, and I thine eremite:
Open thine eyes, for meek St. Agnes' sake,
Or I shall drowse beside thee, so my soul doth ache."

267

Thus whispering, his warm, unnerved arm
Sank in her pillow. Shaded was her dream
By the dusk curtains:—'twas a midnight charm
Impossible to melt as iced stream:
The lustrous salvers in the moonlight gleam:
Broad golden fringe upon the carpet lies:
It seemed he never, never could redeem
From such a stedfast spell his lady's eyes;
So mused awhile, entoiled in woofed phantasies.

Awakening up, he took her hollow lute,—
Tumultuous,—and, in chords that tenderest be,
He played an ancient ditty, long since mute,
In Provence called, "La belle dame sans mercy":
Close to her ear touching the melody;—
Wherewith disturbed, she uttered a soft moan:
He ceased—she panted quick—and suddenly
Her blue affrayed eyes wide open shone:
Upon his knees he sank, pale as smooth-sculptured stone.

Her eyes were open, but she still beheld,
Now wide awake, the vision of her sleep:
There was a painful change, that nigh expelled
The blisses of her dream so pure and deep
At which fair Madeline began to weep,
And moan forth witless words with many a sigh;
While still her gaze on Porphyro would keep;
Who knelt, with joined hands and piteous eye,
Fearing to move or speak, she looked so dreamingly.

"Ah, Porphyro!" said she, "but even now
Thy voice was at sweet tremble in mine ear,
Made tuneable with every sweetest vow;
And those sad eyes were spiritual and clear:
How changed thou art! how pallid, chill, and drear!

Give me that voice again, my Porphyro,
Those looks immortal, those complainings dear!
Oh leave me not in this eternal woe,
For if thou diest, my Love, I know not where to go."

Beyond a mortal man impassioned far
At these voluptuous accents, he arose,
Ethereal, flushed, and like a throbbing star
Seen mid the sapphire heaven's deep repose;
Into her dream he melted, as the rose
Blendeth its odor with the violet,—
Solution sweet: meantime the frost wind blows
Like Love's alarum pattering the sharp sleet
Against the window-panes; St. Agnes' moon hath set.

'Tis dark: quick pattereth the flaw-blown sleet.
"This is no dream, my bride, my Madeline!"
'Tis dark: the iced gusts still rave and beat:
"No dream, alas! alas! and woe is mine!
Porphyro will leave me here to fade and pine.
Cruel! what traitor could thee hither bring?
I curse not for my heart is lost in thine,
Though thou forsakest a deceived thing;—
A dove forlorn and lost with sick unpruned wing."

"My Madeline! sweet dreamer! lovely bride!
Say, may I be for aye thy vassal blest?
Thy beauty's shield, heart-shaped and vermeil-dyed?
Ah, silver shrine, here will I take my rest
After so many hours of toil and quest,
A famished pilgrim,—saved by miracle.
Though I have found, I will not rob thy nest,
Saving of thy sweet self; if thou think'st well
To trust, fair Madeline, to no rude infidel.

"Hark! 'tis an elfin-storm from faery land,
Of haggard seeming, but a boon indeed:
Arise—arise! the morning is at hand;—
The bloated wassailers will never heed;—
Let us away, my love, with happy speed;
There are no ears to hear, or eyes to see,—
Drowned all in Rhenish and the sleepy mead:
Awake! arise! my love, and fearless be,
For o'er the southern moors I have a home for thee."

She hurried at his words, beset with fears,
For there were sleeping dragons all around,
At glaring watch, perhaps, with ready spears—
Down the wide stairs a darkling way they found;
In all the house was heard no human sound.
A chain-drooped lamp was flickering by each door;
The arras, rich with horseman, hawk, and hound,
Fluttered in the besieging wind's uproar;
And the long carpets rose along the gusty floor.

They glide, like phantoms, into the wide hall;
Like phantoms, to the iron porch they glide,
Where lay the Porter, in uneasy sprawl,
With a huge empty flagon by his side:
The wakeful bloodhound rose, and shook his hide,
But his sagacious eye an inmate owns:
By one, and one, the bolts full easy slide:—
The chains lie silent on the footworn stones;
The key turns, and the door upon its hinges groans.

And they are gone; aye, ages long ago
These lovers fled away into the storm.
That night the Baron dreamt of many a woe,
And all his warrior-guests with shade and form
Of witch, and demon, and large coffin-worm,
270

Were long be-nightmared. Angela the old
Died palsy-twitched, with meager face deform;
The Beadsman, after thousand aves told,
For aye unsought-for slept among his ashes cold.

JOHN KEATS

FAIR PHYLLIS

FAIR Phyllis I saw sitting all alone,
   Feeding her flocks near to the mountain-side.
The shepherds knew not whither she was gone,
   But after her, lover Amyntas hied.
Up and down he wandered whilst she was missing;
When he found her, O, then they fell a-kissing.

BEN JONSON

LOVE

ALL thoughts, all passions, all delights,
Whatever stirs this mortal frame,
All are but ministers of Love,
    And feed his sacred flame.

Oft in my waking dreams do I
Live o'er again that happy hour,
When midway on the mount I lay,
    Beside the ruin'd tower.

The moonshine, stealing o'er the scene,
Had blended with the lights of eve;
And she was there, my hope, my joy,
    My own dear Genevieve!

She lean'd against the armèd man,
The statue of the armèd Knight;
She stood and listen'd to my lay,
    Amid the lingering light.

Few sorrows hath she of her own,
My hope! my joy! my Genevieve!
She loves me best whene'er I sing
    The songs that make her grieve.

I play'd a soft and doleful air;
I sang an old and moving story—
An old rude song, that suited well
    That ruin wild and hoary.

She listen'd with a flitting blush,
With downcast eyes and modest grace;
For well she knew I could not choose
    But gaze upon her face.

I told her of the Knight that wore
Upon his shield a burning brand;
And that for ten long years he woo'd
    The Lady of the Land.

I told her how he pined: and ah!
The deep, the low, the pleading tone
With which I sang another's love,
    Interpreted my own.

She listened with a flitting blush,
With downcast eyes, and modest grace;
And she forgave me, that I gazed
    Too fondly on her face!

But when I told the cruel scorn
That crazed that bold and lovely Knight,
And that he cross'd the mountain-woods,
    Nor rested day nor night;

That sometimes from the savage den,
And sometimes from the darksome shade,
And sometimes starting up at once
    In green and sunny glade—

There came and look'd him in the face
An angel beautiful and bright;
And that he knew it was a Fiend,
    This miserable Knight!

And that, unknowing what he did,
He leap'd amid a murderous band,
And saved from outrage worse than death
    The Lady of the Land;—

And how she wept and clasp'd his knees;
And how she tended him in vain—
And ever strove to expiate
    The scorn that crazed his brain;—

And that she nursed him in a cave;
And how his madness went away,
When on the yellow forest leaves
    A dying man he lay;—

His dying words—but when I reach'd
That tenderest strain of all the ditty,
My faltering voice and pausing harp
    Disturb'd her soul with pity!

All impulses of soul and sense
Had thrill'd my guileless Genevieve;
The music and the doleful tale,
    The rich and balmy eve;

And hopes, and fears that kindle hope,
An undistinguishable throng,
And gentle wishes long subdued,
    Subdued and cherish'd long!

She wept with pity and delight,
She blush'd with love and virgin shame;
And like the murmur of a dream,
    I heard her breathe my name.

Her bosom heaved—she stepp'd aside,
As conscious of my look she stept—
Then suddenly, with timorous eye
    She fled to me and wept.

She half enclosed me with her arms,
She press'd me with a meek embrace;
And bending back her head, look'd up,
    And gazed upon my face.

'Twas partly love, and partly fear,
And partly 'twas a bashful art,
That I might rather feel, than see,
    The swelling of her heart.

I calm'd her fears, and she was calm,
And told her love with virgin pride;
And so I won my Genevieve,
    My bright and beauteous Bride.

SAMUEL TAYLOR COLERIDGE

SONG FROM AELLA

O SING unto my roundelay,
O drop the briny tear with me;
Dance no more at holyday,
Like a running river be:
    My love is dead,
      Gone to his death-bed
All under the willow-tree.

Black his cryne as the winter night,
White his rode as the summer snow,
Red his face as the morning light,
Cold he lies in the grave below:
    My love is dead,
      Gone to his death-bed
All under the willow-tree.

Sweet his tongue as the throstle's note,
Quick in dance as thought can be,
Deft his tabor, cudgel stout;
O he lies by the willow-tree!
    My love is dead,
      Gone to his death-bed
All under the willow-tree.

Hark! the raven flaps his wing
In the brier'd dell below;
Hark! the death-owl loud doth sing
To the nightmares, as they go:
    My love is dead,
      Gone to his death-bed
All under the willow-tree.

See! the white moon shines on high;
Whiter is my true-love's shroud:
Whiter than the morning sky,
Whiter than the evening cloud:
    My love is dead,
      Gone to his death-bed
All under the willow-tree.

Here upon my true-love's grave
Shall the barren flowers be laid;
Not one holy saint to save
All the coldness of a maid:
    My love is dead,
      Gone to his death-bed
All under the willow-tree.

With my hands I'll dent the briers
Round his holy corse to gre:
Ouph and fairy, light your fires,
Here my body still shall be:
    My love is dead,
      Gone to his death-bed
All under the willow-tree.

Come, with acorn-cup and thorn,
Drain my heartès blood away;
Life and all its good I scorn,
Dance by night, or feast by day:
    My love is dead,
      Gone to his death-bed
All under the willow-tree.

THOMAS CHATTERTON

THE TWA CORBIES

As I was walking all alane
I heard twa corbies making a mane:
The tane unto the tither did say,
"Whar sall we gang and dine the day?"

"—In behint yon auld fail dyke
I wot there lies a new-slain knight;
And naebody kens that he lies there
But his hawk, his hound, and his lady fair.

"His hound is to the hunting gane,
His hawk to fetch the wild-fowl hame,
His lady's ta'en anither mate,
So we may mak our dinner sweet.

"Ye'll sit on his white hause-bane,
And I'll pike out his bonny blue e'en:
Wi' ae lock o' his gowden hair
We'll theek our nest when it grows bare.

"Mony a one for him maks mane,
But nane sall ken whar he is gane:
O'er his white banes, when they are bare,
The wind sall blaw for evermair."

ANONYMOUS

MARIANA

WITH blackest moss the flower-plots
  Were thickly crusted, one and all;
The rusted nails fell from the knots
  That held the pear to the gable-wall.
The broken sheds looked sad and strange:
  Unlifted was the clinking latch;
  Weeded and worn the ancient thatch
Upon the lonely moated grange.
  She only said, "My life is dreary,
  He cometh not," she said;
She said, "I am aweary, aweary,
  I would that I were dead."

Her tears fell with the dews at even;
  Her tears fell ere the dews were dried;
She could not look on the sweet heaven,
  Either at morn or eventide.
After the flitting of the bats,
  When thickest dark did trace the sky,
  She drew her casement-curtain by,
And glanced athwart the glooming flats.
  She only said, "The night is dreary,
  He cometh not," she said.
She said, "I am aweary, aweary,
  I would that I were dead."

Upon the middle of the night
  Waking she heard the night-fowl crow;
The cock sung out an hour ere light;
  From the dark fen the oxen's low
Came to her; without hope of change,
  In sleep she seemed to walk forlorn,

Till cold winds woke the gray-eyed morn
About the lonely moated grange.
She only said, "The day is dreary,
    He cometh not," she said;
  She said, "I am aweary, aweary,
    I would that I were dead."

About a stone-cast from the wall
  A sluice with blackened waters slept,
And o'er it many, round and small,
  The clustered marish-mosses crept.
Hard by a poplar shook alway,
  All silver-green with gnarlèd bark;
  For leagues no other tree did mark
The level waste, the rounding gray.
  She only said, "My life is dreary,
    He cometh not," she said;
  She said, "I am aweary, aweary,
    I would that I were dead."

And ever when the moon was low,
  And the shrill winds were up and away,
In the white curtain, to and fro,
  She saw the gusty shadow sway.
But when the moon was very low,
  And wild winds bound within their cell,
  The shadow of the poplar fell
Upon her bed, across her brow.
  She only said, "The night is dreary,
    He cometh not," she said;
  She said, "I am aweary, aweary,
    I would that I were dead."

All day within the dreamy house,
  The doors upon their hinges creaked;

279

The blue fly sung in the pane; the mouse
　　Behind the mouldering wainscot shrieked,
Or from the crevice peered about.
　　Old faces glimmered through the doors,
　　Old footsteps trod the upper floors,
Old voices called her from without
　　She only said, "My life is dreary,
　　　　He cometh not," she said;
　　She said, "I am aweary, aweary,
　　　　I would that I were dead!"

The sparrow's chirrup on the roof,
　　The slow clock ticking, and the sound
Which to the wooing wind aloof
　　The poplar made, did all confound
Her sense; but most she loathed the hour
　　When the thick-moted sunbeam lay
　　Athwart the chambers, and the day
Was sloping toward his western bower.
　　Then said she, "I am very dreary,
　　　　He will not come," she said;
　　She wept, "I am aweary, aweary,
　　　　O God, that I were dead!"

ALFRED, LORD TENNYSON

LORD RANDALL

"O WHERE hae ye been, Lord Randall, my son?
　O where hae ye been, my handsome young man?"
"I hae been to the wild wood; mother, make my bed
　　soon,
　For I'm weary wi hunting, and fain wald lie down."

"Where gat ye your dinner, Lord Randall, my son?
  Where gat ye your dinner, my handsome young man?"
"I dined wi my true-love; mother, make my bed soon,
  For I'm weary wi hunting, and fain wald lie down."

"What gat ye to your dinner, Lord Randall, my son?
  What gat ye to your dinner, my handsome young man?"
"I gat eels boiled in broo; mother, make my bed soon,
  For I'm weary wi hunting, and fain wald lie down."

"What became of your bloodhounds, Lord Randall, my
      son?
  What became of your bloodhounds, my handsome
      young man?"
"O they swelld and they died; mother, make my bed
      soon,
  For I'm weary wi hunting, and fain wald lie down."

"O I fear ye are poisond, Lord Randall, my son!
  O I fear ye are poisond, my handsome young man!"
"O yes! I am poisond; mother, make my bed soon,
  For I'm sick at the heart, and I fain wald lie down."

ANONYMOUS

STRANGE FITS OF PASSION
HAVE I KNOWN

STRANGE fits of passion have I known:
And I will dare to tell,
But in the lover's ear alone,
What once to me befell.

281

When she I loved looked every day
Fresh as a rose in June,
I to her cottage bent my way,
Beneath an evening moon.

Upon the moon I fixed my eye,
All over the wide lea;
With quickening pace my horse drew nigh
Those paths so dear to me.

And now we reached the orchard-plot;
And, as we climbed the hill,
The sinking moon to Lucy's cot
Came near, and nearer still.

In one of those sweet dreams I slept,
Kind Nature's gentlest boon!
And all the while my eyes I kept
On the descending moon.

My horse moved on; hoof after hoof
He raised, and never stopped:
When down behind the cottage roof,
At once, the bright moon dropped.

What fond and wayward thoughts will slide
Into a lover's head!
"O mercy!" to myself I cried,
"If Lucy should be dead!"

WILLIAM WORDSWORTH

BONNY BARBARA ALLAN

It was in and about the Martinmas time,
  When the green leaves were a falling,
That Sir John Graeme, in the West country
  Fell in love with Barbara Allan.

He sent his man down through the town,
  To the place where she was dwelling:
"O haste and come to my master dear,
  Gin ye be Barbara Allan."

O hooly, hooly rose she up,
  To the place where he was lying,
And when she drew the curtain by,
  "Young man, I think you're dying."

"O it's I'm sick, and very, very sick,
  And 't is a' for Barbara Allan:"
"O the better for me ye's never be,
  Tho your heart's blood were a spilling.

"O dinna ye mind, young man," said she,
  "When ye was in the tavern a drinking,
That ye made the healths gae round and round,
  And slighted Barbara Allan?"

He turned his face unto the wall,
  And death was with him dealing:
"Adieu, adieu, my dear friends all,
  And be kind to Barbara Allan."

And slowly, slowly raise she up,
  And slowly, slowly left him,

And sighing said, she could not stay,
   Since death of life had reft him.

She had not gane a mile but twa,
   When she heard the dead-bell ringing,
And every jow that the dead-bell geid,
   It cryd, Woe to Barbara Allan!

"O mother, mother, make my bed!
   O make it saft and narrow!
Since my love died for me today,
   I'll die for him tomorrow."

ANONYMOUS

THE TRUE LOVER

THE lad came to the door at night,
   When lovers crown their vows,
And whistled soft and out of sight
   In shadow of the boughs.

I shall not vex you with my face
   Henceforth, my love, for aye;
So take me in your arms a space
   Before the east is grey.

When I from hence away am past
    I shall not find a bride,
And you shall be the first and last
    I ever lay beside.

She heard and went and knew not why;
    Her heart to his she laid;
Light was the air beneath the sky
    But dark under the shade.

"Oh do you breathe, lad, that your breast
    Seems not to rise and fall,
And here upon my bosom prest
    There beats no heart at all?"

"Oh loud, my girl, it once would knock,
    You should have felt it then;
But since for you I stopped the clock
    It never goes again."

"Oh lad, what is it, lad, that drips
    Wet from your neck on mine?
What is it falling on my lips,
    My lad, that tastes of brine?"

"Oh like enough 'tis blood, my dear,
    For when the knife has slit
The throat across from ear to ear
    'Twill bleed because of it."

Under the stars the air was light
    But dark below the boughs,
The still air of the speechless night,
    When lovers crown their vows.

A. E. HOUSMAN

285

QUIA AMORE LANGUEO

In a valley of this restless mind
   I sought in mountain and in mead,
Trusting a true love for to find.
   Upon an hill then took I heed;
   A voice I heard (and near I yede)
In great dolour complaining tho:
   "See, dear soul, how my sides bleed
      Quia amore langueo."

Upon this hill I found a tree,
   Under a tree a man sitting;
From head to foot wounded was he;
   His hearté blood I saw bleeding:
   A seemly man to be a king,
A gracious face to look unto.
   I askèd why he had paining:—
      "Quia amore langueo.

"I am true love that false was never;
   My sister, man's soul, I loved her thus.
Because we would in no wise dissever
   I left my kingdom glorious.
   I purveyed her a palace full precious;
She fled, I followed, I loved her so
   That I suffered this pain piteous
      Quia amore langueo.

"My fair love and my spouse bright!
   I saved her from beating, and she hath me bet;
I clothed her in grace and heavenly light;
   This bloody shirt she hath on me set;

yede—went, drew.

286

For longing of love yet would I not let;
Sweetè strokes are thesè: lo!
I have loved her ever as I her het
    Quia amore langueo.

"I crowned her with bliss, and she me with thorn;
    I led her to chamber, and she me to die;
I brought her to worship, and she me to scorn;
    I did her reverence, she me villany.
    To love that loveth is no maistry;
Her hate made never my love her foe:
    Askè me then no question why—
        Quia amore langueo.

"Look unto mine handès, man!
    These gloves were given me when I her sought;
They be not white, but red and wan;
    Embroidered with blood my spouse them brought.
    They will not off; I loose hem nought;
I woo her with hem wherever she go.
    These hands for her so friendly fought
        Quia amore langueo.

"Marvel not, man, though I sit still.
    See, love hath shod me wonder strait:
Buckled my feet, as was her will,
    With sharpè nails (well thou may'st wait!).
    In my love was never desait;
All my members I have opened her to;
    My body I made her hertè's bait
        Quia amore langueo.

"In my side I have made her nest;
    Look in, how wet a wound is here!

het—promised; *bait*—haven, resting-place.

This is her chamber, here shall she rest,
    That she and I may sleep in fere.
Here may she wash, if any filth were;
Here is seat for all her woe;
    Come when she will, she shall have cheer
        Quia amore langueo.

"I will abide till she be ready,
    I will her sue if she say nay;
If she be reckless I will be greedy,
    If she be dangerous I will her pray;
    If she weep, then bide I ne may:
Mine arms ben spread to clip her me to,
    Cry once, 'I come: now, soul, assay!'
        Quia amore langueo.

"I sit on this hill for to see far;
    I look into the valley my spouse to see;
Now runneth she awayward, yet come she me near,
    For out of my sight may she not flee.
    Some wait her prey to make her to flee;
I run before, and fleme her foe.
    'Return, my spouse, again to me,
        Quia amore langueo.

" 'Fair love, let us go play:
    Apples ben ripe in my gardayne.
I shall thee clothe in a new array,
    Thy meat shall be milk, honey and wine.
    Fair love, let us go dine:
Thy sustenance is in my crippe, lo!
    Tarry thou not, my fair spouse mine,
        Quia amore langueo.

in fere—together; *reckless*—heedless, indifferent; *dangerous*
—disdainful, unyielding; *fleme*—discomfit, put to flight; *crippe*
—script.

" 'If thou be foul, I shall make thee clean;
 If thou be sick, I shall thee heal;
If thou mourn aught, I shall thee mene;
 Why wilt thou not, fair love, with me deal?
 Foundest thou ever love so leal?
What wouldst thou, spouse, that I should do?
 I may not unkindly thee appeal,
  Quia amore langueo.'

"What shall I do now with my spouse
 But abide her of my gentleness,
Till that she look out of her house
 Of fleshly affection? love mine she is;
 Her bed is made, her bolster is bliss,
Her chamber is chosen; is there none mo.
 Look out on me at the window of kindness,
  Quia amore langueo.

"My love's in her chamber: hold your peace!
 Make ye no noise, but let her sleep.
My babe I would not were in disease,
 I may not hear my dear child weep.
 With my pap I shall her keep;
Ne marvel ye not though I tend her to:
 This wound in my side had ne'er been so deep
  But *quia amore langueo.*

" 'Long thou for love never so high,
 My love is more than thine may be.
Thou weepest, thou gladdest, I sit thee by:
 Yet wouldst thou once, lief, look unto me!
 Shoudė I always feedė thee
With children meat? Nay, love, not so!

mene—care for, cherish.

I will prove thy love with adversity,
    Quia amore langueo.

" 'Wax not weary, mine ownė wife!
    What mede is it ever to live in comfort?
In tribulation I reign more rife
    Oftėtimes than in disport.
    In weal and in woe I am aye to support:
Mine ownė wife, go not me fro!
    Thy mede is markėd when thou art mort:
        Quia amore langueo.' "

mede—recompense. *markėd*—assured, (?) signed with the sign of the cross.

ANONYMOUS

A PURITAN'S BALLAD

MY love came up from Barnegat,
    The sea was in his eyes;
He trod as softly as a cat
    And told me terrible lies.

His hair was yellow as new-cut pine
    In shavings curled and feathered;
I thought how silver it would shine
    By cruel winters weathered.

But he was in his twentieth year,
  This time I'm speaking of;
We were head over heels in love with fear
  And half a-feared of love.

His feet were used to treading a gale
  And balancing thereon;
His face was brown as a foreign sail
  Threadbare against the sun.

His arms were thick as hickory logs
  Whittled to little wrists;
Strong as the teeth of terrier dogs
  Were the fingers of his fists.

Within his arms I feared to sink
  Where lions shook their manes,
And dragons drawn in azure ink
  Leapt quickened by his veins.

Dreadful his strength and length of limb
  As the sea to foundering ships;
I dipped my hands in love for him
  No deeper than their tips.

But our palms were welded by a flame
  The moment we came to part,
And on his knuckles I read my name
  Enscrolled within a heart.

And something made our wills to bend
  As wild as trees blown over;
We were no longer friend and friend,
  But only lover and lover.

291

"In seven weeks or seventy years—
 God grant it may be sooner!—
I'll make the handkerchief for your tears
 From the sails of my captain's schooner.

"We'll wear our loves like wedding rings
 Long polished to our touch;
We shall be busy with other things
 And they cannot bother us much.

"When you are skimming the wrinkled cream
 And your ring clinks on the pan,
You'll say to yourself in a pensive dream,
 'How wonderful a man!'

"When I am slitting a fish's head
 And my ring clanks on the knife,
I'll say with thanks, as a prayer is said,
 'How beautiful a wife!'

"And I shall fold my decorous paws
 In velvet smooth and deep
Like a kitten that covers up its claws
 To sleep and sleep and sleep.

"Like a little blue pigeon you shall bow
 Your bright alarming crest;
In the crook of my arm you'll lay your brow
 To rest and rest and rest."

Will he never come back from Barnegat
 With thunder in his eyes,
Treading as soft as a tiger cat
 To tell me terrible lies?

ELINOR WYLIE

ALONG THE FIELD AS WE CAME BY

ALONG the field as we came by
A year ago, my love and I,
The aspen over stile and stone
Was talking to itself alone.
"Oh, who are these that kiss and pass?
A country lover and his lass;
Two lovers looking to be wed;
And time shall put them both to bed,
But she shall lie with earth above,
And he beside another love."

And sure enough beneath the tree
There walks another love with me,
And overhead the aspen heaves
Its rainy-sounding silver leaves;
And I spell nothing in their stir,
But now perhaps they speak to her,
And plain for her to understand
They talk about a time at hand
When I shall sleep with clover clad,
And she beside another lad.

A. E. HOUSMAN

WRAGGLE TAGGLE GIPSIES

THREE gipsies stood at the Castle gate,
They sang so high, they sang so low;
The lady sate in her chamber late,
Her heart it melted away as snow.

293

They sang so sweet, they sang so shrill,
That fast her tears began to flow.
And she laid down her silken gown,
Her golden rings, and all her show.

She's taken off her high-heeled shoes
All made of the Spanish leather, O.
She would in the street with her bare, bare feet
All out in the wind and weather, O.

"O saddle to me my milk-white steed,
And go and fetch my pony, O!
That I may ride and seek my bride
Who is gone with the wraggle taggle gipsies, O!"

O he rode high, and he rode low,
He rode thro' wood and copses too,
Until he came to an open field,
And there he espied his lady, O!

"What makes you leave your house and land?
Your golden treasures to forego?
What makes you leave your new-wedded lord,
To follow the wraggle taggle gipsies, O?"

"What care I for my house and my land?
What care I for my treasure, O?
What care I for my new-wedded lord,—
I'm off with the wraggle taggle gipsies, O!"

"Last night you slept on a goose-feather bed,
With the sheet turned down so bravely, O?
But tonight you'll sleep in a cold open field,
Along with the wraggle taggle gipsies, O!"

"What care I for a goose-feather bed,
With the sheet turned down so bravely, O?
For tonight I shall sleep in a cold open field,
Along with the wraggle taggle gipsies, O!"

ANONYMOUS

LOVE-IN-IDLENESS

He: "Shall I be your first love, lady, shall I be your first?
　Oh! then I'll fall before you down on my velvet knee
　And deeply bend my rosy head and press it upon thee,
And swear that there is nothing more for which my
　　heart doth thirst,
　　But a downy kiss and pink
　　Between your lips' soft chink."

She: "Yes, you shall be my first love, boy, and you shall
　　be my first,
　And I will raise you up again unto my bosom's fold;
　And when you kisses many a one on lip and cheek
　　have told,
I'll let you loose upon the grass, to leave me if you durst;
　　And so we'll toy away
　　The night beside the day."

He: "But let me be your second love, but let me be your
　　second,
　For then I'll tap so gently, dear, upon your window
　　pane,
　And creep between the curtains in, where never man
　　has lain,
And never leave thy gentle side till the morning star
　　hath beckoned,

295

Within the silken lace
Of thy young arms' embrace."

She: "Well thou shalt be my second love, yes, gentle
boy, my second,
    And I will wait at eve for thee within my lonely
    bower,
    And yield unto thy kisses, like a bud to April's shower,
From moonset till the tower-clock the hour of dawn
hath reckoned,
        And lock thee with my arms
        All silent up in charms."

He: "No, I will be thy third love, lady, aye, I will be the
third,
    And break upon thee, bathing, in woody place alone,
    And catch thee to my saddle and ride o'er stream and
    stone,
And press thee well, and kiss thee well, and never speak
a word,
        Till thou hast yielded up
        The first taste of love's cup."

She: "Then thou shalt not be my first love, boy, nor my
second, nor my third;
    If thou'rt the first, I'll laugh at thee and pierce thy
    flesh with thorns;
    If the second, from my chamber pelt with jeering
    laugh and scorns;
And if thou darest be the third, I'll draw my dirk un-
heard
        And cut thy heart in two,—
        And then die, weeping you."

THOMAS LOVELL BEDDOES

296

THE THREE BUSHES

*(An incident from the "Historia mei Temporis" of the
Abbe Michel de Bourdeille)*

SAID lady once to lover,
"None can rely upon
A love that lacks its proper food;
And if your love were gone
How could you sing those songs of love?
I should be blamed, young man."
      O my dear, O my dear.

"Have no lit candles in your room,"
That lovely lady said,
"That I at midnight by the clock
May creep into your bed,
For if I saw myself creep in
I think I should drop dead."
      O my dear, O my dear.

"I love a man in secret,
Dear chambermaid," said she.
"I know that I must drop down dead
If he stop loving me,
Yet what could I but drop down dead
If I lost my chastity?"
      O my dear, O my dear.

"So you must lie beside him
And let him think me there,
And maybe we are all the same
Where no candles are,
And maybe we are all the same
That strip the body bare."
      O my dear, O my dear.

But no dogs barked, and midnights chimed,
And through the chime she'd say,
"That was a lucky thought of mine,
My lover looked so gay";
But heaved a sigh if the chambermaid
Looked half asleep all day.
     O my dear, O my dear.

"No, not another song," said he,
"Because my lady came
A year ago for the first time
At midnight to my room,
And I must lie between the sheets
When the clock begins to chime."
     O my dear, O my dear.

"A laughing, crying, sacred song,
A leching song," they said.
Did ever men hear such a song?
No, but that day they did.
Did ever man ride such a race?
No, not until he rode.
     O my dear, O my dear.

But when his horse had put its hoof
Into a rabbit-hole
He dropped upon his head and died.
His lady saw it all
And dropped and died thereon, for she
Loved him with her soul.
     O my dear, O my dear.

The chambermaid lived long, and took
Their graves into her charge,
And there two bushes planted

That when they had grown large
Seemed sprung from but a single root
So did their roses merge.
  O my dear, O my dear.

When she was old and dying,
The priest came where she was;
She made a full confession.
Long looked he in her face,
And O he was a good man
And understood her case.
  O my dear, O my dear.

He bade them take and bury her
Beside her lady's man,
And set a rose-tree on her grave,
And now none living can,
When they have plucked a rose there,
Know where its roots began.
  O my dear, O my dear.

WILLIAM BUTLER YEATS

THE HAYSTACK IN THE FLOODS

HAD she come all the way for this,
To part at last without a kiss?
Yea, had she borne the dirt and rain
That her own eyes might see him slain
Beside the haystack in the floods?

Along the dripping leafless woods,
The stirrup touching either shoe,
She rode astride as troopers do;
With kirtle kilted to her knee,
To which the mud splashed wretchedly;
And the wet dripped from every tree
Upon her head and heavy hair,
And on her eyelids broad and fair;
The tears and rain ran down her face.
By fits and starts they rode apace,
And very often was his place
Far off from her; he had to ride
Ahead, to see what might betide
When the roads crossed; and sometimes, when
There rose a murmuring from his men,
Had to turn back with promises.
Ah me! she had but little ease;
And often for pure doubt and dread
She sobbed, made giddy in the head
By the swift riding; while, for cold,
Her slender fingers scarce could hold
The wet reins; yea, and scarcely, too,
She felt the foot within her shoe
Against the stirrup: all for this,
To part at last without a kiss
Beside the haystack in the floods.

For when they neared that old soaked hay,
They saw across the only way
That Judas, Godmar, and the three
Red running lions dismally
Grinned from his pennon, under which
In one straight line along the ditch,
They counted thirty heads.

            So then
While Robert turned round to his men,
She saw at once the wretched end,
And, stooping down, tried hard to rend
Her coif the wrong way from her head,
And hid her eyes; while Robert said:
"Nay, love, 'tis scarcely two to one;
At Poictiers where we made them run
So fast—why, sweet my love, good cheer,
The Gascon frontier is so near,
Nought after us."

            But: "O!" she said
"My God! my God! I have to tread
The long way back without you; then
The court at Paris; those six men;
The gratings of the Chatelet;
The swift Seine on some rainy day
Like this, and people standing by,
And laughing, while my weak hands try
To recollect how strong men swim.
All this, or else a life with him,
For which I should be damned at last,
Would God that this next hour were past!"

He answered not, but cried his cry,
"St. George for Marny!" cheerily;
And laid his hand upon her rein.
Alas! no man of all his train

Gave back that cheery cry again;
And, while for rage his thumb beat fast
Upon his sword-hilt, some one cast
About his neck a kerchief long,
And bound him.

       Then they went along
To Godmar, who said: "Now, Jehane,
Your lover's life is on the wane
So fast, that, if this very hour
You yield not as my paramour,
He will not see the rain leave off:
Nay, keep your tongue from gibe and scoff,
Sir Robert, or I slay you now."
She laid her hand upon her brow,
Then gazed upon the palm, as though
She thought her forehead bled, and: "No!"
She said, and turned her head away,
As there was nothing else to say,
And everything was settled: red
Grew Godmar's face from chin to head:
"Jehane, on yonder hill there stands
My castle, guarding well my lands;
What hinders me from taking you,
And doing that I list to do
To your fair wilful body, while
Your knight lies dead?"

       A wicked smile
Wrinkled her face, her lips grew thin,
A long way out she thrust her chin:
"You know that I should strangle you
While you were sleeping; or bite through
Your throat, by God's help: ah!" she said,
"Lord Jesus, pity your poor maid!
For in such wise they hem me in,
I cannot choose but sin and sin,

302

Whatever happens: yet I think
They could not make me eat or drink,
And so should I just reach my rest."
"Nay, if you do not my behest,
O Jehane! though I love you well,"
Said Godmar, "would I fail to tell
All that I know?" "Foul lies," she said.
"Eh? lies, my Jehane? by God's head,
At Paris folk would deem them true!

Do you know, Jehane, they cry for you:
'Jehane the brown! Jehane the brown!
Give us Jehane to burn or drown!'
Eh! gag me Robert—sweet my friend,
This were indeed a piteous end
For those long fingers, and long feet,
And long neck, and smooth shoulders sweet;
An end that few men would forget
That saw it. So, an hour yet:
Consider, Jehane, which to take
Of life or death!"
                        So, scarce awake,
Dismounting, did she leave that place,
And totter some yards: with her face
Turned upward to the sky she lay,
Her head on a wet heap of hay,
And fell asleep: and while she slept,
And did not dream, the minutes crept
Around to twelve again; but she,
Being waked at last, sighed quietly,
And strangely childlike came, and said:
"I will not." Straightway Godmar's head,
As though it hung on strong wires, turned
Most sharply round, and his face burned.

For Robert, both his eyes were dry,
He could not weep, but gloomily
He seemed to watch the rain; yea, too,
His lips were firm; he tried once more
To touch her lips; she reached out, sore
And vain desire so tortured them,
The poor gray lips, and now the hem
Of his sleeve brushed them.
                            With a start
Up Godmar rose, thrust them apart;
From Robert's throat he loosed the bands
Of silk and mail. With empty hands
Held out, she stood and gazed, and saw,
The long bright blade without a flaw
Glide out from Godmar's sheath, his hand
In Robert's hair; she saw him bend
Back Robert's head; she saw him send
The thin steel down; the blow told well,
Right backward the knight Robert fell,
And moaned as dogs do, being half dead,
Unwitting, as I deem: so then
Godmar turned grinning to his men,
Who ran, some five or six, and beat
His head to pieces at their feet.
Then Godmar turned again and said:
"So, Jehane, the first fitte is read!
Take note, my lady, that your way
Lies backward to the Chatelet!"
She shook her head and gazed awhile
At her cold hands with a rueful smile,
As though this thing had made her mad.

This was the parting that they had
Beside the haystack in the floods.

                                    WILLIAM MORRIS

304

THE NUT-BROWN MAID

He.   Be it right or wrong, these men among
      On women do complain;
    Affirming this, how that it is
      A labour spent in vain
    To love them well; for never a deal
      They love a man again,
    For let a man do what he can
      Their favor to attain,
    Yet if a new to them pursue,
      Their first true lover then
    Laboureth for nought, for from their thought
      He is a banished man.

She. I say not nay, but that all day
      It is both writ and said
    That woman's faith is, as who saith,
      All utterly decayed:
    But nevertheless, right good witnèss
      In this case might be laid,
    That they love true, and continùe,—
      Record the Nut-brown Maid;
    Which from her love, when her to prove,
      He came to make his moan,
    Would not depart, for in her heart
      She loved but him alone.

He.   Then between us let us discuss
      What was all the manner
    Between them two: we will also
      Tell all the pain and fear,
    That she was in; now I begin,
      So that ye me answèr:

Wherefore all ye that present be,
 I pray you give an ear.
I am the knight, I come by night,
 As secret as I can,
Saying, Alas! thus standeth the case,
 I am a banished man!

She. *And I your will for to fulfil*
  In this will not refuse,
 Trusting to show, in wordes few,
  That men have an ill use,
 To their own shame, women to blame,
  And causeless them accuse:
 Therefore to you I answer now,
  All women to excuse,
 Mine own heart dear, with you what cheer
  I pray you tell anon:
 For in my mind, of all mankind
  I love but you alone.

He. It standeth so: a deed is done
  Whereof much harm shall grow.
 My destiny is for to die
  A shameful death, I trow,
 Or else to flee,—the one must be:
  None other way I know,
 But to withdraw as an outlàw,
  And take me to my bow.
 Wherefore, adieu, my own heart true,
  None other rede I can;
 For I must to the green-wood go,
  Alone, a banished man.

She. O Lord, what is this worldis bliss,
  That changeth as the moon!

My summer's day in lusty May
    Is derked before the noon.
I hear you say, farewell: Nay, nay,
    We dèpart not so soon.
Why say ye so? whither will ye go?
    Alas! what have ye done?
All my welfàre to sorrow and care
    Should change, if you were gone:
For in my mind, of all mankind
    I love but you alone.

He.   I can believe it shall you grieve,
    And somewhat you distrain;
But afterward your paines hard
    Within a day or twain
Shall soon aslake, and ye shall take
    Comfort to you again.
Why should ye nought? for, to make thought,
    Your labour were in vain,
And thus I do, and pray you, too,
    As heartily as I can:
For I must to the green-wood go,
    Alone, a banished man.

She. Now sith that ye have showed to me
    The secret of your mind,
I shall be plain to you again,
    Like as ye shall me find:
Sith it is so that ye will go,
    I will not live behind;
Shall never be said that Nut-brown Maid
    Was to her love unkind.
Make you ready, for so am I,
    Although it were anon;
For in my mind, of all mankind
    I love but you alone.

307

He.   Yet I you rede to take good heed
        What men will think and say;
    Of young and old it shall be told,
        That ye be gone away
    Your wanton will for to fulfil,
        In green-wood you to play;
    And that ye might from your delight
        No longer make delay.
    Rather than ye should thus for me
        Be called an ill womàn
    Yet would I to the green-wood go
        Alone, a banished man.

She.   Though it be sung of old and young
        That I should be to blame,
    Theirs be the charge that speak so large
        In hurting of my name.
    For I will prove that faithful love
        It is devoid of shame,
    In your distress and heaviness
        To part with you the same;
    And sure all those that do not so,
        True lovers are they none;
    But in my mind, of all mankind
        I love but you alone.

He.   I counsel you remember how
        It is no maiden's law,
    Nothing to doubt, but to run out
        To wood with an outlàw.
    For ye must there in your hand bear
        A bow ready to draw,
    And as a thief thus must ye live,
        Ever in dread and awe;
    By which to you great harm might grow;—

Yet had I liever then
That I had to the green-wood go,
Alone, a banished man.

She. I think not nay, but as ye say,
It is no maiden's lore;
But love may make me for your sake,
As ye have said before,
To come on foot, to hunt and shoot,
To get us meat and store;
For so that I your company
May have, I ask no more;
From which to part it maketh my heart,
As cold as any stone;
For in my mind, of all mankind
I love but you alone.

He. For an outlàw this is the law,
That men him take and bind,
Without pity, hangèd to be,
And waver with the wind.
If I had need, as God forbid,
What succours could ye find?
Forsooth, I trow, you and your bow
Should draw for fear behind;
And no marvèl; for little avail
Were in your counsel then;
Wherefore I to the wood will go,
Alone, a banished man.

She. Full well know ye that women be
Full feeble for to fight;
No womanhead is it, indeed,
To be bold as a knight.
Yet in such fear if that ye were

309

Among enemies day and night,
I would withstand, with bow in hand,
  To grieve them as I might,
And you to save, as women have
  From death many a one:
For in my mind, of all mankind
  I love but you alone.

He. Yet take good heed; for ever I dread
    That ye could not sustain
  The thorny ways, the deep vallèys,
    The snow, the frost, the rain,
  The cold, the heat; for, dry or wet,
    We must lodge on the plain;
  And us above no other roof
    But a brake bush or twain;
  Which soon should grieve you, I believe,
    And ye would gladly then
  That I had to the green-wood go,
    Alone, a banished man.

She. Sith I have here been partynère
    With you of joy and bliss,
  I must alsò part of your woe
    Endure, as reason is;
  Yet am I sure of one pleasùre,
    And shortly, it is this;
  That where ye be, me seemeth, pardè,
    I could not fare amiss.
  Without more speech, I you beseech
    That we were soon agone;
  For in my mind, of all mankind
    I love but you alone.

He. If you go thyder, ye must consider,
    When ye have lust to dine,
There shall no meat be for to get,
    Nor drink, beer, ale, nor wine;
No sheetes clean, to lie between,
    Made of thread and twine;
None other house but leaves and boughs,
    To cover your head and mine.
Lo, mine heart sweet, this evil diét
    Should make you pale and wan:
Wherefore I to the wood will go,
    Alone, a banishèd man.

She. Among the wild deer such an archèr
    As men say that ye be,
Ne may not fail of good vitayle
    Where is so great plentỳ:
And water clear of the rivèr
    Shall be full sweet to me;
With which in hele I shall right wele
    Endure, as ye shall see;
And, or we go, a bed or two
    I can provide anon;
For in my mind, of all mankind
    I love but you alone.

He. Lo, yet before, ye must do more,
    If ye will go with me,
As cut your hair up by your ear,
    Your kirtle by the knee;
With bow in hand for to withstand
    Your enemies, if need be;
And this same night, before daylight,

To woodward will I flee;
And if ye will all this fulfil
  Do it shortly as ye can:
Else will I to the green-wood go,
  Alone, a banished man.

She. I shall as now do more for you
      Than 'longeth to womanhead,
    To short my hair, a bow to bear,
      To shoot in time of need:
    O my sweet mother, before all other,
      For you have I most dread!
    But now, adieu! I must ensue
      Where fortune doth me lead.
    All this make ye: now let us flee;
      The day cometh fast upon;
    For in my mind, of all mankind
      I love but you alone.

He. Nay, nay, not so; ye shall not go,
      And I shall tell you why;
    Your appetite is to be light
      Of love, I well espy:
    For right as ye have said to me,
      In likewise, hardily,
    Ye would answer, whosoever it were,
      In way of company.
    It is said of old, soon hot, soon cold,
      And so is a womàn;
    Wherefore I to the wood will go,
      Alone, a banished man.

She. If ye take heed, it is no need
      Such words to say by me;

312

For oft ye prayed, and long assayed,
   Or I you loved, pardè:
And though that I of ancestry
   A baron's daughter be,
Yet have you proved how I you loved,
   A squire of low degree;
And ever shall, whatso befall,
   To die therefore anon;
For in my mind, of all mankind
   I love but you alone.

He. A baron's child to be beguiled,
   It were a cursèd deed!
To be felàwe with an outlàw—
   Almighty God forbid!
Yet better were the poor squyère
   Alone to forest yede
Than ye shall say another day,
   That by my wicked deed
Ye were betrayed; wherefore, good maid,
   The best rede that I can,
Is, that I to the green-wood go,
   Alone, a banished man.

She. Whatsoever befall, I never shall
   Of this thing you upbraid:
But if ye go, and leave me so,
   Then have ye me betrayed.
Remember you well, how that ye deal,
   For if ye, as ye said,
Be so unkind to leave behind
   Your love, the Nut-brown Maid,
Trust me truly, that I shall die,
   Soon after ye be gone;

313

For in my mind, of all mankind
    I love but you alone.

He.   If that ye went, ye should repent,
    For in the forest now
I have purveyed me of a maid,
    Whom I love more than you:
Another fairer than ever ye were,
    I dare it well avow;
And of you both each should be wroth
    With other, as I trow.
It were mine ease to live in peace;
    So will I, if I can:
Wherefore I to the wood will go,
    Alone, a banished man.

She.   Though in the wood I understood
    Ye had a paramour,
All this may nought remove my thought,
    But that I will be your;
And she shall find me soft and kind
    And courteous every hour,
Glad to fulfil all that she will
    Command me, to my power:
For had ye, lo, an hundred mo,
    Yet would I be that one.
For in my mind, of all mankind
    I love but you alone.

He.   Mine own dear love, I see the prove
    That ye be kind and true;
Of maid, and wife, in all my life,
    The best that ever I knew.

Be merry and glad, be no more sad,
    The case is changèd new;
For it were ruth that for your truth
    Ye should have cause to rue.
Be not dismayed: whatsoever I said
    To you when I began,
I will not to the green-wood go;
    I am no banished man.

She. These tidings be more glad to me
    Than to be made a queen,
If I were sure they should endure;
    But it is often seen,
When men will break promise, they speak
    The wordes on the spleen.
Ye shape some wile me to beguile,
    And steal from me, I ween:
Then were the case worse than it was,
    And I more wobegone;
For in my mind, of all mankind
    I love but you alone.

He. Ye shall not need further to dread:
    I will not disparàge
You, God defend, sith ye descend
    Of so great a lineàge.
Now understand: to Westmoreland,
    Which is my heritage,
I will you bring, and with a ring,
    By way of marriàge,
I will you take, and lady make,
    As shortly as I can:
Thus have you won an Earl's son
    And not a banished man.

Here may ye see that women be
    In love meek, kind, and stable:
Let never man reprove them than,
    Or call them variable;
But rather pray God that we may
    To them be comfortable;
Which sometimes proveth such as loveth,
    If they be charitable.
For sith men would that women should
    Be meek to them each one,
Much more ought they to God obey,
    And serve but Him alone.

ANONYMOUS

XII

The Secret Wounds:

Renunciation

SONG

When lovely woman stoops to folly
    And finds too late that men betray,
What charm can soothe her melancholy?
    What art can wash her guilt away?

The only art her guilt to cover,
    To hide her shame from every eye,
To give repentance to her lover,
    And wring his bosom, is—to die.

Oliver Goldsmith

THE TIME I'VE LOST IN WOOING

The time I've lost in wooing
In watching and pursuing
    The light, that lies
    In woman's eyes,
Has been my heart's undoing.
Though Wisdom oft has sought me,
I scorned the lore she brought me,
    My only books
    Were woman's looks,
And folly's all they've taught me.

Her smile when Beauty granted,
I hung with gaze enchanted,
    Like him the Sprite,
    Whom maids by night

Oft meet in glen that's haunted.
Like him, too, Beauty won me,
But while her eyes were on me,
    If once their ray
    Was turned away,
O, winds could not outrun me.

And are those follies going?
And is my proud heart growing
    Too cold or wise
    For brilliant eyes
Again to set it glowing?
No, vain, alas! th' endeavor
From bonds so sweet to sever;—
    Poor Wisdom's chance
    Against a glance
Is now as weak as ever.

THOMAS MOORE

PRIVATE WORSHIP

SHE lay there in the stone folds of his life
Like a blue flower in granite—this he knew;
And knew how now inextricably the petals
Clung to the rock; recessed beyond his hand-thrust;
More deeply in, past more forgotten windings
Than his rude tongue could utter, praising her.

He praised her with his eyes, beholding oddly
Not what another saw, but what she added—
Thinning today and shattering with a slow smile—
To the small flower within, to the saved secret.
She was not his to have—except that something,
Always like petals falling, entered him.

320

She was not his to keep—except the brightness,
Flowing from her, that lived in him like dew;
And the kind flesh he could remember touching,
And the unconscious lips, and both her eyes:
These lay in him like leaves—beyond the last turn
Breathing the rocky darkness till it bloomed.

It was not large, this chamber of the blue flower,
Nor could the scent escape; nor the least color
Ebb from that place and stain the outer stone.
Nothing upon his grey sides told the fable,
Nothing of love or lightness, nothing of song;
Nothing of her at all. Yet he could fancy—

Oh, he could feel where petals spread their softness,
Gathered from windfalls of her when she smiled;
Growing some days, he thought, as if to burst him—
Oh, he could see the split halves, and the torn flower
Fluttering in sudden sun; and see the great stain—
Oh, he could see what tears had done to stone.

MARK VAN DOREN

THE CONTRARIOUS PASSIONS
IN A LOVER

I FIND no peace, and all my war is done;
I fear and hope, I burn, and freeze like ice;
I fly above the wind, yet can I not arise;
And nought I have, and all the world I seize on,
That loseth nor locketh, holdeth me in prison,
And holdeth me not, yet can I escape no wise;
Nor letteth me live, nor die, at my devise,

321

At yet of death it giveth me occasion.
Without eye I see; and without tongue I plain:
I desire to perish, and yet I ask health;
I love another, and thus I hate myself;
I feed me in sorrow, and laugh in all my pain.
Likewise displeaseth me both death and life,
And my delight is causer of this strife.

SIR THOMAS WYATT

RENOUNCEMENT

I MUST not think of thee; and, tired yet strong,
I shun the love that lurks in all delight—
   The love of thee—and in the blue heaven's height,
And in the dearest passage of a song.
Oh, just beyond the sweetest thoughts that throng
   This breast, the thought of thee waits hidden yet
      bright;
But it must never, never come in sight;
I must stop short of thee the whole day long.
But when sleep comes to close each difficult day,
   When night gives pause to the long watch I keep,
And all my bonds I needs must loose apart,
Must doff my will as raiment laid away,—
   With the first dream that comes with the first sleep
I run, I run, I am gather'd to thy heart.

ALICE MEYNELL

THE DARK MEMORY

It was our love's Gethsemane, and you wept.
    Around us, in the drab twilight, the little room
That had known our love, that had known our tears and
        our laughter, kept
    Shamed silence. Silently round us rose the gloom—

And in the street the first few lamps were gleaming—
        day's
    Last fire on garish windows glared. The light
Feebled; over the huddled city's wastes and ways
    Gravely and pitifully came the night.

Darkness—and from far-off a siren mourned. The sands
    Of time drew downward, but still no word was said,
No word—only your poor hands lying in my hands,
    So hopeless, against my shoulder your poor head.

You were so tired, you were so hushed, so fain,
    Poor love, all blind with weeping; pinched and small
Your face shone in the glimmer—but I, who felt no pain
    Save pity, I was so eager to end it all.

And I could not endure it; suddenly my heart grew old,
    In the gray evening, in the drab twilight—while, one
        by one,
Your hot tears ached along my hands. Oh, stern and cold
    I sat beside you, in that last hour, and you wept alone.

            .   .   .   .

Brief was our parting, very brief, and without a word.
    With a mute kiss we parted—you turned, and I,
Closing the door, in the outer hall-way heard,
    Already as if from far away, your sudden cry.

That cry! What silences followed—what silences haunt
the space
Of the years grown wide between us! On barren
rhyme
I have wreaked my youth; I have followed a phantom
loveliness—your face
Fades in the hungry darknesses of time.

But now, in my nights, now in my loneliness, I know
The bitter passion that moved those tears—and why,
When my life went home to you, when the tides groped,
you shuddered so—
And the agony of that love, the dolor of that cry.

Had you foreseen, O wise and sad, the unkinder ways
My feet must wander, on strange roads? Did you
foresee,
Beyond that wilful hour, the desolate nights and days—
And the tears that I pitied so, were they shed for me?

O fatuous dream, that like a sword clove us apart!
Dear room, where once your sorrowing lips on mine
Trembled—where humbly for my proud and ignorant
heart
You broke the bread and poured the living wine!

Love, I have heard it told, is God, and once Love found
me—
Across my heart his very heart was bowed—
He came to me out of the darkness, his arms were laid
around me:
But I was stubborn, I was foolish, and very proud.

Often, often now, in the silence of the after-years,
  In the night, I remember your weeping. O my own,
In the darkness I have remembered them, your sacred
    tears
  Shed for my sake—and how you wept alone.

JOHN HALL WHEELOCK

WHEN YOU ARE OLD

WHEN you are old and gray and full of sleep,
And nodding by the fire, take down this book,
And slowly read, and dream of the soft look
Your eyes had once, and of their shadows deep;

How many loved your moments of glad grace,
And loved your beauty with love false or true;
But one man loved the pilgrim soul in you,
And loved the sorrows of your changing face.

And bending down beside the glowing bars,
Murmur, a little sadly, how love fled
And paced upon the mountains overhead
And hid his face amid a crowd of stars.

WILLIAM BUTLER YEATS

HEART, WE WILL FORGET HIM!

HEART, we will forget him!
　　You and I, to-night!
You may forget the warmth he gave,
　　I will forget the light.

When you have done, pray tell me,
　　That I my thoughts may dim;
Haste! lest while you're lagging,
　　I may remember him!

EMILY DICKINSON

HYMN TO HER UNKNOWN

IN despair at not being able to rival the creations of God
I thought on her
Whom I saw on the twenty-fourth of August nineteen
　　thirty-four
Having tea on the fifth story of Swan and Edgar's
In Piccadilly Circus.

She sat facing me with an older woman and a younger
And a little boy aged about five;
I could see that she was his mother,
Also she wore a wedding-ring and one set with dia-
　　monds.

She was about twenty-five years old,
Slim, graceful, disciplined;
She had none of the mannerisms of the suburbs,

No affectations, a low clear speech, good manners,
Hair thick and undyed.
She knew that she was beautiful and exceedingly attrac-
tive,
Every line of her dress showed it;
She was cool and determined and laughed heartily,
A wide mouth with magnificent teeth.

And having said this I come to the beginning of my
despair,
Despair that I in no way can describe her
Or bring before the eyes of the present or the future
This image that I saw.

Hundreds and hundreds of women do I see
But rarely a woman on whom eyes linger
As the eyes of Venus lingered on Adonis.

What is the use of being a poet?
Is it not a farce to call an artist a creator,
Who can create nothing, not even re-present what his
eyes have seen?

She never showed a sign that she saw me
But I knew and she knew that I knew—
Our eyes fleeting past, never meeting directly
Like that vernal twinkling of butterflies
To which Coleridge compared Shakespeare's *Venus and
Adonis.*

And, like Venus, I lavished my love upon her
I dallied with her hair, her delicate skin and smooth
limbs,
On her arms were heavy thick bangles
Like the ropes of my heart's blood.

327

Could I express the ecstasy of my adoration?
Mating with her were itself a separation!
Only our bodies fusing in a flame of crystal
Burning in an infinite empyrean
Until all the blue of the limitless heaven were drunken
In one globe of united perfection
Like a bubble that is all the oceans of the world ascend.
  ing
To the fire that is the fire of fires, transcending
The love of God, the love of God, the love of God—
Ah! my pitiful efforts now ending
I remember a bough of coral
Flower of the transparent sea
Delicate pink as though a ray of the sun descending
Pathless into the ocean
Printed the foot of Venus
Where bloomed this asphodel.

W. J. Turner

SONG

Give me more love or more disdain,
    The torrid or the frozen zone
Bring equal ease unto my pain,
    The temperate affords me none;
Either extreme of love or hate
Is sweeter than a calm estate.

Give me a storm; if it be love,
    Like Danaë in that golden shower
I swim in pleasure; if it prove
    Disdain, that torrent will devour

My vulture hopes; and he's possessed
Of heaven that's but from hell released.
Then crown my joys or cure my pain,
Give me more love or more disdain.

THOMAS CAREW

SONNET

THUS ends my love, but this doth grieve me most
    That so it ends; but that ends too; this yet
Besides the wishes, hopes and time I lost
    Troubles my mind awhile, that I am set
Free, worse than denied. I can neither boast
    Choice nor success, as my case is, nor get
Pardon from myself that I loved not
    A better mistress, or her worse. This debt
Only's her due still, that she be forgot
    Ere changed lest I love none; this done, the taint
Of foul inconstancy is cleared at least
    In me. There only rests but to unpaint
Her form in my mind, that so dispossest
    It be a temple, but without a saint.

LORD HERBERT *of Cherbury*
329

FIFE TUNE

(6/8) for Sixth Platoon, 308th I.T.C.

One morning in spring
We marched from Devizes
All shapes and all sizes
Like beads on a string,
But yet with a swing
We trod the bluemetal
And full of high fettle
We started to sing.

She ran down the stair
A twelve-year-old darling
And laughing and calling
She tossed her bright hair;
Then silent to stare
At the men flowing past her—
There were all she could master
Adoring her there.

It's seldom I'll see
A sweeter or prettier;
I doubt we'll forget her
In two years or three,
And lucky he'll be
She takes for a lover
While we are far over
The treacherous sea.

John Manifold

THE SOLITARY REAPER

BEHOLD her, single in the field,
Yon solitary Highland Lass!
Reaping and singing by herself;
Stop here, or gently pass!
Alone she cuts and binds the grain,
And sings a melancholy strain;
O listen! for the vale profound
Is overflowing with the sound.

No nightingale did ever chaunt
More welcome notes to weary bands
Of travelers in some shady haunt,
Among Arabian sands;
A voice so thrilling ne'er was heard,
In springtime from the cuckoo bird,
Breaking the silence of the seas
Among the farthest Hebrides.

Will no one tell me what she sings?—
Perhaps the plaintive numbers flow
For old, unhappy, far-off things,
And battles long ago:
Or is it some more humble lay,
Familiar matter of to-day?
Some natural sorrow, loss or pain,
That has been, and may be again?

Whate'er the theme, the maiden sang
As if her song could have no ending;
I saw her singing at her work,
And o'er the sickle bending;—
I listened, motionless, and still;
And, as I mounted up the hill,

The music in my heart I bore,
Long after it was heard no more.
WILLIAM WORDSWORTH

FAIR IS MY LOVE

FAIR is my Love, and cruel as she's fair:
Her brow shades frowns, although her eyes are sunny;
Her smiles are lightning, though her pride despair,
And her disdains are gall, her favors honey.
A modest maid, decked with a blush of honor,
Whose feet do tread green paths of youth and love;
The wonder of all eyes that look upon her,
Sacred on earth, designed a Saint above.
Chastity and Beauty, which were deadly foes,
Live reconcilèd friends within her brow;
And had she Pity to conjoin with those,
Then who had heard the plaints I utter now?
   O had she not been fair, and thus unkind,
   My Muse had slept, and none had known my mind.
SAMUEL DANIEL

WHEN MEN SHALL FIND

WHEN men shall find thy flower, thy glory pass,
And thou, with careful brow, sitting alone,
Receivèd hast this message from thy glass,
That tells the truth, and says that *All is gone;*
Fresh shalt thou see in me the wounds thou madest,
Though spent thy flame, in me the heat remaining:
I that have loved thee thus before thou fadest,
My faith shall wax, when thou art in thy waning!
332

The world shall find this miracle in me,
That fire can burn when all the matter's spent:
Then what my faith hath been, thyself shalt see,
And that thou wast unkind, thou may'st repent!
    Thou may'st repent that thou hast scorned my tears,
    When Winter snows upon thy golden hairs.

SAMUEL DANIEL

A RENOUNCING OF LOVE

FAREWELL, love, and all thy laws for ever,
Thy baited hooks shall tangle me no more;
Senec and Plato call me from thy lore
To perfect wealth, my wit for to endeavor;
In blind error when I did persever,
Thy sharp repulse that pricketh aye so sore
Taught me in trifles that I set no store,
But scape forth thence since liberty is lever.
Therefore, farewell! Go trouble younger hearts,
And in me claim no more authority;
With idle youth go use thy property,
And thereon spend thy many brittle darts.
For hitherto though I have lost my time,
Me list no longer rotten boughs to climb.

SIR THOMAS WYATT

WHEN I LOVED THEE

THOUGH when I lov'd thee thou wert fair,
    Thou art no longer so;
Those glories all the pride they wear
    Unto opinion owe;
Beauties, like stars, in borrow'd lustre shine;
And 'twas my love that gave thee thine.

333

The flames that dwelt within thine eye
    Do now, with mine, expire;
Thy brightest graces fade and die
    At once with my desire;
Love's fires thus mutual influence return;
    Thine cease to shine when mine to burn.

Then, proud Celinda, hope no more
    To be implor'd or woo'd,
Since by thy scorn thou dost restore
    The wealth my love bestow'd;
And thy despis'd disdain too late shall find
    That none are fair but who are kind.

THOMAS STANLEY

I LOVED, I LOVE YOU

I LOVED, I love you, for this love have lost
    State, station, heaven, mankind's, my own esteem,
And yet can not regret what it hath cost,
    So dear is still the memory of that dream;
Yet, if I name my guilt, 'tis not to boast,
    None can deem harshlier of me than I deem:
I trace this scrawl because I cannot rest—
I've nothing to reproach, or to request.
Man's love is of man's life a thing apart,
    'Tis woman's whole existence; man may range
The court, camp, church, the vessel, and the mart;
    Sword, gown, gain, glory, offer in exchange
Pride, fame, ambition, to fill up his heart,
    And few there are whom these cannot estrange;
Men have all these resources, we but one,
To love again, and be again undone.

GEORGE GORDON, LORD BYRON

XIII

Kiss and Part:

Separation, Absence, Loss

THE PARTING

SINCE there's no help, come let us kiss and part—
Nay, I have done, you get no more of me;
And I am glad, yea, glad with all my heart,
That thus so cleanly I myself can free.
Shake hands for ever, cancel all our vows,
And when we meet at any time again,
Be it not seen in either of our brows
That we one jot of former love retain.
Now at the last gasp of Love's latest breath,
When, his pulse failing, Passion speechless lies,
When Faith is kneeling by his bed of death,
And Innocence is closing up his eyes,
—Now if thou wouldst, when all have given him over,
From death to life thou might'st him yet recover.

MICHAEL DRAYTON

BREAK OF DAY

'TIS true, 'tis day; what though it be?
Oh, wilt thou therefore rise from me?
Why should we rise because 'tis light?
Did we lie down because 'twas night?
Love which in spite of darkness brought us hither,
Should in despite of light keep us together.

Light hath no tongue, but is all eye;
If it could speak as well as spy,
This were the worst that it could say,
That being well I fain would stay,

337

And that I loved my heart and honour so
That I would not from him, that had them, go.

Must business thee from hence remove?
Oh, that's the worst disease of love,
The poor, the foul, the false, love can
Admit, but not the busied man.
He which hath business, and makes love, doth do
Such wrong as when a married man doth woo.

JOHN DONNE

PARTING WITHOUT A SEQUEL

SHE has finished and sealed the letter
At last, which he so richly deserved,
With characters venomous and hatefully curved,
And nothing could be better.

But even as she gave it,
Saying to the blue-capped functioner of doom,
'Into his hands,' she hoped the leering groom
Might somewhere lose and leave it.

Then all the blood
Forsook the face. She was too pale for tears,
Observing the ruin of her younger years.
She went and stood

Under her father's vaunting oak
Who kept his peace in wind and sun, and glistened
Stoical in the rain; to whom she listened
If he spoke.

And now the agitation of the rain
Rasped his sere leaves, and he talked low and gentle,
Reproaching the wan daughter by the lintel;
Ceasing, and beginning again.

Away went the messenger's bicycle,
His serpent's track went up the hill forever,
And all the time she stood there hot as fever
And cold as any icicle.

JOHN CROWE RANSOM

DEAR, WHY SHOULD YOU COMMAND ME?

DEAR, why should you command me to my rest
When now the night doth summon all to sleep?
Methinks this time becometh lovers best;
Night was ordained together friends to keep.
How happy are all other living things,
Which though the day disjoin by several flight,
The quiet evening yet together brings,
And each returns unto his love at night!
O thou that are so courteous else to all,
Why shouldst thou, Night, abuse me only thus,
That every creature to his kind dost call,
And yet 'tis thou dost only sever us?
Well could I wish it would be ever day,
If, when night comes, you bid me go away.

MICHAEL DRAYTON

I HEAR AN ARMY

I HEAR an army charging upon the land,
  And the thunder of horses plunging, foam about their
    knees:
Arrogant, in black armor, behind them stand,
  Disdaining the reins, with fluttering whips, the
    charioteers.

They cry unto the night their battle-name:
  I moan in sleep when I hear afar their whirling
    laughter.
They cleave the gloom of dreams, a blinding flame,
  Clanging, clanging upon the heart as upon an anvil.

They come shaking in triumph their long green hair:
  They come out of the sea and run shouting by the
    shore.
My heart, have you no wisdom thus to despair?
  My love, my love, my love, why have you left me
    alone?

JAMES JOYCE

PARTING

My life closed twice before its close;
It yet remains to see
If Immortality unveil
A third event to me,

So huge, so hopeless to conceive,
As these that twice befell.
Parting is all we know of heaven,
And all we need of hell.

EMILY DICKINSON

340

AN EARNEST SUIT TO HIS UNKIND MISTRESS NOT TO FORSAKE HIM

AND wilt thou leave me thus?
Say nay, say nay, for shame!
To save thee from the blame
Of all my grief and grame.
And wilt thou leave me thus?
Say nay! say nay!

And wilt thou leave me thus,
That hath loved thee so long
In wealth and woe among:
And is thy heart so strong
As for to leave me thus?
Say nay! say nay!

And wilt thou leave me thus,
That hath given thee my heart
Never for to depart
Neither for pain nor smart:
And wilt thou leave me thus?
Say nay! say nay!

And wilt thou leave me thus,
And have no more pity
Of him that loveth thee?
Alas, thy cruelty!
And wilt thou leave me thus?
Say nay! say nay!

SIR THOMAS WYATT

LOVE'S SNARE

TANGLED was I in Love's snare,
Oppressed with pain, torment with care;
Of grief right sure, of joy quite bare,
Clean in despair by cruelty.
But ha! ha! ha! full well is me,
For I am now at liberty.

The woeful days so full of pain,
The weary nights all spent in vain,
The labour lost for so small gain,
To write them all it will not be.
But ha! ha! ha! full well is me,
For I am now at liberty.

With feignèd words which were but wind
To long delays was I assigned;
Her wily looks my wits did blind;
Whate'er she would I would agree.
But ha! ha! ha! full well is me,
For I am now at liberty.

Was never bird tangled in lime
That broke away in better time,
Than I, that rotten boughs did climb
And had no hurt but 'scapèd free.
But ha! ha! ha! full well is me,
For I am now at liberty.

SIR THOMAS WYATT

ASHES OF LIFE

LOVE has gone, and left me and the days are all alike.
　　Eat I must, and sleep I will—and would that night
　　　　were here!
But ah, to lie awake and hear the slow hours strike!
　　Would that it were day again, with twilight near!

Love has gone and left me, and I don't know what to do;
　　This or that or what you will is all the same to me;
But all the things that I begin I leave before I'm
　　　　through—
　　There's little use in anything as far as I can see.

Love has gone and left me, and the neighbors knock and
　　　　borrow,
　　And life goes on forever like the gnawing of a mouse.
And tomorrow and tomorrow and tomorrow and to-
　　　　morrow
　　There's this little street and this little house.

EDNA ST. VINCENT MILLAY

A MAN WALKS IN THE WIND

BEING so tired, it is hard to hide from you;
It is hard to walk any longer in the night and the wind.
I have gone among brown trees, I have crunched the
     blue
Frost-bitten grass under my feet, I have stood
In parted thickets, caught in the crackling leaves,
I have seen the brushpiles on the ridges fired,
I have watched the twisted smoke that weaves
Blue strands in the black branches of the wood;
And now, being tired,
Being tired now and worn enough for rest,
Would it not be safe, would it not be very good
Tonight, to find it in your breast,
In your wise breast where this is understood?

Do you remember another night of wind,
Moonlight and wind, when it was all
The sky could do to keep from reeling upon us in shame,
When, breathless, we held it there
From slipping down about us with your hair?
Do you remember a night last fall
When the wind whirled us and whetted us to flame,
And whirled the leaves and whetted us to flame,
Whipped out your dress and would not let us be,
And drove us along the prairie, two shadows clinging,
And dropped us at the foot of a tree:
That was September before the frost:
In the morning the prairie was gray with mist
And the grass was matted white where we had lain.
And the arms of the elm, the grizzled arms of the elm,
Pawed at the wind for something that was lost,
And knotted up with pain.

Fall comes to fall again,
And I walk alone, I walk alone in the wind. . . .
I cannot master the beauty of the night.
I walk alone. The poplar fingers rise
Tall and awful among white glittering stars.
Surely this is the most sorrowful delight
Of any man, to walk alone with a dream.
Do you hear the ripple singing in the stream?
The beauty of the poplars strikes me down.
The wind over the grass—I had not known
The wind was such a lonely thing.
The wind cleaves me with beauty to the bone,
And the gray clouds that brush the fields and fling
Gray darkness on to the driven prairie, and fold
Their lonely silence around the hills, and fly
On to the upper night, to the upper air—
They have beat me clear, they have beat my body cold
With beauty. Do you hear the wild geese cry?

And now the dark is heavy in my head,
And in my heart all the sorrows have come home.
I am tired—you do not know how tired I come.
You would not care tonight? You would not care,
But let your hand wander through my hair?
There would be no hurt now, we are both too tired.
I would finger the soft silk of your dress the same
As long ago, when you were first desired,
As long ago, when the wind whirled us to flame.

For we know the bitter tune the wind sings;
There will be silence now, there will be rest,
And eyes will heal after the wind stings,
And I shall hear your heart under your breast
Moving across time with a great flow.

And we shall hear no more the wind's calling,
But only the silence of it falling and falling;
And always the room will throb quietly and slow.

MAURICE LESEMANN

SONG

SWEETEST love, I do not go
   For weariness of thee,
Nor in hope the world can show
   A fitter love for me;
     But since that I
Must die at last, 'tis best,
To use myself in jest,
   Thus by feigned deaths to die.

Yesternight the sun went hence,
   And yet is here to-day;
He hath no desire nor sense,
   Nor half so short a way:
     Then fear not me,
But believe that I shall make
Speedier journeys, since I take
   More wings and spurs than he.

O how feeble is man's power,
   That, if good fortune fall,
Cannot add another hour,
   Nor a lost hour recall!
     But come bad chance,
And we join to it our strength,
And we teach it art and length,
   Itself o'er us to advance.

When thou sigh'st, thou sigh'st not wind,
  But sigh'st my soul away;
When thou weep'st, unkindly kind,
  My life's blood doth decay.
    It cannot be
That thou lov'st me as thou say'st,
If in thine my life thou waste;
  Thou art the best of me.

Let not thy divining heart
  Forethink me any ill;
Destiny may take thy part,
  And may thy fears fulfil.
    But think that we
Are but turned aside to sleep;
They who one another keep
  Alive, ne'er parted be.

JOHN DONNE

OH, WHEN I WAS IN LOVE WITH YOU

OH, when I was in love with you,
  Then I was clean and brave,
And miles around the wonder grew
  How well did I behave.

And now the fancy passes by,
  And nothing will remain,
And miles around they'll say that I
  Am quite myself again.

A. E. HOUSMAN

347

MADRIGAL

Like the Idalian Queen,
Her hair about her eyne,
With neck and breasts' ripe apples to be seen,
At first glance of the Morn
In Cyprus' gardens gathering those fair flowers
Which of her blood were born,
I saw, but fainting saw, my paramours.
The Graces naked danced about the place,
The winds and trees amazed
With silence on her gazed,
The flowers did smile, like those upon her face,
And as their aspen stalks those fingers band,
That she might read my case,
A hyacinth I wished me in her hand.

WILLIAM DRUMMOND OF HAWTHORNDEN

I ENVY NOT IN ANY MOODS

I envy not in any moods
      The captive void of noble rage,
      The linnet born within the cage,
That never knew the summer woods:

I envy not the beast that takes
      His license in the field of time,
      Unfetter'd by the sense of crime,
To whom a conscience never wakes;

Nor, what may count itself as blest,
      The heart that never plighted troth

But stagnates in the weeds of sloth,
Nor any want-begotten rest.

I hold it true, whate'er befall;
    I feel it, when I sorrow most;
    'Tis better to have loved and lost
Than never to have loved at all.

ALFRED, LORD TENNYSON

LONG BETWIXT LOVE & FEAR

LONG betwixt love and fear Phillis tormented
Shunned her own wish, yet at last she consented;
But loath that day should her blushes discover:
    Come gentle night, she said,
    Come quickly to my aid,
    And a poor shamefaced maid
    Hide from her lover.

Now cold as ice I am, now hot as fire,
I dare not tell myself my own desire,
But let day fly away and let night haste her.
    Grant, ye kind powers above,
    Slow hours to parting love,
    But when to bliss we move,
    Bid them fly faster.

How sweet it is to love when I discover
That fire which burns my heart warming my lover;
'Tis pity love so true should be mistaken.
    But if this night he be
    False or unkind to me,
    Let me die ere I see
    That I'm forsaken.

JOHN DRYDEN

349

MUSIC I HEARD

Music I heard with you was more than music,
And bread I broke with you was more than bread;
Now that I am without you, all is desolate;
All that was once so beautiful is dead.

Your hands once touched this table and this silver,
And I have seen your fingers hold this glass.
These things do not remember you, beloved,
And yet your touch upon them will not pass.

For it was in my heart you moved among them,
And blessed them with your hands and with your eyes;
And in my heart they will remember always,—
They knew you once, O beautiful and wise.

CONRAD AIKEN

TO MYRA

I, with whose colors Myra dressed her head,
I, that wear posies of her own hand-making,
I, that mine own name in the chimneys read
By Myra finely wrought ere I was waking;
350

Must I look on, in hope time coming may
With change bring back my turn again to play?

I, that on Sunday at the church-stile found
A garland sweet with true-love knots in flowers,
Which I to wear about mine arms was bound,
That each of us might know that all was ours;
    Must I now lead an idle life in wishes,
    And follow Cupid for his loaves and fishes?

I, that did wear the ring her mother left,
I, for whose love she gloried to be blamed,
I, with whose eyes her eyes committed theft,
I, who did make her blush when I was named;
    Must I lose ring, flowers, blush, theft, and go naked,
    Watching with sighs till dead love be awakéd?

I, that when drowsy Argus fell asleep,
Like jealousy o'erwatchéd with desire,
Was ever warnéd modesty to keep,
While her breath speaking kindled Nature's fire;
    Must I look on a-cold, while others warm them?
    Do Vulcan's brothers in such fine nets arm them?

Was it for this that I might Myra see
Washing the water with her beauties white?
Yet would she never write her love to me,
Thinks wit of change while thoughts are in delight?
    Mad girls must safely love, as they may leave;
    No man can print a kiss; lines may deceive.

FULKE GREVILLE, LORD BROOKE
351

THE LOVER SENDETH SIGHS
TO MOVE HIS SUIT

Go, burning sighs, unto the frozen heart,
Go break the ice which pity's painful dart
Might never pierce, and if that mortal prayer
In heaven be heard at least, yet I desire
That death, or mercy, end my woful smart.
Take with thee pain whereof I have my part,
And eke the flame from which I cannot start,
And leave me then in rest, I you require.
Go, burning sighs, fulfil that I desire,
I must go work, I see, by craft and art,
For truth and faith in her is laid apart:
Alas! I cannot therefore now assail her,
With pitiful complaint and scalding fire,
That from my breast deceivably doth start.

Sir Thomas Wyatt

WHEN WE TWO PARTED

When we two parted
    In silence and tears,
Half broken-hearted
    To sever for years,
Pale grew thy cheek and cold,
    Colder thy kiss;
Truly that hour foretold
    Sorrow to this.

The dew of the morning
    Sank chill on my brow—

It felt like the warning
  Of what I feel now.
Thy vows are all broken,
  And light is thy fame:
I hear thy name spoken,
  And share in its shame.

They name thee before me,
  A knell to mine ear;
A shudder comes o'er me—
  Why wert thou so dear?
They know not I knew thee,
  Who knew thee too well:—
Long, long shall I rue thee,
  Too deeply to tell.

In secret we met—
  In silence I grieve,
That thy heart could forget,
  Thy spirit deceive.
If I should meet thee
  After long years,
How should I greet thee?—
  With silence and tears.

GEORGE GORDON, LORD BYRON

LOVE'S ABSENCE IN THE SPRING

THOUGH you be absent here, I needs must say
The trees as beauteous are, and flowers as gay,
  As ever they were wont to be;
  Nay, the birds' rural music too

Is as melodious and free,
   As if they sung to pleasure you:
I saw a rose-bud ope this morn; I'll swear
The blushing morning opened not more fair. . . .

How could it be so fair, and you away?
How could the trees be beauteous, flowers so gay?
   Could they remember but last year,
   How you did them, they you delight,
   The sprouting leaves which saw you here,
   And called their fellows to the sight,
Would, looking round for the same sight in vain,
Creep back into their silent barks again. . . .

But who can blame them now? for, since you're gone,
They're here the only fair, and shine alone.
   You did their natural rights invade;
   Where ever you did walk or sit,
   The thickest boughs could make no shade,
   Although the sun had granted it:
The fairest flowers could please no more, near you,
Than painted flowers, set next to them, could do.

When e'er then you come hither, that shall be
The time, which this to others is, to me.
   The little joys which here are now,
   The name of punishments do bear;
   When by their sight they let us know
   How we deprived of greater are.
'Tis you the best of seasons with you bring;
This is for beasts, and that for men the Spring.

                                        ABRAHAM COWLEY

354

SINCE SHE IS GONE

So shuts the marigold her leaves
    At the departure of the sun;
So from the honeysuckle sheaves
    The bee goes when the day is done;
So sits the turtle when she is but one,
And so all woe, as I, since she is gone.

To some few birds kind Nature hath
    Made all the summer as one day;
Which once enjoyed, cold winter's wrath
    As night they sleeping pass away.
Those happy creatures are that know not yet
The pain to be deprived or to forget.

I oft have heard men say there be
    Some that with confidence profess
The helpful Art of Memory;
    But could they teach forgetfulness
I'd learn, and try what further art could do
To make me love her and forget her too.

                                        WILLIAM BROWNE

ABSENCE

ABSENCE, hear thou my protestation
        Against thy strength,
        Distance, and length;
Do what thou canst for alteration,
        For hearts of truest mettle
        Absence doth join and time doth settle.

Who loves a mistress of such quality,
    His mind hath found
    Affection's ground
Beyond time, place, and all mortality;
    To hearts that cannot vary
    Absence is present, Time doth tarry.

My senses want their outward motion,
    Which now within
    Reason doth win,
Redoubled by her secret notion;
    Like rich men that take pleasure
    In hiding more than handling treasure.

By absence this good means I gain,
    That I can catch her,
    Where none can watch her,
In some close corner of my brain;
    There I embrace and kiss her,
    And so I both enjoy and miss her.

                    JOHN DONNE

WITH A FLOWER

I HIDE myself within a flower
That wearing on your breast,
You, unsuspecting, wear me too—
And angels know the rest.

I hide myself within my flower,
That, fading from your vase,
You, unsuspecting, feel for me
Almost a loneliness.

                    EMILY DICKINSON

KISSES MAKE MEN LOATH
TO GO

MY Love bound me with a kiss.
    That I should no longer stay;
When I felt so sweet a bliss
    I had less power to part away:
Alas! that women do not know
Kisses make men loath to go.

Yes, she knows it but too well,
    For I heard when Venus' dove
In her ear did softly tell
    That kisses were the seals of love:
O muse not then though it be so,
Kisses make men loath to go.

Wherefore did she thus inflame
    My desires, heat my blood,
Instantly to quench the same
    And starve whom she had given food?
Ay, ay, the common sense can show,
Kisses make men loath to go.

Had she bid me go at first
    It would ne'er have grieved my heart
Hope delayed had been the worst;
    But ah to kiss and then to part!
How deep it struck, speak, gods! you know
Kisses make men loath to go.

ANONYMOUS

357

ARCITE'S FAREWELL

THE woeful spirit in my heart may not
Declare, of my heart's bitterness, one jot
To you, my lady, that I love the most,
But I bequeath the service of my ghost
To you alone and to none other one,
Now that my life its earthly course has run.
Alas, the woe! alas, the pain so strong
That I for you have suffered, and so long!
Alas, for death! alas, mine Emily!
Alas, the parting of our company!
Alas, my heart's own queen! alas, my wife!
My heart's dear lady, ender of my life!
What is this world? what shall man ask to have?
Now with his love, now in the cold grave
Alone, with never any company.
Farewell, my sweetest foe, mine Emily!

GEOFFREY CHAUCER

(Modern English by John Hall Wheelock)

PARTING

DARLING, this is good-bye. The words are ordinary
But love is rare. So let it go tenderly
As the sound of violins into silence.

Parting is sad for us, because something is over,
But for the thing we have ended, it is a beginning—
Let love go like a young bird flying from the nest,

Like a new star, airborne into the evening,
Watched out of sight, or let fall gently as a tear,
Let our love go out of the world, like the prayer for a
　　soul's rest.

Let the roses go, that you fastened in my hair
One summer night in a garden, and the song
That we heard from another house, where a piano was
　　playing;
The shadow a street lamp cast through the net curtain,
The river at night, smooth and silent Thames, flowing
　　through London.

For two years Ullswater was silver with my love of you,
The golden birch-leaves were holy, the wild cherry was
　　sweet
On the fell-sides, scenting the spring for you.
The bees, drunk with the lime-flowers, dropped like
　　grapes on the road,
And the silence was yours, over all Westmorland at
　　night.

I raised the mountains for you, and set the streams
Running down the hills for love. I saw the moss grow

359

And the ferns unroll their croziers for love of you,
The snowdrops, the primrose, the heron, the martin,
    the sheep on the fells.

The snow was yours in winter, and the frost crystals
That shone like amethyst and sapphire in the starlight,
That grew their geometric beauty on the trees' animate
    branches,
The frozen waterfall, the coral caves of ice,
The noise of water rushing from the thawing springs.

The wind on the mountain, the shelter of the garden,
The stone seat under the yew-tree, the fire in the eve-
    ning,
Home-baked loaves, and apples, trout from the beck
I loved for you, held holy for you, my darling.

That was erotic. That was one with the grass,
One with the night, the animals and the stars,
All that is mortal in us, and must pass,
Creatures whose own death is their unguessed secret,
Loving in one another the rose that must fade.

Yours, too, was the anteroom of the angels,
When I could hear a pin drop, or a drop of rain,
Or the creak of a beam, or the butterfly caught in the
    rafters.
I wrestled with angels for you, and in my body
Endured the entire blessing of love's pain.

All this is true. These things, my dear, are a life
Lived for love of you. The fire in the heart, the fire on
    the hearth,
And children's stories in the evening, even hope's death
Were precious for you. Precious all things in time

And outside time. The poem I know, and the wisdom
That is not mine, the poem that can never be written.

To you, one man among all men, I dedicate
The world I have known, my days and nights, my
     flowers,
The angels, the sorrows, the forms of life I consecrate
In your name, far beyond ourselves, or any selves—
These attributes are God's.

To you, once loved and for ever, from whom I part
Not because fate is blind, or the heart cold,
But because the world is neither yours nor mine,
Not even ourselves, not even what is dearest,
I offer what I can, my living moment,
My human span.

KATHLEEN RAINE

A FAREWELL

WITH all my will, but much against my heart,
We two now part.
My Very Dear,
Our solace is, the sad road lies so clear.

It needs no art,
With faint, averted feet
And many a tear,
In our opposed paths to persevere.
Go thou to East, I West.
We will not say
There's any hope, it is so far away.
But, O, my Best,
When the one darling of our widowhead,
The nursling Grief,
Is dead,
And no dews blur our eyes
To see the peach-bloom come in evening skies,
Perchance we may,
Where now this night is day,
And even through faith of still averted feet,
Making full circle of our banishment,
Amazed meet;
The bitter journey to the bourne so sweet
Seasoning the termless feast of our content
With tears of recognition never dry.

COVENTRY PATMORE

XIV

Whose Holy Fire:

Married Love, Domestic

A SONG TO AMORET

IF I were dead, and in my place
    Some fresher youth designed
To warm thee with new fires, and grace
    Those arms I left behind;

Were he as faithful as the sun,
    That's wedded to the sphere;
His blood as chaste and temp'rate run,
    As April's mildest tear;

Or were he rich, and with his heaps
    And spacious share of earth,
Could make divine affection cheap,
    And court his golden birth:

For all these arts I'd not believe,
    No, though he should be thine—
The mighty amorist could not give
    So rich a heart as mine.

Fortune and beauty thou might'st find,
    And greater men than I;
But my true resolvéd mind
    They never shall come nigh.

For I not for an hour did love,
    Or for a day desire,
But with my soul had from above
    This endless, holy fire.

HENRY VAUGHAN

365

AS THRO' THE LAND AT EVE WE WENT

As thro' the land at eve we went,
　And pluck'd the ripen'd ears,
We fell out, my wife and I,
O we fell out I know not why,
　And kiss'd again with tears.
And blessings on the falling out
　That all the more endears,
When we fall out with those we love
　And kiss again with tears!
For when we came where lies the child
　We lost in other years,
There above the little grave,
O there above the little grave,
　We kiss'd again with tears.

ALFRED, LORD TENNYSON

SHE WAS A PHANTOM OF DELIGHT

SHE was a phantom of delight
When first she gleamed upon my sight;
A lovely apparition, sent
To be a moment's ornament;
Her eyes as stars of twilight fair;
Like twilight's, too, her dusky hair;
But all things else about her drawn
From May-time and the cheerful dawn;
A dancing shape, an image gay,
To haunt, to startle, and way-lay.

I saw her upon nearer view,
A spirit, yet a woman too!
Her household motions light and free,
And steps of virgin-liberty;
A countenance in which did meet
Sweet records, promises as sweet;
A creature not too bright or good
For human nature's daily food;
For transient sorrows, simple wiles,
Praise, blame, love, kisses, tears, and smiles.

And now I see with eye serene
The very pulse of the machine;
A being breathing thoughtful breath,
A traveller between life and death;
The reason firm, the temperate will,
Endurance, foresight, strength, and skill;
A perfect woman, nobly planned,
To warm, to comfort, and command;
And yet a spirit still, and bright
With something of angelic light.

WILLIAM WORDSWORTH

OF THE UNSCATHING FIRE

SITTING in our garden you cannot escape symbols,
    Take them how you will.
  Here on the lawn like an island where the wind is still,
    Circled by tides in the field and swirling trees,
    It is of love I muse:
This designs the coloured fronds and heavy umbels,
        Second-hand marriage, not for passion but business,
        Brought on by the obliging bees.

This hedge is a cool perch for the brown turtle-dove
    His phoenix unseen:
  Such was their love that they had grown into one;
    At first the mystical making one in marriage
    Had all my heart and my homage:
A fire and a fusion were what I wanted of love,
      But bodies are separate, and her fanatic bliss
      Left the phoenix bodiless.

Frosty burning cloud, delectable gate
    Of heaven hopelessly far,
  Though tilting almost to touch, whose holy fire
    Has no corrosive property unless
    Despair of it destroys us;
When we love, towards you our faces are set.
      Once I would win by the pain of passion alone,
      Aim at you still, that method outgrown.

If daily love now takes from these earlier ones
    The sweetness without the pain,
  The burning nights, the breathless fears gone,
    Peace in their place I never hoped to be given
    Unless at last in Heaven;
It is your doing, my darling, who have at once
      The unscathing fire and the ease of peace,
      All that I praise and bless.

ANNE RIDLER

MEETING AT NIGHT

THE gray sea and the long black land;
And the yellow half-moon large and low;
And the startled little waves that leap
In fiery ringlets from their sleep,
As I gain the cove with pushing prow,
And quench its speed i' the slushy sand.
Then a mile of warm sea-scented beach;
Three fields to cross till a farm appears;
A tap at the pane, the quick sharp scratch
And blue spurt of a lighted match,
And a voice less loud, through its joys and fears,
Than the two hearts beating each to each!

ROBERT BROWNING

ROMANCE

I WILL make you brooches and toys for your delight
Of bird-song at morning and star-shine at night.
I will make a palace fit for you and me
Of green days in forests and blue days at sea.

I will make my kitchen and you shall keep your room
Where white flows the river and bright blows the broom,
And you shall wash your linen and keep your body
    white
In rainfall at morning and dewfall at night.

And this shall be for music when no one else is near
The fine song for singing, the rare song to hear!
That only I remember, that only you admire,
Of the broad road that stretches and the roadside fire.

ROBERT LOUIS STEVENSON

369

THE RIVER-MERCHANT'S
WIFE: A LETTER

WHILE my hair was still cut straight across my forehead
I played about the front gate, pulling flowers.
You came by on bamboo stilts, playing horse,
You walked about my seat, playing with blue plums.
And we went on living in the village of Chokan:
Two small people, without dislike or suspicion.

At fourteen I married My Lord you.
I never laughed, being bashful.
Lowering my head, I looked at the wall.
Called to, a thousand times, I never looked back.

At fifteen I stopped scowling,
I desired my dust to be mingled with yours
Forever and forever and forever.
Why should I climb the look out?

At sixteen you departed,
You went into far Ku-to-yen, by the river of swirling
    eddies,
And you have been gone five months.
The monkeys make a sorrowful noise overhead.
You dragged your feet when you went out.
By the gate now, the moss is grown, the different mosses,
Too deep to clear them away!
The leaves fall early this autumn, in wind.
The paired butterflies are already yellow with August
Over the grass in the West garden;
They hurt me. I grow older.
If you are coming down through the narrows of the river
    Kiang,

Please let me know beforehand,
And I will come to meet you
        As far as Cho-fu-sa.

EZRA POUND

LUCINDA MATLOCK

I WENT to the dances at Chandlerville,
And played snapout at Winchester.
One time we changed partners,
Driving home in the moonlight of middle June,
And then I found Davis.
We were married and lived together for seventy years,
Enjoying, working, raising the twelve children,
Eight of whom we lost
Ere I had reached the age of sixty.
I spun, I wove, I kept the house, I nursed the sick,
I made the garden, and for holiday
Rambled over the fields where sang the larks,
And by Spoon River gathering many a shell,
And many a flower and medicinal weed—
Shouting to the wooded hills, singing to the green
        valleys.
At ninety-six I had lived enough, that is all,
And passed to a sweet repose.
What is this I hear of sorrow and weariness,
Anger, discontent, and drooping hopes?
Degenerate sons and daughters,
Life is too strong for you—
It takes life to love Life.

EDGAR LEE MASTERS

MY MARY

THE twentieth year is wellnigh past
Since first our sky was overcast;
Ah, would that this might be the last!
        My Mary!

Thy spirits have a fainter flow,
I see thee daily weaker grow;
'Twas my distress that brought thee low,
        My Mary!

Thy needles, once a shining store,
For my sake restless heretofore,
Now rust disused, and shine no more;
        My Mary!

For though thou gladly wouldst fulfil
The same kind office for me still,
Thy sight now seconds not thy will,
        My Mary!

But well thou play'dst the housewife's part,
And all thy threads with magic art
Have wound themselves about this heart,
        My Mary!

Thy indistinct expressions seem
Like language utter'd in a dream;
Yet me they charm, whate'er the theme,
        My Mary!

Thy silver locks, once auburn bright,
Are still more lovely in my sight

Than golden beams of orient light,
                    My Mary!

For could I view nor them nor thee,
What sight worth seeing could I see?
The sun would rise in vain for me,
                    My Mary!

Partakers of thy sad decline,
Thy hands their little force resign;
Yet, gently press'd, press gently mine,
                    My Mary!

Such feebleness of limbs thou prov'st,
That now at every step thou mov'st
Upheld by two; yet still thou lov'st,
                    My Mary!

And still to love, though press'd with ill,
In wintry age to feel no chill,
With me is to be lovely still,
                    My Mary!

But ah! by constant heed I know
How oft the sadness that I show
Transforms thy smiles to looks of woe,
                    My Mary!

And should my future lot be cast
With much resemblance of the past,
Thy worn-out heart will break at last—
                    My Mary!

WILLIAM COWPER

373

POEM IN PROSE

THIS poem is for my wife
I have made it plainly and honestly
The mark is on it
Like the burl on the knife

I have not made it for praise
She has no more need for praise
Than summer has
On the bright days

In all that becomes a woman
Her words and her ways are beautiful
Love's lovely duty
The well-swept room

Wherever she is there is sun
And time and a sweet air
Peace is there
Work done

There are always curtains and flowers
And candles and baked bread
And a cloth spread
And a clean house

Her voice when she sings is a voice
At dawn by a freshening sea
Where the wave leaps in the
Wind and rejoices

Wherever she is it is now
It is here where the apples are

Here in the stars
In the quick hour

The greatest and richest good—
My own life to live—
This she has given me

If giver could

ARCHIBALD MacLEISH

PROTHALAMION

CALM was the day, and through the trembling air
Sweet-breathing Zephyrus did softly play
A gentle spirit, that lightly did delay
Hot Titan's beams, which then did glister fair;
When I (whom sullen care,
Through discontent of my long fruitless stay
In Prince's Court, and expectation vain
Of idle hopes, which still do fly away,
Like empty shadows, did afflict my brain),
Walked forth to ease my pain
Along the shore of silver streaming Thames;
Whose rutty bank, the which his river hems,
Was painted all with variable flowers,
And all the meads adorned with dainty gems,
Fit to deck maidens' bowers,
And crown their paramours
Against the bridal day, which is not long:
    Sweet Thames! run softly, till I end my song.

There, in a meadow, by the river's side,
A flock of nymphs I chancèd to espy,

375

All lovely daughters of the flood thereby,
With goodly greenish locks, all loose untied,
As each had been a bride:
And each one had a little wicker basket,
Made of fine twigs, entrailèd curiously,
In which they gathered flowers to fill their flasket,
And, with fine fingers, cropped full feateously
The tender stalks on high.
Of every sort, which in that meadow grew,
They gathered some; the violet, pallid blue,
The little daisy, that at evening closes,
The virgin lily, and the primrose true,
With store of vermeil roses,
To deck their bridegroom's posies
Against the bridal day, which was not long:
    Sweet Thames! run softly, till I end my song.

With that I saw two swans of goodly hue
Come softly swimming down along the Lee;
Two fairer birds I yet did never see;
The snow, which doth the top of Pindus strew,
Did never whiter shew,
Nor Jove himself, when he a swan would be
For love of Leda, whiter did appear;
Yet Leda was, they say, as white as he,
Yet not so white as these, nor nothing near;
So purely white they were,
That even the gentle stream, the which them bare,
Seemed foul to them, and bade his billows spare
To wet their silken feathers, lest they might
Soil their fair plumes with water not so fair,
And mar their beauties bright,
That shone as heaven's light,
Against their bridal day, which was not long:
    Sweet Thames! run softly, till I end my song.

376

Eftsoons the nymphs, which now had flowers their fill,
Ran all in haste to see that silver brood,
As they came floating on the crystal flood;
Whom when they saw, they stood amazèd still,
Their wondering eyes to fill;
Them seemed they never saw a sight so fair
Of fowls so lovely, that they sure did deem
Them heavenly born, or to be that same pair
Which through the sky draw Venus' silver team;
For sure they did not seem
To be begot of any earthly seed,
But rather angels, or of angels' breed;
Yet were they bred of summer's heat, they say,
In sweetest season, when each flower and weed
The earth did fresh array;
So fresh they seemed as day,
Even as their bridal day, which was not long:
   Sweet Thames! run softly, till I end my song.

Then forth they all out of their baskets drew
Great store of flowers, the honor of the field,
That to the sense did fragrant odors yield,
All which upon those goodly birds they threw
And all the waves did strew,
That like old Peneus' waters they did seem,
When down along by pleasant Tempe's shore,
Scattered with flowers, through Thessaly they stream,
That they appear, through lilies' plenteous store,
Like a bride's chamber floor:
Two of those nymphs, meanwhile, two garlands bound
Of freshest flowers which in that mead they found,
The which presenting all in trim array,
Their snowy foreheads therewithal they crowned,
Whilst one did sing this lay,
Prepared against that day,

Against their bridal day, which was not long:
   Sweet Thames! run softly, till I end my song.

"Ye gentle birds! the world's fair ornament,
And heaven's glory whom this happy hour
Doth lead unto your lover's blissful bower,
Joy may you have, and gentle hearts' content
Of your love's couplement;
And let fair Venus, that is queen of love,
With her heart-quelling son upon you smile,
Whose smile, they say, hath virtue to remove
All love's dislike, and friendship's faulty guile
For ever to assoil;
Let endless peace your steadfast hearts accord,
And blessèd plenty wait upon your board;
And let your bed with pleasures chaste abound,
That fruitful issue may to you afford,
Which may your foes confound,
And make your joys redound
Upon your bridal day, which is not long":
   Sweet Thames! run softly, till I end my song.

So ended she: and all the rest around
To her redoubled that her undersong,
Which said their bridal day should not be long:
And gentle Echo from the neighbor-ground
Their accents did resound.
So forth those joyous birds did pass along,
Adown the Lee, that to them murmured low,
As he would speak, but that he lacked a tongue,
Yet did by signs his glad affection show,
Making his stream run slow.
And all the fowl which in his flood did dwell
'Gan flock about these twain, that did excel
The rest, so far as Cynthia doth shend
378

The lesser stars. So they, enrangèd well,
Did on those two attend,
And their best service lend
Against their wedding day, which was not long:
   Sweet Thames! run softly, till I end my song.

At length they all to merry London came,
To merry London, my most kindly nurse,
That to me gave this life's first native source;
Though from another place I take my name,
An house of ancient fame:
There when they came, whereas those bricky towers
The which on Thames' broad, aged back do ride,
Where now the studious lawyers have their bowers,
There whilom wont the Templar Knights to bide,
Till they decayed through pride:
Next whereunto there stands a stately place,
Where oft I gainèd gifts and goodly grace
Of that great lord, which therein wont to dwell,
Whose want too well now feels my friendless case;
But ah! here fits not well
Old woes, but joys, to tell
Against the bridal day, which is not long:
   Sweet Thames! run softly, till I end my song.

Yet therein now doth lodge a noble peer,
Great England's glory, and the world's wide wonder,
Whose dreadful name late through all Spain did thunder,
And Hercules' two pillars standing near
Did make to quake and fear:
Fair branch of honor, flower of chivalry!
That fillest England with thy triumph's fame,
Joy have thou of thy noble victory,
And endless happiness of thine own name,
That promiseth the same;

That through thy prowess, and victorious arms,
Thy country may be freed from foreign harms;
And great Elisa's glorious name may ring
Through all the world, filled with thy wide alarms,
Which some brave muse may sing
To ages following,
Upon the bridal day, which is not long:
  Sweet Thames! run softly, till I end my song.

From those high towers this noble lord issuing,
Like radiant Hesper, when his golden hair
In the ocean billows he hath bathèd fair,
Descended to the river's open viewing,
With a great train ensuing.
Above the rest were goodly to be seen
Two gentle knights of lovely face and feature
Beseeming well the bower of any queen,
With gifts of wit, and ornaments of nature,
Fit for so goodly stature,
That like the twins of Jove they seemed in sight,
Which deck the baldrick of the heavens bright;
They two, forth pacing to the river's side,
Received those two fair brides, their love's delight;
Which, at the appointed tide,
Each one did make his bride
Against their bridal day, which is not long:
  Sweet Thames! run softly, till I end my song.

EDMUND SPENSER

380

EPITHALAMION

YE learnèd sisters, which have oftentimes
Been to me aiding, others to adorn,
Whom ye thought worthy of your graceful rhymes,
That even the greatest did not greatly scorn
To hear their names sung in your simple lays,
But joyèd in their praise;
And when ye list your own mishaps to mourn,
Which death, or love, or fortune's wreck did raise,
Your string could soon to sadder tenor turn,
And teach the woods and waters to lament
Your doleful dreariment:
Now lay those sorrowful complaints aside;
And, having all your heads with garlands crowned,
Help me mine own love's praises to resound;
Nor let the same of any be envied:
So Orpheus did for his own bride!
So I unto myself alone will sing;
The woods shall to me answer, and my echo ring.

Early, before the world's light-giving lamp
His golden beam upon the hills doth spread,
Having dispersed the night's uncheerful damp,
Do ye awake; and, with fresh lusty-hed,
Go to the bower of my belovèd love,
My truest turtle dove;
Bid her awake; for Hymen is awake,
And long since ready forth his mask to move,
With his bright Tead that flames with many a flake,
And many a bachelor to wait on him,
In their fresh garments trim.
Bid her awake therefore, and soon her dight,
For lo! the wishèd day is come at last,

That shall, for all the pains and sorrows past,
Pay to her usury of long delight:
And, whilst she doth her dight,
Do ye to her of joy and solace sing,
That all the woods may answer, and your echo ring.

Bring with you all the Nymphs that you can hear,
Both of the rivers and the forests green,
And of the sea that neighbors to her near,
All with gay garlands goodly well beseen.
And let them also with them bring in hand
Another gay garland,
For my fair love, of lilies and of roses,
Bound truelove wise with a blue silk riband;
And let them make great store of bridal posies,
And let them eke bring store of other flowers,
To deck the bridal bowers.
And let the ground whereas her foot shall tread,
For fear the stones her tender foot should wrong,
Be strewed with fragrant flowers all along,
And diapered like the discolored mead;
Which done, do at her chamber door await,
For she will waken straight;
The whiles do ye this song unto her sing,
The woods shall to you answer, and your echo ring.

Ye Nymphs of Mulla, which with careful heed
The silver scaly trouts do tend full well,
And greedy pikes which use therein to feed
(Those trouts and pikes all others do excel);
And ye likewise, which keep the rushy lake,
Where none do fishes take;
Bind up the locks the which hang scattered light,
And in his waters, which your mirror make,
Behold your faces as the crystal bright,
382

That when you come whereas my love doth lie,
No blemish she may spy.
And eke, ye lightfoot maids, which keep the deer,
That on the hoary mountain used to tower;
And the wild wolves, which seek them to devour,
With your steel darts do chase from coming near;
Be also present here,
To help to deck her, and to help to sing,
That all the woods may answer, and your echo ring.

Wake, now my love, awake! for it is time;
The rosy morn long since left Tithon's bed,
All ready to her silver coach to climb;
And Phœbus 'gins to show his glorious head.
Hark, how the cheerful birds do chant their lays
And carol of love's praise.
The merry lark her matins sings aloft;
The thrush replies; the mavis descant plays;
The ouzel shrills; the ruddock warbles soft;
So goodly all agree, with sweet consent,
To this day's merriment.
Ah! my dear love, why do ye sleep thus long,
When meeter were that ye should now awake,
To await the coming of your joyous mate,
And hearken to the birds' love-learnèd song,
The dewy leaves among!
For they of joy and pleasance to you sing,
That all the woods them answer, and their echo ring.

My love is now awake out of her dreams,
And her fair eyes, like stars that dimmèd were
With darksome cloud, now show their goodly beams
More bright than Hesperus his head doth rear.
Come now, ye damsels, daughters of delight,
Help quickly her to dight:

383

But first come, ye fair hours, which were begot
In Jove's sweet paradise of Day and Night;
Which do the seasons of the year allot,
And all that ever in this world is fair,
Do make and still repair:
And ye three handmaids of the Cyprian queen,
The which do still adorn her beauty's pride,
Help to adorn my beautifulest bride;
And as ye her array, still throw between
Some graces to be seen,
And, as ye use to Venus, to her sing,
The whiles the woods shall answer, and your echo ring.

Now is my love all ready forth to come:
Let all the virgins therefore well await:
And ye fresh boys, that tend upon her groom,
Prepare yourselves; for he is coming straight;
Set all your things in seemly good array,
Fit for so joyful day:
The joyfulest day that ever sun did see.
Fair Sun! show forth thy favorable ray,
And let thy life-full heat not fervent be,
For fear of burning her sunshiny face,
Her beauty to disgrace.
O fairest Phœbus! father of the Muse!
If ever I did honor thee aright,
Or sing the thing that might thy mind delight,
Do not thy servant's simple boon refuse;
But let this day, let this one day, be mine;
Let all the rest be thine.
Then I thy sovereign praises loud will sing,
That all the woods shall answer, and their echo ring.

Hark! how the Minstrels 'gin to shrill aloud
Their merry music that resounds from far.

The pipe, the tabor, and the trembling croud,
That well agree withouten breach or jar.
But, most of all, the Damsels do delight
When they their timbrels smite,
And thereunto do dance and carol sweet,
That all the senses they do ravish quite;
The whiles the boys run up and down the street,
Crying aloud with strong confusèd noise,
As if it were one voice,
Hymen, iö Hymen, Hymen, they do shout;
That even to the heavens their shouting shrill
Doth reach, and all the firmament doth fill;
To which the people standing all about,
As in approvance, do thereto applaud,
And loud advance her laud;
And evermore they Hymen, Hymen sing,
That all the woods them answer, and their echo ring.

Lo! where she comes along with portly pace,
Like Phœbe, from her chamber of the East,
Arising forth to run her mighty race,
Clad all in white, that seems a virgin best.
So well it her beseems, that ye would ween
Some angel she had been.
Her long loose yellow locks like golden wire,
Sprinkled with pearl, and pearling flowers atween,
Do like a golden mantle her attire;
And, being crownèd with a garland green,
Seem like some maiden queen.
Her modest eyes, abashèd to behold
So many gazers as on her do stare,
Upon the lowly ground affixèd are;
Nor dare lift up her countenance too bold,
But blush to hear her praises sung so loud,
So far from being proud.

Nathless do ye still loud her praises sing,
That all the woods may answer, and your echo ring.

Tell me, ye merchants' daughters, did ye see
So fair a creature in your town before;
So sweet, so lovely, and so mild as she,
Adorned with beauty's grace and virtue's store?
Her goodly eyes like sapphires shining bright,
Her forehead ivory white,
Her cheeks like apples which the sun hath ruddied,
Her lips like cherries charming men to bite,
Her breast like to a bowl of cream uncrudded,
Her paps like lilies budded,
Her snowy neck like to a marble tower;
And all her body like a palace fair,
Ascending up, with many a stately stair,
To honor's seat and chastity's sweet bower.
Why stand ye still, ye virgins, in amaze,
Upon her so to gaze,
Whiles ye forget your former lay to sing,
To which the woods did answer, and your echo ring?

But if ye saw that which no eyes can see,
The inward beauty of her lively spright,
Garnished with heavenly gifts of high degree,
Much more then would ye wonder at that sight,
And stand astonished like to those which read
Medusa's mazeful head.
There dwells sweet love, and constant chastity,
Unspotted faith, and comely womanhood,
Regard of honor, and mild modesty;
There virtue reigns as queen in royal throne,
And giveth laws alone,
The which the base affections do obey,
And yield their services unto her will;

Nor thought of thing uncomely ever may
Thereto approach to tempt her mind to ill.
Had ye once seen these her celestial treasures,
And unrevealèd pleasures,
Then would ye wonder, and her praises sing,
That all the woods should answer, and your echo ring.

Open the temple gates unto my love,
Open them wide that she may enter in,
And all the posts adorn as doth behove,
And all the pillars deck with garlands trim,
For to receive this Saint with honor due,
That cometh in to you.
With trembling steps, and humble reverence,
She cometh in, before the Almighty's view;
Of her ye virgins learn obedience,
When so ye come into those holy places,
To humble your proud faces:
Bring her up to the high altar, that she may
The sacred ceremonies there partake,
The which do endless matrimony make;
And let the roaring organs loudly play
The praises of the Lord in lively notes;
The whiles, with hollow throats,
The Choristers the joyous Anthems sing,
That all the woods may answer, and their echo ring.

Behold, while she before the altar stands,
Hearing the holy priest that to her speaks,
And blesseth her with his two happy hands,
How the red roses flush up in her cheeks,
And the pure snow, with goodly vermill stain
Like crimson dyed in grain:
That even the Angels, which continually
About the sacred altar do remain,

387

Forget their service and about her fly,
Oft peeping in her face, that seems more fair,
The more they on it stare.
But her sad eyes, still fastened on the ground,
Are governèd with goodly modesty,
That suffers not one look to glance awry,
Which may let in a little thought unsound.
Why blush ye, love, to give me your hand,
The pledge of all our band?
Sing, ye sweet Angels, Alleluja sing,
That all the woods may answer, and your echo ring.

Now all is done: bring home the bride again;
Bring home the triumph of our victory:
Bring home with you the glory of her gain;
With joyance bring her and with jollity.
Never had man more joyful day than this,
Whom heaven would heap with bliss.
Make feast therefore now all this live-long day;
This day for ever to me holy is.
Pour out the wine without restraint or stay,
Pour not by cups, but by the belly full,
Pour out to all that will,
And sprinkle all the posts and walls with wine,
That they may sweat, and drunken be withal.
Crown ye God Bacchus with a coronal,
And Hymen also crown with wreaths of vine;
And let the Graces dance unto the rest,
For they can do it best:
The whiles the maidens do their carol sing,
To which the woods shall answer, and their echo ring.

Ring ye the bells, ye young men of the town,
And leave your wonted labors for this day:
This day is holy; do ye write it down,

That ye for ever it remember may.
This day the sun is in his chiefest height,
With Barnaby the bright,
From whence declining daily by degrees,
He somewhat loseth of his heat and light,
When once the Crab behind his back he sees.
But for this time it ill ordainèd was,
To choose the longest day in all the year,
And shortest night, when longest fitter were:
Yet never day so long, but late would pass.
Ring ye the bells, to make it wear away,
And bonfires make all day;
And dance about them, and about them sing,
That all the woods may answer, and your echo ring.

Ah! when will this long weary day have end,
And lend me leave to come unto my love?
How slowly do the hours their numbers spend?
How slowly does sad Time his feathers move?
Haste thee, O fairest Planet, to thy home,
Within the Western foam:
Thy tirèd steeds long since have need of rest.
Long though it be, at last I see it gloom,
And the bright evening-star with golden crest
Appear out of the East.
Fair child of beauty! glorious lamp of love!
That all the host of heaven in ranks dost lead,
And guidest lovers through the night's sad dread,
How cheerfully thou lookest from above,
And seems to laugh atween thy twinkling light,
As joying in the sight
Of these glad many, which for joy do sing,
That all the woods them answer, and their echo ring!

Now, cease, ye damsels, your delights fore-past;

Enough is it that all the day was yours:
Now day is done, and night is nighing fast,
Now bring the bride into the bridal bowers.
The night is come, now soon her disarray,
And in her bed her lay;
Lay her in lilies and in violets,
And silken curtains over her display,
And odored sheets, and Arras coverlets.
Behold how goodly my fair love does lie,
In proud humility!
Like unto Maia, when as Jove her took
In Tempe, lying on the flowery grass,
'Twixt sleep and wake, after she weary was,
With bathing in the Acidalian brook.
Now it is night, ye damsels may be gone,
And leave my love alone,
And leave likewise your former lay to sing:
The woods no more shall answer, nor your echo ring.

Now welcome, night! thou night so long expected,
That long day's labor dost at last defray,
And all my cares, which cruel Love collected,
Hast summed in one, and cancellèd for aye:
Spread thy broad wing over my love and me,
That no man may us see;
And in thy sable mantle us enwrap,
From fear of peril and foul horror free.
Let no false treason seek us to entrap,
Nor any dread disquiet once annoy
The safety of our joy;
But let the night be calm, and quietsome,
Without tempestuous storms or sad affray:
Like as when Jove with fair Alcmena lay,
When he begot the great Tirynthian groom:
Or like as when he with thyself did lie
390

And begot Majesty.
And let the maids and young men cease to sing;
Nor let the woods them answer, nor their echo ring.

Let no lamenting cries, nor doleful tears,
Be heard all night within, nor yet without:
Nor let false whispers, breeding hidden fears,
Break gentle sleep with misconceivèd doubt.
Let no deluding dreams, nor dreadful sights,
Make sudden sad affrights;
Nor let house-fires, nor lightning's helpless harms,
Nor let the Puck, nor other evil sprites,
Nor let mischievous witches with their charms,
Nor let hobgoblins, names whose sense we see not,
Fray us with things that be not:
Let not the screech-owl nor the stork be heard,
Nor the night raven, that still deadly yells;
Nor damnèd ghosts, called up with mighty spells,
Nor grizzly vultures, make us once afraid:
Nor let the unpleasant choir of frogs still croaking
Make us to wish their choking.
Let none of these their dreary accents sing;
Nor let the woods them answer, nor their echo ring.

But let still Silence true night-watches keep,
That sacred Peace may in assurance reign,
And timely Sleep, when it is time to sleep,
May pour his limbs forth on your pleasant plain;
The whiles an hundred little wingèd loves,
Like divers-feathered doves,
Shall fly and flutter round about your bed,
And in the secret dark, that none reproves,
Their pretty stealths shall work, and snares shall spread
To filch away sweet snatches of delight,
Concealed through covert night.

Ye sons of Venus, play your sports at will!
For greedy pleasure, careless of your toys,
Thinks more upon her paradise of joys,
Then what ye do, albeit good or ill.
All night therefore attend your merry play,
For it will soon be day:
Now none doth hinder you, that say or sing;
Nor will the woods now answer, nor your echo ring.

Who is the same, which at my window peeps?
Or whose is that fair face that shines so bright?
Is it not Cynthia, she that never sleeps,
But walks about high heaven all the night?
O! fairest goddess, do thou not envy
My love with me to spy:
For thou likewise didst love, though now unthought,
And for a fleece of wool, which privily
The Latmian shepherd once unto thee brought,
His pleasures with thee wrought.
Therefore to us be favorable now;
And since of women's labors thou hast charge,
And generation goodly dost enlarge,
Incline thy will to effect our wishful vow,
And the chaste womb inform with timely seed,
That may our comfort breed:
Till which we cease our hopeful hap to sing;
Nor let the woods us answer, nor our echo ring.

And thou, great Juno! which with awful might
The laws of wedlock still dost patronize,
And the religion of the faith first plight
With sacred rites hast taught to solemnize;
And eke for comfort often callèd art
Of women in their smart;
Eternally bind thou this lovely band,

And all thy blessings unto us impart.
And thou, glad Genius! in whose gentle hand
The bridal bower and genial bed remain,
Without blemish or stain;
And the sweet pleasures of their love's delight
With secret aid dost succor and supply,
Till they bring forth the fruitful progeny;
Send us the timely fruit of this same night.
And thou, fair Hebe! and thou, Hymen free!
Grant that it may so be.
Till which we cease your further praise to sing;
Nor any woods shall answer, nor your echo ring.

And ye high heavens, the temple of the gods,
In which a thousand torches flaming bright
Do burn, that to us wretched earthly clods
In dreadful darkness lend desirèd light;
And all ye powers which in the same remain,
More than we men can feign,
Pour out your blessing on us plenteously,
And happy influence upon us rain,
That we may raise a large posterity,
Which from the earth, which they may long possess
With lasting happiness,
Up to your haughty palaces may mount;
And, for the guerdon of their glorious merit,
May heavenly tabernacles there inherit,
Of blessèd Saints for to increase the count.
So let us rest, sweet love, in hope of this,
And cease till then our timely joys to sing:
The woods no more us answer, nor our echo ring!

Song! made in lieu of many ornaments,
With which my love should duly have been decked,
Which cutting off through hasty accidents,

Ye would not stay your due time to expect,
But promised both to recompense;
Be unto her a goodly ornament,
And for short time an endless monument.

EDMUND SPENSER

CHORUS FROM 'MARIAM'

'Tis not enough for one that is a wife
   To keep her spotless from an act of ill;
But from suspicion she should free her life,
   And bare herself of power as well as will.
'Tis not so glorious for her to be free,
As by her proper self restrain'd to be.

When she hath spacious ground to walk upon,
   Why on the ridge should she desire to go?
It is no glory to forbear alone
   Those things that may her honour overthrow:
But 'tis thankworthy, if she will not take
All lawful liberties for honour's sake.

394

That wife her hand against her fame doth rear,
  That more than to her lord alone will give
A private word to any second ear;
  And though she may with reputation live,
Yet tho' most chaste, she doth her glory blot,
And wounds her honour, tho' she kills it not.

When to their husbands they themselves do bind,
  Do they not wholly give themselves away?
Or give they but their body, not their mind,
  Reserving that, tho' best, for others' prey?
No, sure, their thought no more can be their own,
And therefore should to none but one be known.

Then she usurps upon another's right,
  That seeks to be by public language grac'd;
And tho' her thoughts reflect with purest light
  Her mind, if not peculiar, is not chaste.
For in a wife it is no worse to find
A common body, than a common mind.

LADY ELIZABETH CAREW

WEDLOCK

ALAS! my son, you little know,
The sorrows which from wedlock flow:
Farewell, sweet hours of mirth and ease,
When you have gotten a wife to please.
    Sae bide ye yet, and bide ye yet,
    Ye little ken what's to betide ye yet,
    The half o' that will gane you yet
    If a wayward wife obtain you yet.

Your hopes are high, your wisdom small,
Woe has not had you in its thrall;
The black cow on your foot ne'er trod,
Which makes you sing along the road.

When I, like you, was young and free,
I valued not the proudest she;
Like you my boast was bold and vain,
That men alone were born to reign.

Great Hercules and Sampson too
Were stronger far than I or you,
Yet they were baffled by their dears,
And felt the distaff and the shears.

Stout gates of brass, and well-built walls,
Are proof 'gainst swords and cannon-balls;
But nought is found, by sea or land,
That can a wayward wife withstand.

JENNY GRAHAME

WHY SHOULD A FOOLISH
MARRIAGE VOW

WHY should a foolish marriage vow
    Which long ago was made
Oblige us to each other now,
    When passion is decayed?
We loved, and we loved, as long as we could,
    Till our love was loved out in us both;
But our marriage is dead when the pleasure is fled;
    'Twas pleasure first made it an oath.

If I have pleasures for a friend
   And further love in store,
What wrong has he whose joys did end,
   And who could give no more?
'Tis a madness that he should be jealous of me,
Or that I should bar him of another;
For all we can gain is to give ourselves pain
When neither can hinder the other.

JOHN DRYDEN

A LETTER

LYING in bed this morning, just a year
   since our first days, I was trying to assess—
against my natural caution—by desire
   and how the fact outdid it, my happiness:
and finding the awkwardness of keeping clear
   numberless flamingo thoughts and memories,
     my dear and dearest husband, in this kind
     of rambling letter, I'll disburse my mind.

Technical problems have always given me trouble:
   a child stiff at the fiddle, my ear had praise
and my intention only; so, as was natural,
   coming to verse, I hid my lack of ease

397

by writing only as I thought myself able,
   escaped the crash of the bold by salt originalities.
      This is one reason for writing far from one's heart,
      a better is, that one fears it may be hurt.

By an inadequate style one fears to cheapen
   glory, and that it may be blurred if seen
through the eye's used centre, not the new margin.
   It is the hardest thing with love to burn
and write it down, for what was the real passion
   left to its own words will seem trivial and thin.
      We can in making love look face to face:
      in poetry, crooked, and with no embrace.

Tolstoy's hero found in his newborn child
   only another aching, vulnerable part;
and it is true our first joy hundredfold
   increased our dangers, pricking in every street
in accidents and wars: yet this is healed
   not by reason, but the endurance of delight
      since our marriage, which, once thoroughly known,
      is known for good, though in time it were gone.

You, hopeful baby with the erring toes,
   grew, it seems to me, to a natural pleasure
in the elegant strict machine, from the abstruse
   science of printing to the rich red and azure
it plays on hoardings, rusty industrial noise,
   all these could add to your inherited treasure:
      a poise which many wish for, writing the machine
      poems of laboured praise, but few attain.

And loitered up your childhood to my arms.
   I would hold you there for ever, and know
certainly now, that though the vacuum glooms,

quotidian dullness, in these beams don't die,
they're wrong who say that happiness never comes
on earth, that has spread here its crystal sea.
  And since you, loiterer, did compose this wonder,
  be with me still, and may God hold his thunder.

ANNE RIDLER

THE LETTER

THE night is measureless, no voice, no cry
Pierces the dark in which the planet swings—
It is the shadow of her bulk that flings
So deep a gloom on the enormous sky;
This timorous dust, this phantom that is I,
Cowers in shelter, while the evening brings
A sense of mystery and how all things
Waver like water and are gliding by.

Now, while the stars in heaven like blowing sand
Drift to their darkness, while oblivion
Hushes the fire of some fading sun,
I turn the page again—and there they stand,
Traced by love's fleeting but victorious hand,
The words: "My darling, my belovéd one."

JOHN HALL WHEELOCK

AFTER LONG SILENCE

SPEECH after long silence; it is right,
All other lovers being estranged or dead,
Unfriendly lamplight hid under its shade,
The curtains drawn upon unfriendly night,
That we descant and yet again descant
Upon the supreme theme of Art and Song:
Bodily decrepitude is wisdom; young
We loved each other and were ignorant.

WILLIAM BUTLER YEATS

RESTATEMENT OF ROMANCE

THE night knows nothing of the chants of night.
It is what it is as I am what I am:
And in perceiving this I best perceive myself

And you. Only we two may interchange
Each in the other what each has to give.
Only we two are one, not you and night.

Nor night and I, but you and I, alone,
So much alone, so deeply by ourselves,
So far beyond the casual solitudes,

That night is only the background of our selves,
Supremely true each to its separate self,
In the pale light that each upon the other throws.

WALLACE STEVENS

THE RECONCILEMENT

COME, let us now resolve at last
  To live and love in quiet;
We'll tie the knot so very fast
  That Time shall ne'er untie it.

The truest joys they seldom prove
  Who free from quarrels live:
'Tis the most tender part of love
  Each other to forgive.

When least I seemed concerned, I took
  No pleasure nor no rest;
And when I feigned an angry look,
  Alas, I loved you best.

Own but the same to me—you'll find
  How blest will be our fate.
O to be happy—to be kind
  Sure never is too late!

> JOHN SHEFFIELD,
> *Duke of Buckinghamshire*

TRUE LOVE

TRUE love is but an humble, low-born thing,
And hath its food served up in earthern ware;
It is a thing to walk with hand in hand
Through the every-dayness of this work-day world,

Baring its tender feet to every flint,
Yet letting not one heart-beat go astray;
A simple, fire-side thing, whose quiet smile
Can warm earth's poorest hovel to a home.

Such is true love, which steals into the heart
With feet as silent as the lightsome dawn,
That kisses smooth the rough brows of the dark,
And hath its will through blissful gentleness:

A love that gives and takes, that seeth faults,
Not with flaw-seeing eyes like needle points,
But loving-kindly ever looks them down,
With the o'ercoming faith that still forgives;

A love that shall be new and fresh each hour,
As is the sunset's golden mystery,
Or the sweet coming of the evening star.

JAMES RUSSELL LOWELL

A WOMAN'S LAST WORD

LET's contend no more, Love,
    Strive nor weep:
All be as before, Love,
    —Only sleep!

What so wild as words are?
    I and thou
In debate, as birds are,
    Hawk on bough!

See the creature stalking
    While we speak!

Hush and hide the talking,
  Cheek on cheek!

What so false as truth is,
  False to thee?
Where the serpent's tooth is
  Shun the tree—

Where the apple reddens
  Never pry—
Lest we lose our Edens,
  Eve and I.

Be a god and hold me
  With a charm!
Be a man and fold me
  With thine arm!

Teach me, only teach, Love!
  As I ought
I will speak thy speech, Love,
  Think thy thought—

Meet, if thou require it,
  Both demands,
Laying flesh and spirit
  In thy hands.

That shall be to-morrow
  Not to-night:
I must bury sorrow
  Out of sight:

—Must a little weep, Love,
  (Foolish me!)
And so fall asleep, Love,
  Loved by thee.

ROBERT BROWNING

403

MY WIFE'S A WINSOME WEE THING

She is a winsome wee thing,
She is a handsome wee thing,
She is a lo'esome wee thing,
    This sweet wee wife o' mine.

I never saw a fairer,
I never lo'ed a dearer,
And neist my heart I'll wear her,
    For fear my jewel tine.

The warld's wrack, we share o't,
The warstle and the care o't;
Wi' her I'll blythely bear it,
    And think my lot divine.

She is a winsome wee thing,
She is a handsome wee thing,
She is a lo'esome wee thing,
    This sweet wee wife o' mine.

ROBERT BURNS

THE MARRIED LOVER

Why, having won her, do I woo?
    Because her spirit's vestal grace
Provokes me always to pursue,
    But, spirit-like, eludes embrace. . . .

Because, although in act and word
    As lowly as a wife can be,
Her manners, when they call me lord,
    Remind me 'tis by courtesy.

Because her gay and lofty brows,
    When all is won which hope can ask,
Reflect a light of hopeless snows
    That bright in virgin ether bask;

Because, tho' free of the outer court
    I am, this Temple keeps its shrine
Sacred to Heaven; because in short,
    She's not, and never can be mine.

COVENTRY PATMORE

whose holy rites Married Love, Domestic

Because, although in act and word
As lowly as a wife can be,
Her manners when they call me lord,
Remind me 'tis by courtesy.

Because her gay and lofty brows,
When all is won which hope can ask,
Reflect a light of hopeless snows
That bright in virgin ether bask:

Because, tho' free of the outer court
I am, this Temple keeps its shrine
Sacred to Heaven; because, in short,

XV

The One Bell Only:

Love's Elegies

WHEN OUR TWO SOULS STAND UP

WHEN our two souls stand up erect and strong,
Face to face, silent, drawing nigh and nigher,
Until the lengthening wings break into fire
At either curvèd point,—what bitter wrong
Can the earth do to us, that we should not long
Be here contented? Think! In mounting higher,
The angels would press on us and aspire
To drop some golden orb of perfect song
Into our deep, dear silence. Let us stay
Rather on earth, Beloved,—where the unfit
Contrarious moods of men recoil away
And isolate pure spirits, and permit
A place to stand and love in for a day,
With darkness and the death-hour rounding it.

ELIZABETH BARRETT BROWNING

FAIR HELEN

I WISH I were where Helen lies;
Night and day on me she cries;
O that I were where Helen lies
    On fair Kirconnell lea!

Curst be the heart that thought the thought,
And curst the hand that fired the shot,
When in my arms burd Helen dropt,
    And died to succour me!

409

O think no but my heart was sair
When my Love dropt down and spake nae mair!
I laid her down wi' meikle care
 On fair Kirconnell lea.

As I went down the water-side,
None but my foe to be my guide,
None but my foe to be my guide,
 On fair Kirconnell lea;

I lighted down my sword to draw,
I hacked him in pieces sma',
I hacked him in pieces sma',
 For her sake that died for me.

O Helen fair, beyond compare!
I'll make a garland of thy hair
Shall bind my heart for evermair
 Until the day I die.

O that I were where Helen lies!
Night and day on me she cries;
Out of my bed she bids me rise,
 Says, "Haste and come to me!"

O Helen fair! O Helen chaste!
If I were with thee, I were blest,
Where thou lies low and takes thy rest
 On fair Kirconnell lea.

I wish my grave were growing green,
A winding-sheet drawn ower my een,
And I in Helen's arms lying,
 On fair Kirconnell lea.

I wish I were where Helen lies;
Night and day on me she cries;
And I am weary of the skies,
 Since my Love died for me.   ANON.

410

HOW SHOULD I YOUR TRUE LOVE KNOW

How should I your true love know
   From another one?
By his cockle hat and staff
   And his sandal shoon.

He is dead and gone, lady,
   He is dead and gone;
At his head a grass-green turf,
   At his heels a stone.

White his shroud as the mountain snow,
   Larded with sweet flowers;
Which bewept to the grave did go
   With true-love showers.

WILLIAM SHAKESPEARE

SHE DWELT AMONG THE UNTRODDEN WAYS

SHE dwelt among the untrodden ways
   Beside the springs of Dove,
A Maid whom there were none to praise
   And very few to love:

A violet by a mossy stone
   Half hidden from the eye!
—Fair as a star, when only one
   Is shining in the sky.

411

She lived unknown, and few could know
　　When Lucy ceased to be;
But she is in her grave, and, oh,
　　The difference to me!

WILLIAM WORDSWORTH

LUCY

I

THREE years she grew in sun and shower;
Then Nature said, "A lovelier flower
　　On earth was never sown;
This child I to myself will take;
She shall be mine, and I will make
　　A lady of my own.

"Myself will to my darling be
Both law and impulse: and with me
　　The girl, in rock and plain,
In earth and heaven, in glade and bower,
Shall feel an overseeing power
　　To kindle or restrain.

"She shall be sportive as the fawn
That wild with glee across the lawn
　　Or up the mountain springs;
And hers shall be the breathing balm,
And hers the silence and the calm
　　Of mute insensate things.

"The floating clouds their state shall lend
To her; for her the willow bend;
　　Nor shall she fail to see

Even in the motions of the storm
Grace that shall mold the maiden's form
  By silent sympathy.

"The stars of midnight shall be dear
To her; and she shall lean her ear
  In many a secret place
Where rivulets dance their wayward round
And beauty born of murmuring sound
  Shall pass into her face.

"And vital feelings of delight
Shall rear her form to stately height,
  Her virgin bosom swell;
Such thoughts to Lucy I will give
While she and I together live
  Here in this happy dell."

Thus Nature spake—The work was done—
How soon my Lucy's race was run!
  She died, and left to me
This heath, this calm and quiet scene;
The memory of what has been,
  And never more will be.

II

A slumber did my spirit seal;
  I had no human fears:
She seemed a thing that could not feel
  The touch of earthly years.

No motion has she now, or force;
  She neither hears nor sees;
Rolled round in earth's diurnal course,
  With rocks, and stones, and trees.

WILLIAM WORDSWORTH

WHEN I HAVE SEEN BY TIME'S FELL HAND DEFACED

WHEN I have seen by Time's fell hand defaced
The rich proud cost of outworn buried age;
When sometime lofty towers I see down-razed
And brass eternal slave to mortal rage;
When I have seen the hungry ocean gain
Advantage on the kingdom of the shore,
And the firm soil win of the watery main,
Increasing store with loss and loss with store;
When I have seen such interchange of state,
Or state itself confounded to decay;
Ruin hath taught me thus to ruminate,
That Time will come and take my love away.
This thought is as a death, which cannot choose
But weep to have that which it fears to lose.

WILLIAM SHAKESPEARE

NATURAL CAUSES

I DIED, and they looked in my head: 2 plus 2
Equals 3, and the faucet that dripped unmended,
The cracked gauge on the furnace, the fraying cuff

—These they found, and ten unpaid bills, and
2 plus 2 equals 2; certain marbles I lost as a child
Through a board walk; a flamingo feather I kept

For years but had nothing it went with, a
Foreign thing; one copy of *Huck Finn*; 20 boxes
Of empty pay envelopes, and pseudo-sheep diploma.

There was talk of heartbreak via the nerves; matter of
    fact
The autopsy was notable for the splendid tone of the
    aorta,
And legally bled I lay there in my own ice water.

But they missed the scrap of film—and anyway
Had no unionman, nor a projector if they'd had—
Of the girl running toward me forever through the
    cloversunned field.

W. T. SCOTT

BREDON HILL

IN summer time on Bredon
    The bells they sound so clear;
Round both the shires they ring them
    In steeples far and near,
    A happy noise to hear.

Here of a Sunday morning
    My love and I would lie,
And see the colored counties,
    And hear the larks so high
    About us in the sky.

The bells would ring to call her
    In valleys miles away:
"Come all to church, good people;
    Good people, come and pray."
    But here my love would stay.

415

And I would turn and answer
    Among the springing thyme,
"Oh, peal upon our wedding,
    And we will hear the chime,
    And come to church in time."

But when the snows at Christmas
    On Bredon top were strown,
My love rose up so early
    And stole out unbeknown
    And went to church alone.

They tolled the one bell only,
    Groom there was none to see,
The mourners followed after,
    And so to church went she,
    And would not wait for me.

The bells they sound on Bredon,
    And still the steeples hum.
"Come all to church, good people,—"
    Oh, noisy bells, be dumb;
    I hear you, I will come.

A. E. HOUSMAN

EXEQUY ON HIS WIFE

ACCEPT, thou shrine of my dead saint,
    Instead of dirges this complaint;
And for sweet flowers to crown thy herse
Receive a strew of weeping verse
From thy grieved friend, whom thou might'st see
Quite melted into tears for thee.

Dear loss! since thy untimely fate,
My task hath been to meditate
On thee, on thee! Thou art the book,
The library whereon I look,
Tho' almost blind. For thee, loved clay,
I languish out, not live, the day. . . .
Thou hast benighted me; thy set
This eve of blackness did beget,
Who wast my day (tho' overcast
Before thou hadst thy noontide past):
And I remember must in tears
Thou scarce hadst seen so many years
As day tells hours. By thy clear sun
My love and fortune first did run;
But thou wilt never more appear
Folded within my hemisphere,
Since both thy light and motion,
Like a fled star, is fall'n and gone,
And 'twixt me and my soul's dear wish
The earth now interposèd is. . . .

I could allow thee for a time
To darken me and my sad clime;
Were it a month, a year, or ten,
I would thy exile live till then,
And all that space my mirth adjourn—
So thou wouldst promise to return,
And putting off thy ashy shroud
At length disperse this sorrow's cloud.

But woe is me! the longest date
Too narrow is to calculate
These empty hopes: never shall I
Be so much blest as to descry
A glimpse of thee, till that day come
Which shall the earth to cinders doom,
And a fierce fever must calcine

417

The body of this world—like thine,
My little world! That fit of fire
Once off, our bodies shall aspire
To our souls' bliss: then we shall rise
And view ourselves with clearer eyes
In that calm region where no night
Can hide us from each other's sight.

Meantime thou hast her, earth: much good
May my harm do thee! Since it stood
With Heaven's will I might not call
Her longer mine, I give thee all
My short-lived right and interest
In her whom living I loved best.
Be kind to her, and prithee look
Thou write into thy Doomsday book
Each parcel of this rarity
Which in thy casket shrined doth lie,
As thou wilt answer Him that lent—
Not gave—thee my dear monument.
So close the ground, and 'bout her shade
Black curtains draw: my bride is laid.

Sleep on, my Love, in thy cold bed
Never to be disquieted!
My last good-night! Thou wilt not wake
Till I thy fate shall overtake:
Till age, or grief, or sickness must
Marry my body to that dust
It so much loves; and fill the room
My heart keeps empty in thy tomb.
Stay for me there: I will not fail
To meet thee in that hollow vale.
And think not much of my delay:
I am already on the way.
And follow thee with all the speed
Desire can make, or sorrows breed.

Each minute is a short degree
And every hour a step towards thee. . . .
   'Tis true—with shame and grief I yield—
Thou, like the van, first took'st the field;
And gotten hast the victory
In thus adventuring to die
Before me, whose more years might crave
A just precedence in the grave.
But hark! my pulse, like a soft drum,
Beats my approach, tells thee I come;
And slow howe'er my marches be
I shall at last sit down by thee.
   The thought of this bids me go on
And wait my dissolution
With hope and comfort. Dear—forgive
The crime—I am content to live
Divided, with but half a heart,
Till we shall meet and never part.

HENRY KING

THE FUNERAL

WHOEVER comes to shroud me, do not harm
    Nor question much
That subtle wreath of hair about mine arm;
The mystery, the sign you must not touch,
    For 'tis my outward soul,
Viceroy to that which, unto heav'n being gone,
    Will leave this to control
And keep these limbs, her provinces, from dissolution.

For if the sinewy thread my brain lets fall
    Through every part
Can tie those parts, and make me one of all;
Those hairs, which upward grew, and strength and art
    Have from a better brain,
Can better do't; except she meant that I
    By this should know my pain,
As prisoners then are manacled, when they're con-
    demned to die.

Whate'er she meant by 't, bury it with me,
    For since I am
Love's martyr, it might breed idolatry
If into other hands these reliques came
    As 't was humility
To afford to it all that a soul can do,
    So 'tis some bravery
That, since you would have none of me, I bury some
    of you.

JOHN DONNE

REQUIESCAT

STREW on her roses, roses,
    And never a spray of yew!
In quiet she reposes;
    Ah, would that I did too!

Her mirth the world required;
    She bathed it in smiles of glee.
But her heart was tired, tired,
    And now they let her be.

Her life was turning, turning,
    In mazes of heat and sound.
But for peace her soul was yearning,
    And now peace laps her round.

Her cabined, ample spirit,
    It fluttered and failed for breath.
To-night it doth inherit
    The vasty hall of death.

MATTHEW ARNOLD

SONG

WHEN I am dead, my dearest,
    Sing no sad songs for me;
Plant thou no roses at my head,
    Nor shady cypress tree:
Be the green grass above me
    With showers and dewdrops wet;

And if thou wilt, remember,
   And if thou wilt, forget.

I shall not see the shadows,
   I shall not feel the rain;
I shall not hear the nightingale
   Sing on, as if in pain;
And dreaming through the twilight
   That doth not rise nor set,
Haply I may remember,
   And haply may forget.

CHRISTINA ROSSETTI

THE PHOENIX AND THE TURTLE

LET the bird of loudest lay,
On the sole Arabian tree,
Herald sad and trumpet be,
To whose sound chaste wings obey.

But thou shrieking harbinger,
Foul precurrer of the fiend,
Augur of the fever's end,
To this troop come thou not near!

From this session interdict
Every fowl of tyrant wing,
Save the eagle, feather'd king:
Keep the obsequy so strict.

Let the priest in surplice white,
That defunctive music can,

Be the death-divining swan,
Lest the requiem lack his right.

And thou treble-dated crow,
That thy sable gender makest
With the breath thou givest and takest,
'Mongst our mourners shalt thou go.

Here the anthem doth commence:
Love and constancy is dead;
Phoenix and the turtle fled
In a mutual flame from hence.

So they loved, as love in twain
Had the essence but in one;
Two distincts, division none:
Number there in love was slain.

Hearts, remote, yet not asunder;
Distance, and no space was seen
'Twixt the turtle and his queen:
But in them it were a wonder.

So between them love did shine,
That the turtle saw his right
Flaming in the phoenix' sight;
Either was the other's mine.

Property was thus appalled,
That the self was not the same;
Single nature's double name
Neither two nor one was called.

Reason in itself confounded,
Saw division grow together,

To themselves yet either neither,
Simple were so well compounded;

That it cried, How true a twain
Seemeth this concordant one!
Love hath reason, reason none,
If what parts can so remain.

Whereupon it made this threne
To the phoenix and the dove,
Co-supremes and stars of love,
As chorus to their tragic scene.

THRENOS.

Beauty, truth, and rarity,
Grace in all simplicity,
Here enclosed in cinders lie.

Death is now the phoenix' nest;
And the turtle's loyal breast
To eternity doth rest,

Leaving no posterity:
'Twas not their infirmity,
It was married chastity.

Truth may seem, but cannot be;
Beauty brag, but 'tis not she;
Truth and beauty buried be.

To this urn let those repair
That are either true or fair;
For these dead birds sigh a prayer.

WILLIAM SHAKESPEARE

ROSE AYLMER

Ah, what avails the sceptred race!
   Ah, what the form divine!
What every virtue, every grace!
   Rose Aylmer, all were thine.

Rose Aylmer, whom these wakeful eyes
   May weep, but never see,
A night of memories and sighs
   I consecrate to thee.

WALTER SAVAGE LANDOR

WITH RUE MY HEART IS LADEN

With rue my heart is laden
   For golden friends I had,
For many a rose-lipt maiden
   And many a lightfoot lad.

By brooks too broad for leaping
   The lightfoot boys are laid;
The rose-lipt girls are sleeping
   In fields where roses fade.

A. E. HOUSMAN

WITH A KISS I DIE

O, how may I
Call this a lightning? O my love! my wife!
Death, that hath suckt the honey of thy breath,
Hath had no power yet upon thy beauty:
Thou art not conquer'd; beauty's ensign yet
Is crimson in thy lips and in thy cheeks,
And death's pale flag is not advanced there.
Tybalt, liest thou there in thy bloody sheet:
O, what more favour can I do to thee,
Than with that hand that cut thy youth in twain
To sunder his that was thine enemy?
Forgive me, cousin!—Ah, dear Juliet,
Why art thou yet so fair? shall I believe
That unsubstantial Death is amorous;
And that the lean abhorred monster keeps
Thee here in dark to be his paramour?
For fear of that, I still will stay with thee;
And never from this palace of dim night
Depart again: here, here will I remain
With worms that are thy chamber-maids; O, here
Will I set up my everlasting rest;
And shake the yoke of inauspicious stars
From this world-wearied flesh.—Eyes, look your last!
Arms, take your last embrace! and, lips, O you
The doors of breath, seal with a righteous kiss
A dateless bargain to engrossing death!—
Come, bitter conduct, come, unsavoury guide!
Thou desperate pilot, now at once run on
The dashing rocks thy sea-sick weary bark!
Here's to my love!—O true apothecary!
Thy drugs are quick. Thus with a kiss I die.

WILLIAM SHAKESPEARE

ANNABEL LEE

IT was many and many a year ago,
   In a kingdom by the sea,
That a maiden there lived whom you may know
   By the name of Annabel Lee;—
And this maiden she lived with no other thought
   Than to love and be loved by me.

She was a child and I was a child,
   In this kingdom by the sea,
But we loved with a love that was more than love—
   I and my Annabel Lee—
With a love that the winged seraphs of Heaven
   Coveted her and me.

And this was the reason that, long ago,
   In this kingdom by the sea,
A wind blew out of a cloud, by night
   Chilling my Annabel Lee;
So that her highborn kinsmen came
   And bore her away from me,
To shut her up in a sepulchre
   In this kingdom by the sea.

The angels, not half so happy in Heaven,
   Went envying her and me:
Yes! that was the reason (as all men know,
   In this kingdom by the sea)
That the wind came out of the cloud, chilling
   And killing my Annabel Lee.

But our love it was stronger by far than the love
   Of those who were older than we—

Of many far wiser than we—
And neither the angels in Heaven above
  Nor the demons down under the sea,
Can ever dissever my soul from the soul
  Of the beautiful Annabel Lee:—

For the moon never beams without bringing me dreams
  Of the beautiful Annabel Lee;
And the stars never rise but I see the bright eyes
  Of the beautiful Annabel Lee;
And so, all the night-tide, I lie down by the side
Of my darling, my darling, my life and my bride,
  In her sepulchre there by the sea—
  In her tomb by the sounding sea.

EDGAR ALLAN POE

AN EPITAPH ON HUSBAND AND WIFE WHO DIED AND WERE BURIED TOGETHER

To these whom death again did wed
This grave's the second marriage-bed.
For though the hand of Fate could force
'Twixt soul and body a divorce,
It could not sever man and wife,
Because they both lived but one life.
Peace, good reader, do not weep;
Peace, the lovers are asleep.
They, sweet turtles, folded lie
In the last knot that love could tie.
Let them sleep, let them sleep on,
Till the stormy night be gone,

And the eternal morrow dawn;
Then the curtains will be drawn,
And they wake into a light
Whose day shall never die in night.

RICHARD CRASHAW

IF THOU SURVIVE MY
WELL-CONTENTED DAY

IF thou survive my well-contented day
When that churl Death my bones with dust shall cover,
And shalt by fortune once more re-survey
These poor rude lines of thy deceasèd lover,
Compare them with the bettering of the time,
And though they be outstripped by every pen,
Reserve them for my love, not for their rhyme,
Exceeded by the height of happier men.
O, then vouchsafe me but this loving thought:
"Had my friend's Muse grown with this growing age,
A dearer birth than this his love had brought,
To march in ranks of better equipage:
    But since he died, and poets better prove,
    Theirs for their style I'll read, his for his love."

WILLIAM SHAKESPEARE
429

EPITAPH ON THE LADY VILLIERS

THIS little vault, this narrow room,
Of love and beauty is the tomb;
The dawning beam that gan to clear
Our clouded sky, lies darkened here,
Forever set to us, by death
Sent to inflame the world beneath.
'Twas but a bud, yet did contain
More sweetness than shall spring again;
A budding star that might have grown
Into a sun, when it had blown.
This hopeful beauty did create
New life in love's declining state;
But now his empire ends, and we
From fire and wounding darts are free;
His brand, his bow, let no man fear,—
The flames, the arrows, all lie here.

THOMAS CAREW

XVI

Till A' The Seas Gang Dry:

Love-Eternal

FEAR NOT, DEAR LOVE

FEAR not, dear love, that I'll reveal
Those hours of pleasure we two steal;
No eye shall see, nor yet the sun
Descry, what thou and I have done;
No ear shall hear our love, but we
Silent as the night will be;
The god of love himself (whose dart
Did first wound mine, and then thy heart)
Shall never know, that we can tell,
What sweets in stol'n embraces dwell.
This only means may find it out:
If, when I die, physicians doubt
What caus'd my death, and there to view
Of all their judgements which was true,
Rip up this heart, O then, I fear,
The world will see thy picture there.

THOMAS CAREW

BRIGHT STAR

BRIGHT STAR! would I were steadfast as thou art—
Not in lone splendour hung aloft the night,
And watching, with eternal lids apart,
Like Nature's patient sleepless Eremite,
The moving waters at their priestlike task
Of pure ablution round earth's human shores,
Or gazing on the new soft fallen mask
Of snow upon the mountains and the moors:—
No—yet still steadfast, still unchangeable,
Pillow'd upon my fair Love's ripening breast

433

To feel for ever its soft fall and swell,
Awake for ever in a sweet unrest;
Still, still to hear her tender-taken breath,
And so live ever,—or else swoon to death.

JOHN KEATS

THERE IS A LADY SWEET
AND KIND

THERE is a Lady sweet and kind,
Was never face so pleased my mind;
I did but see her passing by,
And yet I love her till I die.

Her gesture, motion, and her smiles,
Her wit, her voice my heart beguiles,
Beguiles my heart, I know not why,
And yet I love her till I die.

Cupid is wingèd and doth range,
Her country so my love doth change:
But change she earth, or change she sky,
Yet will I love her till I die.

ANONYMOUS

LOVE'S NOT TIME'S FOOL

LET me not to the marriage of true minds
Admit impediments. Love is not love
Which alters when it alteration finds,
Or bends with the remover to remove:

434

O, no! it is an ever-fixèd mark
That looks on tempests and is never shaken;
It is the star to every wandering bark,
Whose worth's unknown, although his height be taken.
Love's not Time's fool, though rosy lips and cheeks
Within his bending sickle's compass come;
Love alters not with his brief hours and weeks,
But bears it out even to the edge of doom.
If this be error and upon me proved,
I never writ, nor no man ever loved.

WILLIAM SHAKESPEARE

LOVE NOT ME FOR COMELY GRACE

LOVE not me for comely grace,
For my pleasing eye or face,
Nor for any outward part,
No, nor for a constant heart:
    For these may fail or turn to ill,
      So thou and I shall sever:
Keep, therefore, a true woman's eye,
And love me still but know not why—
    So hast thou the same reason still
      To doat upon me ever!

ANONYMOUS

435

PROSPICE

FEAR death?—to feel the fog in my throat,
  The mist in my face,
When the snows begin, and the blasts denote
  I am nearing the place,
The power of the night, the press of the storm,
  The post of the foe;
Where he stands, the Arch Fear in a visible form,
  Yet the strong man must go:
For the journey is done and the summit attained,
  And the barriers fall,
Though a battle's to fight ere the guerdon be gained,
  The reward of it all.
I was ever a fighter, so—one fight more,
  The best and the last!
I would hate that death bandaged my eyes, and fore-
      bore,
  And bade me creep past.
No! let me taste the whole of it, fare like my peers
  The heroes of old,
Bear the brunt, in a minute pay glad life's arrears
  Of pain, darkness and cold.
For sudden the worst turns the best to the brave,
  The black minute's at end,
And the elements' rage, the fiend-voices that rave,
  Shall dwindle, shall blend,
Shall change, shall become first a peace out of pain,
  Then a light, then thy breast,
O thou soul of my soul! I shall clasp thee again,
  And with God be the rest!

ROBERT BROWNING

436

MUSIC, WHEN SOFT VOICES DIE

Music, when soft voices die,
Vibrates in the memory—
Odors, when sweet violets sicken,
Live within the sense they quicken.
Rose leaves, when the rose is dead,
Are heaped for the beloved's bed;
And so thy thoughts, when thou art gone,
Love itself shall slumber on.

PERCY BYSSHE SHELLEY

REMEMBRANCE

Cold in the earth, and the deep snow piled above thee!
Far, far removed, cold in the dreary grave!
Have I forgot, my only Love, to love thee,
Severed at last by Time's all-wearing wave?

Now, when alone, do my thoughts no longer hover
Over the mountains, on Angora's shore,
Resting their wings where heath and fern-leaves cover
That noble heart for ever, ever more?

Cold in the earth, and fifteen wild Decembers
From those brown hills, have melted into spring:
Faithful, indeed, is the spirit that remembers
After such years of change and suffering!

Sweet Love of youth, forgive, if I forget thee,
While the world's tide is bearing me along:

437

Sterner desires and darker hopes beset me,
Hopes which obscure, but cannot do thee wrong.

No later light has lightened up my heaven,
No second moon has ever shone for me;
All my life's bliss from thy dear life was given,
All my life's bliss is in the grave with thee.

But, when the days of golden dreams had perished,
And ev'n Despair was powerless to destroy;
Then did I learn how existence could be cherished,
Strengthened, and fed without the aid of joy.

Then did I check the tears of useless passion—
Weaned my young soul from yearning after thine;
Sternly denied its burning wish to hasten
Down to that tomb already more than mine.

And, even yet, I dare not let it languish,
Dare not indulge in memory's rapturous pain;
Once drinking deep of that divinest anguish,
How could I seek the empty world again?

EMILY BRONTE

LEGEND

WHERE are you hid from me, belovèd one
That I am seeking through the lonely world—
A wanderer, on my way home to you?
Dark is the night, and perilous the road:
At many a breast in longing have I leaned,
At many a wayside worshipped—and my heart
Is tired from long travelling. Perhaps

438

In centuries to come you wait for me,
And are, as yet, an iris by the stream
Lifting her single blossom, or the soft
Tremulous haze upon the hills—and we
Have missed each other. Oh, if it be so,
Then may this song reach to the verge of doom,
Ages unborn—to find you where you are,
My lonely one—and like a murmuring string,
Faint with one music, endlessly repeat
To you, not even knowing I was yours,
Her plaintive burden from the dolorous past
Of dusty legend, her archaic woe—
Telling of one upon a hopeless quest,
How, in the dark of time, he lost his way.

JOHN HALL WHEELOCK

ON HIS DECEASED WIFE

METHOUGHT I saw my late espousèd saint
    Brought to me like Alcestis from the grave,
    Whom Jove's great son to her glad husband gave,
    Rescued from Death by force, though pale and faint.
Mine, as whom washed from spot of child-bed taint
    Purification in the old law did save,
    And such as yet once more I trust to have
    Full sight of her in heaven without restraint,
Came vested all in white, pure as her mind.
    Her face was veiled; yet to my fancied sight
    Love, sweetness, goodness, in her person shined
So clear as in no face with more delight.
    But O, as to embrace me she inclined,
    I waked, she fled, and day brought back my night.

JOHN MILTON

439

TO LUCASTA, GOING BEYOND THE SEAS

IF to be absent were to be
    Away from thee;
  Or that when I am gone,
    You or I were alone;
  Then, my Lucasta, might I crave
Pity from blustering wind, or swallowing wave.

  But I'll not sigh one blast or gale
    To swell my sail,
  Or pay a tear t' assuage
    The foaming blue god's rage;
  For whether he will let me pass
Or no, I'm still as happy as I was.

  Though seas and land betwixt us both,
    Our faith and troth,
  Like separated souls,
    All time and space controls;
  Above the highest sphere we meet
Unseen, unknown, and great as angels greet.

  So then we do anticipate
    Our after-fate,
  And are alive i' the skies,
    If thus our lips and eyes
  Can speak like spirits unconfined
In Heaven, their earthly bodies left behind.

RICHARD LOVELACE

A VOW TO LOVE FAITHFULLY, HOWSOEVER HE BE REWARDED

SET me whereas the sun doth parch the green
Or where his beams do not dissolve the ice;
In temperate heat, where he is felt and seen;
In presence prest of people, mad or wise;
Set me in high, or yet in low degree;
In longest night, or in the shortest day;
In clearest sky, or where clouds thickest be;
In lusty youth, or when my hairs are grey:
Set me in heaven, in earth, or else in hell,
In hill, or dale, or in the foaming flood;
Thrall, or at large, alive whereso I dwell,
Sick, or in health, in evil fame or good,
Hers will I be; and only with this thought
Content myself, although my chance be nought.

HENRY HOWARD, *Earl of Surrey*

ECHO

COME to me in the silence of the night;
    Come in the speaking silence of a dream;
Come with soft rounded cheeks and eyes as bright
    As sunlight on a stream;
        Come back in tears,
O memory, hope, love of finished years.

O dream how sweet, too sweet, too bitter sweet,
    Whose wakening should have been in Paradise,

441

Where souls brimfull of love abide and meet;
   Where thirsty longing eyes
     Watch the slow door
That opening, letting in, lets out no more.

Yet come to me in dreams, that I may live
   My very life again though cold in death:
Come back to me in dreams, that I may give
   Pulse for pulse, breath for breath:
     Speak low, lean low,
As long ago, my love, how long ago.

Christina Rossetti

AN ODE

Upon a Question Moved, Whether Love Should Continue for Ever?

O no, beloved, I am most sure
   Those virtuous habits we acquire,
   As being with the Soul entire,
Must with it evermore endure.

For if where sins and vice reside
   We find so foul a guilt remain,
   As never dying in his stain
Still punished in the Soul doth bide;

Much more that true and real joy
   Which in a virtuous love is found
   Must be more solid in its ground
Than Fate or Death can e'er destroy.

442

Else should our Souls in vain elect,
   And vainer yet were Heaven's laws,
   When to an everlasting Cause
They gave a perishing Effect.

Nor here on earth, then, nor above,
   Our good affection can impair;
   For where God doth admit the fair,
Think you that he excludeth Love?

LORD HERBERT *of Cherbury*

TO ONE IN PARADISE

THOU wast all that to me, love,
   For which my soul did pine—
A green isle in the sea, love,
   A fountain and a shrine,
All wreathed with fairy fruits and flowers,
   And all the flowers were mine.

Ah, dream too bright to last!
   Ah, starry Hope! that didst arise
But to be overcast!
   A voice from out the Future cries,
"On! on!"—but o'er the Past
   (Dim gulf!) my spirit hovering lies
Mute, motionless, aghast!

For, alas! alas! with me
   The light of Life is o'er!
   "No more—no more—no more—"
(Such language holds the solemn sea
   To the sands upon the shore)
Shall bloom the thunder-blasted tree
   Or the stricken eagle soar!

443

And all my days are trances,
    And all my nightly dreams
Are where thy grey eye glances,
    And where thy footstep gleams—
In what ethereal dances,
    By what eternal streams.

EDGAR ALLAN POE

FAIN WOULD I CHANGE

FAIN would I change that note
To which fond love hath charm'd me
Long long to sing by rote,
Fancying that that harm'd me:
Yet when this thought doth come,
"Love is the perfect sum
Of all delight,"
I have no other choice
Either for pen or voice
To sing or write.

O Love, they wrong thee much
That say thy sweet is bitter,
When thy rich fruit is such
As nothing can be sweeter.
Fair house of joy and bliss,
Where truest pleasure is,
I do adore thee;
I know thee what thou art,
I serve thee with my heart,
And fall before thee.

ANONYMOUS

LOVE'S REMORSE

I FEEL remorse for all that Time has done
To you, my love, as if myself, not Time,
Had set on you the never-resting sun
And the little deadly days, to work this crime.
For not to guard what by such grace was given,
But leave it for the idle hours to take,
Let autumn bury away our summer heaven:
To such a charge what answer can I make

But the old saw still by the heart retold,
"Love is exempt from Time." And that is true,
But we, the loved and the lover, we grow old:
Only the truth, the truth is always new:
"Eternity alone our wrong can right,
That makes all young again in Time's despite."

EDWIN MUIR

TURN ALL THY THOUGHTS
TO EYES

TURN all thy thoughts to eyes,
Turn all thy hairs to ears,
Change all thy friends to spies
And all thy joys to fears;
    True love will yet be free
    In spite of jealousy.

Turn darkness into day,
Conjectures into truth,
Believe what th' envious say,
Let age interpret youth:
    True love will yet be free
    In spite of jealousy.

Wrest every word and look,
Rack every hidden thought,
Or fish with golden hook;
True love cannot be caught:
    For that will still be free
    In spite of jealousy.

THOMAS CAMPION

IF THOU MUST LOVE ME

IF thou must love me, let it be for naught
Except for love's sake only. Do not say,
"I love her for her smile—her look—her way
Of speaking gently,—for a trick of thought
That falls in well with mine, and certes brought
A sense of pleasant ease on such a day"—
For these things in themselves, Belovèd, may
Be changed, or change for thee—and love, so wrought,
May be unwrought so. Neither love me for
Thine own dear pity's wiping my cheeks dry:
A creature might forget to weep, who bore
Thy comfort long, and lose thy love thereby!
But love me for love's sake, that evermore
Thou mayst love on, through love's eternity.

ELIZABETH BARRETT BROWNING

SINCE BRASS, NOR STONE, NOR EARTH

Since brass, nor stone, nor earth, nor boundless sea,
But sad mortality o'er-sways their power,
How with this rage shall beauty hold a plea,
Whose action is no stronger than a flower?
O, how shall summer's honey breath hold out
Against the wreckful siege of battering days,
When rocks impregnable are not so stout,
Nor gates of steel so strong, but Time decays?
O fearful meditation! where, alack,
Shall Time's best jewel from Time's chest lie hid?
Or what strong hand can hold his swift foot back?
Or who his spoil of beauty can forbid?
    O, none, unless this miracle have might,
    That in black ink my love may still shine bright.

WILLIAM SHAKESPEARE

LIKE AS THE WAVES MAKE TOWARDS THE PEBBLED SHORE

Like as the waves make towards the pebbled shore,
So do our minutes hasten to their end;
Each changing place with that which goes before,
In sequent toil all forwards do contend.
Nativity, once in the main of light,
Crawls to maturity, wherewith being crowned,
Crooked eclipses 'gainst his glory fight,
And Time that gave doth now his gift confound.

447

Time doth transfix the flourish set on youth
And delves the parallels in beauty's brow,
Feeds on the rarities of nature's truth,
And nothing stands but for his scythe to mow:
    And yet to times in hope my verse shall stand,
    Praising thy worth, despite his cruel hand.

WILLIAM SHAKESPEARE

AT HER FAIR HANDS

At her fair hands how have I grace entreated,
    With prayers oft repeated!
    Yet still my love is thwarted:
Heart, let her go, for she 'll not be converted.
    Say, shall she go?
    Oh, no, no, no, no, no!
She is most fair, though she be marble-hearted.

How often have my sighs declared mine anguish,
    Wherein I daily languish!
    Yet still she doth procure it:
Heart, let her go, for I cannot endure it.
    Say, shall she go?

O, no, no, no, no, no!
She gave the wound, and she alone must cure it.

The trickling tears that down my cheeks have flowed
    My love have often showed;
      Yet still unkind I prove her:
Heart, let her go, for nought I do can move her.
    Say, shall she go?
      O, no, no, no, no, no!
Though me she hate I cannot choose but love her.

But shall I still a true affection owe her,
    Which prayers, sighs, tears do show her,
      And shall she still disdain me?
Heart, let her go, if they no grace can gain me.
    Say, shall she go?
      O, no, no, no, no, no!
She made me hers, and hers she will retain me.

But if the love that hath and still doth burn me
    No love at length return me,
      Out of my thoughts I 'll set her:
Heart, let her go, O heart, I pray thee, let her.
    Say, shall she go?
      O, no, no, no, no, no!
Fixed in the heart, how can the heart forget her?

But if I weep and sigh and often wail me
    Till tears, sighs, prayers fail me,
      Shall yet my love persèver?
Heart, let her go, if she will right thee never.
    Say, shall she go?
      O, no, no, no, no, no!
Tears, sighs, prayers fail, but true love lasteth ever.

ANONYMOUS

449

YOU NEVER CAN BE OLD

To me, fair friend, you never can be old;
For as you were when first your eye I eyed,
Such seems your beauty still. Three Winters cold
Have from the forest shook three Summers' pride;
Three beauteous Springs to yellow Autumn turned
In process of the seasons have I seen,
Three April perfumes in three hot Junes burned,
Since first I saw you fresh, which yet are green.

Ah! yet doth beauty, like a dial-hand,
Steal from his figure, and no pace perceived;
So your sweet hue, which methinks still doth stand,
Hath motion, and mine eye may be deceived:
    For fear of which, hear this, thou age unbred:
    Ere you were born was beauty's Summer dead.

WILLIAM SHAKESPEARE

XVII

The Great Love Songs

AULD LANG SYNE

SHOULD auld acquaintance be forgot
    And never brought to mind?
Should auld acquaintance be forgot,
    And auld lang syne!

Chorus

For auld lang syne, my dear,
    For auld lang syne,
We'll tak a cup o' kindness yet,
    For auld lang syne!

We twa hae run about the braes,
    And pu'd the gowans fine;
But we've wandered monie a weary foot
    Sin' auld lang syne.

We twa hae paidled i' the burn
    Frae mornin' sun till dine;
But seas between us braid hae roared
    Sin' auld lang syne.

And there's a hand, my trusty fiere,
    And gie's a hand o' thine;
And we'll tak a right guid-willie waught,
    For auld lang syne.

ROBERT BURNS

453

DRINK TO ME ONLY WITH THINE EYES

DRINK to me only with thine eyes,
    And I will pledge with mine;
Or leave a kiss but in the cup,
    And I'll not look for wine.
The thirst that from the soul doth rise
    Doth ask a drink divine;
But might I of Jove's nectar sup,
    I would not change for thine.

I sent thee late a rosy wreath,
    Not so much honoring thee
As giving it a hope that there
    It could not withered be.
But thou thereon didst only breathe,
    And sent'st it back to me;
Since when it grows, and smells, I swear,
    Not of itself but thee.

                BEN JONSON

ANNIE LAURIE

MAXWELTON'S braes are bonnie
Where early fa's the dew,
And it's there that Annie Laurie
Gie'd me her promise true;
Gie'd me her promise true,
Which ne'er forgot will be;
And for bonnie Annie Laurie
I'd lay me doun and dee.

Her brow is like the snaw drift;
Her throat is like the swan;
Her face it is the fairest
That e'er the sun shone on—
That e'er the sun shone on—
And dark blue is her e'e;
And for bonnie Annie Laurie
I'd lay me doun and dee.

Like dew on the gowan lying
Is the fa' o' her fairy feet;
And like winds in summer sighing,
Her voice is low and sweet—
Her voice is low and sweet—
And she's a' the world to me;
And for bonnie Annie Laurie
I'd lay me doun and dee.

WILLIAM DOUGLAS (?)

THE TWELVE DAYS OF CHRISTMAS

THE twelfth day of Christmas,
My true love gave to me
Twelve lords a leaping,
Eleven ladies dancing,
Ten pipers piping,
Nine drummers drumming,
Eight maids a milking,
Seven swans a swimming,
Six geese a laying,
Five gold rings,

455

Four colly birds,
Three French hens,
Two turtle doves, and
A partridge in a pear-tree.

ANONYMOUS

NOBODY

I HAVE a wife of my own,
    I'll partake with nobody;
I'll take cuckold from none,
    I'll give cuckold to nobody.

I have a penny to spend,
    There—thanks to nobody;
I have nothing to lend,
    I'll borrow from nobody.

I am nobody's lord,
    I'll be slave to nobody;
I have a good broad sword,
    I'll take blows from nobody.

I'll be merry and free,
    I'll be sad for nobody;
If nobody care for me,
    I'll care for nobody.

ROBERT BURNS

O MY LUVE IS LIKE A RED, RED ROSE

O my Luve is like a red, red rose
    That's newly sprung in June:
O my Luve is like the melodie
    That's sweetly play'd in tune.

As fair art thou, my bonnie lass,
    So deep in luve am I:
And I will luve thee still, my dear,
    Till a' the seas gang dry.

Till a' the seas gang dry, my dear,
    And the rocks melt wi' the sun:
And I will luve thee still, my dear,
    While the sands o' life shall run.

And fare thee weel, my only Luve,
    And fare thee weel a while!
And I will come again, my Luve,
    Tho' it were ten thousand mile.

ROBERT BURNS

BELIEVE ME, IF ALL THOSE ENDEARING YOUNG CHARMS

BELIEVE me, if all those endearing young charms,
    Which I gaze on so fondly today,
Were to change by tomorrow, and fleet in my arms,
    Like fairy-gifts fading away,
Thou wouldst still be adored, as this moment thou art,
    Let thy loveliness fade as it will,

457

And around the dear ruin each wish of my heart
  Would entwine itself verdantly still.

It is not while beauty and youth are thine own,
  And thy cheeks unprofaned by a tear,
That the fervour and faith of a soul can be known,
  To which time will but make thee more dear;
No, the heart that has truly loved never forgets,
  But as truly loves on to the close,
As the sunflower turns on her god, when he sets,
  The same look which she turned when he rose.

THOMAS MOORE

JOHN ANDERSON, MY JO

JOHN ANDERSON, my jo, John,
  When we were first acquent;
Your locks were like the raven,
  Your bonie brow was brent;
But now your brow is bald, John,
  Your locks are like the snow;
But blessings on your frosty pow,
  John Anderson, my jo.

John Anderson, my jo, John,
  We clamb the hill thegither:
And mony a cantie day, John,
  We've had wi' ane anither:
Now we maun totter down, John,
  And hand in hand we'll go,
And sleep thegither at the foot,
  John Anderson, my jo.

ROBERT BURNS

SWEET AFTON

FLOW gently, sweet Afton! among thy green braes,
Flow gently, I'll sing thee a song in thy praise;
My Mary's asleep by thy murmuring stream,
Flow gently, sweet Afton, disturb not her dream.

Thou stock-dove whose echo resounds through the glen,
Ye wild whistling blackbirds in yon thorny den,
Thou green-crested lapwing, thy screaming forbear,
I charge you, disturb not my slumbering fair.

How lofty, sweet Afton, thy neighboring hills,
Far marked with the courses of clear, winding rills;
There daily I wander as noon rises high,
My flocks and my Mary's sweet cot in my eye.

How pleasant thy banks and green valleys below,
Where, wild in the woodlands, the primroses blow;
There oft, as mild ev'ning weeps over the lea,
The sweet-scented birk shades my Mary and me.

Thy crystal stream, Afton, how lovely it glides,
And winds by the cot where my Mary resides;
How wanton thy waters her snowy feet lave,
As, gathering sweet flowerets, she stems thy clear wave.

Flow gently, sweet Afton, among thy green braes,
Flow gently, sweet river, the theme of my lays;
My Mary's asleep by thy murmuring stream,
Flow gently, sweet Afton, disturb not her dream.

ROBERT BURNS

GREEN GROW THE RASHES

GREEN grow the rashes, O;
'Green grow the rashes, O;
The sweetest hours that e'er I spend,
    Are spent amang the lasses, O.

There's nought but care on every han',
    In every hour that passes, O:
What signifies the life o' man,
    An 'twere na for the lasses, O.

The war'ly race may riches chase,
    An' riches still may fly them, O;
An' though at last they catch them fast,
    Their hearts can ne'er enjoy them, O.

But gie me a cannie hour at e'en,
    My arms about my dearie, O,
An' war'ly cares, an' war'ly men
    May a' gae tapsalteerie, O!

For you sae douce, ye sneer at this;
    Ye're nought but senseless asses, O;
The wisest man the warl' e'er saw,
    He dearly loved the lasses, O.

Auld Nature swears, the lovely dears
    Her noblest work she classes, O:
Her 'prentice han' she tried on man,
    An' then she made the lasses, O.

ROBERT BURNS

MY HEART'S IN THE
HIGHLANDS

FAREWELL to the Highlands, farewell to the North,
The birth-place of valor, the country of worth!
Wherever I wander, wherever I rove,
The hills of the Highlands for ever I love.

My heart's in the Highlands, my heart is not here,
My heart's in the Highlands a-chasing the deer,
A-chasing the wild deer and following the roe—
My heart's in the Highlands, wherever I go.

Farewell to the mountains high-covered with snow,
Farewell to the straths and green valleys below,
Farewell to the forests and wild-hanging woods,
Farewell to the torrents and loud-pouring floods!

My heart's in the Highlands, my heart is not here;
My heart's in the Highlands a-chasing the deer,
A-chasing the wild deer and following the roe—
My heart's in the Highlands, wherever I go!

ROBERT BURNS

TAKE, O TAKE THOSE LIPS AWAY

TAKE, O take those lips away
That so sweetly were forsworn,
And those eyes, like break of day,
Lights that do mislead the morn:

461

But my kisses bring again,
        Bring again—
Seals of love, but seal'd in vain,
        Seal'd in vain!

WILLIAM SHAKESPEARE

WHEN ALL THE WORLD IS YOUNG, LAD

WHEN all the world is young, lad,
    And all the trees are green;
And every goose a swan, lad,
    And every lass a queen;
Then hey for boot and horse, lad,
    And round the world away:
Young blood must have its course, lad,
    And every dog his day.

When all the world is old, lad,
    And all the trees are brown;
And all the sport is stale, lad,
    And all the wheels run down;
Creep home, and take your place there,
    The spent and maimed among:
God grant you find one face there,
    You loved when all was young.

CHARLES KINGSLEY

XVIII

Love:

The Light Side

SALLY IN OUR ALLEY

OF all the girls that are so smart
  There's none like pretty Sally;
She is the darling of my heart,
  And she lives in our alley.
There is no lady in the land
  Is half so sweet as Sally;
She is the darling of my heart,
  And she lives in our alley.

Her father he makes cabbage-nets,
  And through the streets does cry 'em
Her mother she sells laces long
  To such as please to buy 'em:
But sure such folks could ne'er beget
  So sweet a girl as Sally!
She is the darling of my heart,
  And she lives in our alley.

When she is by, I leave my work,
  I love her so sincerely;
My master comes like any Turk,
  And bangs me most severely:
But let him bang his bellyful,
  I'll bear it all for Sally;
She is the darling of my heart,
  And she lives in our alley.

Of all the days that's in the week
  I dearly love but one day—
And that's the day that comes betwixt
  A Saturday and Monday;
For then I'm drest all in my best

To walk abroad with Sally;
She is the darling of my heart,
   And she lives in our alley.

My master carries me to church,
   And often am I blamèd
Because I leave him in the lurch
   As soon as text is namèd;
I leave the church in sermon-time
   And slink away to Sally;
She is the darling of my heart,
   And she lives in our alley.

When Christmas comes about again,
   O, then I shall have money;
I'll hoard it up, and box it all,
   I'll give it to my honey:
I would it were ten thousand pound,
   I'd give it all to Sally;
She is the darling of my heart,
   And she lives in our alley.

My master and the neighbours all,
   Make game of me and Sally,
And, but for her, I'd better be
   A slave and row a galley;
But when my seven long years are out,
   O, then I'll marry Sally;
O, then we'll wed, and then we'll bed—
   But not in our alley!

HENRY CAREY

466

THE PLOUGHMAN'S SONG

In the merry month of May,
In a morn by break of day,
Forth I walked by the wood side,
Whereas May was in his pride.
There I spied all alone
Phyllida and Corydon.
Much ado there was, God wot,
He would love and she would not.
She said, never man was true;
He said, none was false to you.
He said, he had loved her long;
She said, love should have no wrong.
Corydon would kiss her then;
She said, maids must kiss no men,
Till they did for good and all.
Then she made the shepard call
All the heavens to witness truth,
Never loved a truer youth.
Thus with many a pretty oath,
Yea and nay, and faith and troth,
Such as silly shepards use,
When they will not love abuse,
Love, which had been long deluded,
Was with kisses sweet concluded:
And Phyllida with garlands gay
Was made the Lady of the May.

NICHOLAS BRETON

A DESCRIPTION OF LOVE

Now what is love I pray thee, tell?
It is that fountain and that well,
Where pleasure and repentance dwell.
It is perhaps that sauncing bell,
That tolls all in to heaven or hell:
And this is love, as I heard tell.

Yet what is love, I pray thee say?
It is a work on holiday;
It is December matched with May;
When lusty bloods, in fresh array,
Hear ten months after of the play:
And this is love, as I hear say.

Yet what is love? I pray thee sayn?
It is a sunshine mixed with rain;
It is a tooth-ache, or like pain;
It is a game where none doth gain;
The lass saith no, and would full fain:
And this is love, as I hear sayn.

Yet what is love, I pray thee say?
It is a yea, it is a nay,
A pretty kind of sporting fray;
It is a thing will soon away;
Then take the vantage while you may:
And this is love, as I hear say.

Yet what is love, I pray thee show?
A thing that creeps, it cannot go;
A prize that passeth to and fro;

A thing for one, a thing for mo;
And he that proves must find it so:
And this is love, sweet friend, I trow.

SIR WALTER RALEIGH

TO MISTRESS ISABEL PENNELL

By Saint Mary, my lady,
Your mammy and your daddy,
Brought forth a goodly baby!

My maiden Isabel,
Reflaring rosabel,
The fragrant camomel;
    The ruddy rosary,
The sovereign rosemary,
The pretty strawberry;
    The columbine, the nept,
The gillyflower well set,
The proper violet:
    Ennewéd your colour
Is like the daisy flower
After the April shower;

469

Star of the morrow gray,
The blossom on the spray,
The freshest flower of May;
    Maidenly demure,
Of womanhood the lure;
Wherefore I make you sure
    It were an heavenly health,
It were an endless wealth,
A life for God himself,
    To hear this nightingale
Among the birdës smale
Warbling in the vale,
    Dug, dug,
    Jug, jug,
        Good year and good luck,
        With chuck, chuck, chuck, chuck!

JOHN SKELTON

TO ONE ADMIRING HERSELF
IN A LOOKING GLASS

FAIR lady, when you see the grace
Of beauty in your looking glass:
A stately forehead smooth and high
And full of princely majesty;
A sparkling eye, no gem so fair,
Whose lustre dims the Cyprian star;
A glorious cheek divinely sweet
Wherein both roses kindly meet;
A cherry lip that would entice
Even gods to kiss at any price;
You think no beauty is so rare
That with your shadow might compare,

That your reflection is alone
The thing that men most dote upon.
Madam, alas, your glass doth lie,
And you are much deceived; for I
A beauty know of richer grace.
Sweet, be not angry—'tis your face.
Hence then, oh learn more mild to be,
And leave to lay your blame on me;
If me your real substance move
When you so much your shadow love.
Wise nature would not let your eye
Look on her own bright majesty,
Which had you once but gazed upon,
You could except yourself love none.
What then you cannot love, let me,
That face I can, you cannot see.
Now you have what to love, you'll say,
What then is left for me, I pray?
My face, sweetheart, if it please thee;
That which you can, I cannot see.
So either love shall gain his due;
Yours, sweet, in me, and mine in you.

THOMAS RANDOLPH

A LOVE SONNET

I LOVED a lass, a fair one,
    As fair as e'er was seen;
She was indeed a rare one,
    Another Sheba queen.
But fool as then I was,
    I thought she loved me too;

But now, alas! sh' 'as left me,
    Falero, lero, loo.

Her hair like gold did glister,
    Each eye was like a star;
She did surpass her sister,
    Which passed all others far.
She would me honey call;
    She'd, O she'd kiss me too;
But now, alas! sh' 'as left me,
    Falero, lero, loo.

In summer time to Medley,
    My love and I would go;
The boatmen there stood ready,
    My love and I to row.
For cream there would we call,
    For cakes, and for prunes too;
But now, alas! sh' 'as left me,
    Falero, lero, loo.

Many a merry meeting
    My love and I have had;
She was my only sweeting,
    She made my heart full glad.
The tears stood in her eyes,
    Like to the morning dew;
But now, alas! sh' 'as left me,
    Falero, lero, loo.

And as abroad we walked,
    As lovers' fashion is,
Oft as we sweetly talked
    The sun should steal a kiss.
The wind upon her lips

Likewise most sweetly blew;
But now, alas! sh' 'as left me,
   Falero, lero, loo.

Her cheeks were like the cherry,
   Her skin as white as snow;
When she was blithe and merry,
   She angel-like did show.
Her waist exceeding small,
   The fives did fit her shoe;
But now, alas! sh' 'as left me,
   Falero, lero, loo.

In summer time or winter
   She had her heart's desire;
I still did scorn to stint her
   From sugar, sack, or fire.
The world went round about,
   No cares we ever knew;
But now, alas! sh' 'as left me,
   Falero, lero, loo.

As we walked home together
   At midnight through the town,
To keep away the weather
   O'er her I'd cast my gown.
No cold my love should feel,
   Whate'er the heavens could do;
But now, alas! sh' 'as left me,
   Falero, lero, loo.

Like doves we would be billing,
   And clip and kiss so fast;
Yet she would be unwilling
   That I should kiss the last.

473

They're Judas-kisses now,
    Since that they proved untrue;
For now, alas! sh' 'as left me,
    Falero, lero, loo.

To maidens' vows and swearing
    Henceforth no credit give;
You may give them the hearing,
    But never them believe.
They are as false as fair,
    Unconstant, frail, untrue;
For mine, alas! has left me,
    Falero, lero, loo.

'Twas I that paid for all things,
    'Twas others drank the wine;
I cannot now recall things,
    Live but a fool to pine.
'Twas I that beat the bush,
    The bird to others flew;
For she, alas! hath left me,
    Falero, lero, loo.

If ever that dame Nature,
    For this false lover's sake,
Another pleasing creature
    Like unto her would make,
Let her remember this,
    To make the other true;
For this, alas! hath left me,
    Falero, lero, loo.

No riches now can raise me,
    No want make me despair;
No misery amaze me,

Not yet for want I care.
I have lost a world itself.
My earthly heaven, adieu,
Since she, alas! hath left me,
Falero, lero, loo.

GEORGE WITHER

SONG

SYLVIA the fair, in the bloom of fifteen,
Felt an innocent warmth as she lay on the green;
She had heard of a pleasure, and something she guessed
By the towsing and tumbling and touching her breast;
She saw the men eager, but was at a loss
What they meant by their sighing and kissing so close;
  By their praying and whining,
  And clasping and twining,
  And panting and wishing,
  And sighing and kissing,
  And sighing and kissing so close.

Ah, she cried, ah, for a languishing maid
In a country of Christians to die without aid!
Not a Whig or a Tory or Trimmer at least,
Or a Protestant parson or Catholic priest,

475

To instruct a young virgin that is at a loss
What they meant by their sighing and kissing so close;
    By their praying &c.

Cupid in shape of a swain did appear;
He saw the sad wound, and in pity drew near,
Then showed her his arrow and bid her not fear,
For the pain was no more than a maiden may bear;
When the balm was infused, she was not at a loss
What they meant by their sighing and kissing so close;
    By their praying &c.

John Dryden

THE FLEA

MARK but this flea, and mark in this,
How little that which thou deniest me is;
It sucked me first, and now sucks thee,
And in this flea our two bloods mingled be.
Thou know'st that this cannot be said
A sin, nor shame, nor loss of maidenhead;
    Yet this enjoys before it woo,
    And pampered swells with one blood made of two;
    And this, alas! is more than we would do.

Oh stay, three lives in one flea spare,
Where we almost, yea, more than married are.
This flea is you and I, and this
Our marriage bed, and marriage temple is.
Though parents grudge, and you, we're met,
And cloistered in these living walls of jet.
    Though use make you apt to kill me,

Let not to that self-murder added be,
And sacrilege, three sins in killing three.

Cruel and sudden, hast thou since
Purpled thy nail in blood of innocence?
Wherein could this flea guilty be,
Except in that drop which it sucked from thee?
Yet thou triumph'st, and say'st that thou
Find'st not thyself nor me the weaker now.
    'Tis true; then learn how false fears be;
    Just so much honor, when thou yield'st to me,
    Will waste, as this flea's death took life from thee.

JOHN DONNE

I CARE NOT FOR THESE LADIES

I CARE not for these ladies
That must be wooed and prayed,
Give me kind Amaryllis,
The wanton country maid.
Nature art disdaineth,
Her beauty is her own.
    Her when we court and kiss,
    She cries, "Forsooth, let go!"
    But when we come where comfort is,
    She never will say no.

If I love Amaryllis,
She gives me fruit and flowers,
But if we love these ladies,
We must give golden showers.

Give them gold that sell love,
Give me the nut-brown lass,
    Who when we court and kiss,
    She cries, "Forsooth, let go!"
    But when we come where comfort is,
    She never will say no.

These ladies must have pillows
And beds by strangers wrought;
Give me a bower of willows,
Of moss and leaves unbought,
And fresh Amaryllis,
With milk and honey fed,
    Who when we court and kiss,
    She cries, "Forsooth, let go!"
    But when we come where comfort is,
    She never will say no.

                                    THOMAS CAMPION

SONG

O, THAT joy so soon should waste!
    Or so sweet a bliss
        As a kiss
Might not for ever last!
So sugared, so melting, so soft, so delicious,
    The dew that lies on roses,
    When the Morn herself discloses,
        Is not so precious.
O, rather than I would it smother,
Were I to taste such another,
    It should be my wishing
    That I might die kissing.

                                    BEN JONSON

TO CLOE JEALOUS, A BETTER ANSWER

DEAR Cloe, how blubber'd is that pretty face;
  Thy cheek all on fire, and thy hair all uncurl'd:
Prythee quit this caprice; and (as old Falstaff says)
  Let us e'en talk a little like folks of this world.

How canst thou presume, thou hast leave to destroy
  The beauties, which Venus but lent to thy keeping?
Those looks were design'd to inspire love and joy:
  More ord'nary eyes may serve people for weeping.

To be vex'd at a trifle or two that I writ,
  Your judgment at once, and my passion you wrong:
You take that for fact, which will scarce be found wit:
  Odds life! must one swear to the truth of a song?

What I speak, my fair Cloe, and what I write, shows
  The difference there is betwixt nature and art:
I court others in verse; but I love thee in prose:
  And they have my whimsies, but thou hast my heart.

The god of us verse-men (you know, child) the sun,
  How after his journeys he sets up his rest:
If at morning o'er earth 'tis his fancy to run;
  At night he declines on his Thetis's breast.

So when I am wearied with wandering all day,
  To thee, my delight, in the evening I come:
No matter what beauties I saw in my way;
  They were all but my visits, but thou art my home.

479

Then finish, dear Cloe, this pastoral war;
    And let us, like Horace and Lydia, agree:
For thou art a girl as much brighter than her,
    As he was a poet sublimer than me.

MATTHEW PRIOR

SONG

Of all the torments, all the cares,
    With which our lives are cursed;
Of all the plagues a lover bears,
    Sure rivals are the worst!
By partners, in each other kind,
    Afflictions easier grow;
In love alone we hate to find
    Companions of our woe.

Sylvia, for all the pangs you see
    Are labouring in my breast;
I beg not you would favour me,
    Would you but slight the rest!
How great so e'er your rigours are,
    With them alone I'll cope;
I can endure my own despair,
    But not another's hope.

WILLIAM WALSH

HERE'S TO THE MAIDEN

HERE's to the maiden of bashful fifteen;
    Here's to the widow of fifty;
Here's to the flaunting extravagant quean,
    And here's to the housewife that's thrifty.

Chorus.

Let the toast pass,—
Drink to the lass,
I'll warrant she'll prove an excuse for the glass.

Here's to the charmer whose dimples we prize;
    Now to the maid who has none, sir:
Here's to the girl with a pair of blue eyes,
    And here's to the nymph with but *one,* sir.

Chorus.   Let the toast pass, &c.

Here's to the maid with a bosom of snow;
    Now to her that's as brown as a berry:
Here's to the wife with a face full of woe,
    And now to the girl that is merry.

Chorus.   Let the toast pass, &c.

For let 'em be clumsy, or let 'em be slim,
    Young or ancient, I care not a feather;
So fill a pint bumper quite up to the brim,
    And let us e'en toast them together,
        Let the toast pass,—
        Drink to the lass,
    I'll warrant she'll prove an excuse for the glass.

RICHARD BRINSLEY BUTLER SHERIDAN

KISSIN'

SOME say kissin's ae sin,
 But I say, not at a';
For it's been in the warld
 Ever sin' there were twa.

If it werena lawfu',
 Lawyers wadna' 'low it;
If it werena holy,
 Meenisters wadna' dae it;

If it werena modest,
 Maidens wadna' taste it;
If it werena plenty,
 Poor folk couldna' hae it.

ANONYMOUS

THE SUICIDE'S GRAVE

ON a tree by a river a little tom-tit
 Sang "Willow, titwillow, titwillow!"
And I said to him, "Dicky-bird, why do you sit
 Singing 'Willow, titwillow, titwillow'?
Is it a weakness of intellect, birdie?" I cried,
"Or a rather tough worm in your little inside?"
With a shake of his poor little head he replied,
 "Oh, willow, titwillow, titwillow!"

He slapped at his chest, as he sat on that bough,
 Singing "Willow, titwillow, titwillow!"
And a cold perspiration bespangled his brow,
 Oh, willow, titwillow, titwillow!

482

He sobbed and he sighed, and a gurgle he gave,
Then he threw himself into the billowy wave,
And an echo arose from the suicide's grave—
    "Oh, willow, titwillow, titwillow!"

Now, I feel just as sure as I'm sure that my name
    Isn't Willow, titwillow, titwillow,
That 'twas blighted affection that made him exclaim,
    "Oh, willow, titwillow, titwillow!"
And if you remain callous and obdurate, I
Shall perish as he did, and you will know why,
Though I probably shall not exclaim as I die,
    "Oh, willow, titwillow, titwillow!"

SIR W. S. GILBERT

SIGH NO MORE, LADIES

SIGH no more, ladies, sigh no more,
    Men were deceivers ever,
One foot in sea and one on shore,
    To one thing constant never:
Then sigh not so, but let them go,
    And be you blithe and bonny,
Converting all your sounds of woe
    Into Hey nonny, nonny.

Sing no more ditties, sing no more,
    Of dumps so dull and heavy;
The fraud of men was ever so,
    Since summer first was leafy:
Then sigh not so, but let them go,
    And be you blithe and bonny,
Converting all your sounds of woe
    Into Hey nonny, nonny.

WILLIAM SHAKESPEARE

CARDS AND KISSES

CUPID and my Campaspe play'd
At cards for kisses—Cupid paid:
He stakes his quiver, bow, and arrows,
His mother's doves, and team of sparrows;
Loses them too; then down he throws
The coral of his lips, the rose
Growing on's cheek (but none knows how);
With these, the crystal of his brow,
And then the dimple of his chin:
All these did my Campaspe win.
At last he set her both his eyes—
She won, and Cupid blind did rise.
O Love! has she done this for thee?
What shall, alas! become of me?

JOHN LYLY

FRANKIE AND JOHNNY

FRANKIE and Johnny were lovers, great God how they
    could love!
Swore to be true to each other, true as the stars up
    above.
He was her man, but he done her wrong.

Frankie she was his woman, everybody knows.
She spent her forty dollars for Johnny a suit of clothes.
He was her man, but he done her wrong.

Frankie and Johnny went walking, Johnny in his brand
  new suit.
"O good Lawd," said Frankie, "but don't my Johnny
  look cute?"
He was her man, but he done her wrong.

Frankie went down to the corner, just for a bucket of
  beer.
Frankie said, "Mr. Bartender, has my loving Johnny
  been here.
He is my man, he wouldn't do me wrong."

"I don't want to tell you no story, I don't want to tell
  you no lie,
But your Johnny left here an hour ago with that lousy
  Nellie Blye.
He is your man, but he's doing you wrong."

Frankie went back to the hotel, she didn't go there for
  fun,
For under her red kimono she toted a forty-four gun.
He was her man, but he done her wrong.

Frankie went down to the hotel and looked in the
  window so high,
And there was her loving Johnny a-loving up Nellie
  Blye.
He was her man, but he was doing her wrong.

Frankie threw back her kimono, took out that old forty-
  four.
Root-a-toot-toot, three times she shot, right through the
  hardwood door.
He was her man, but he was doing her wrong.

Johnny grabbed off his Stetson, crying, "O, Frankie, don't shoot!"
Frankie pulled that forty-four, went root-a-toot-toot-toot-toot.
He was her man, but he done her wrong.

"Roll me over gently, roll me over slow,
Roll me on my right side, for my left side hurts me so,
I was her man, but I done her wrong."

With the first shot Johnny staggered, with the second shot he fell;
When the last bullet got him, there was a new man's face in hell.
He was her man, but he done her wrong.

"O, bring out your rubber-tired hearses, bring out your rubber-tired hacks;
Gonna take Johnny to the graveyard and ain't gonna bring him back.
He was my man, but he done me wrong."

"O, put me in that dungeon, put me in that cell,
Put me where the northeast wind blows from the southeast corner of hell.
I shot my man, cause he done me wrong!"

ANONYMOUS

486

DUNCAN GRAY

DUNCAN GRAY came here to woo,
    Ha, ha, the wooing o't,
On blythe Yule night when we were fou,
    Ha, ha, the wooing o't.
Maggie coost her head fu' heigh,
Look'd asklent and unco skeigh,
Gart poor Duncan stand abeigh;
    Ha, ha, the wooing o't.

Duncan fleech'd, and Duncan pray'd;
    Ha, ha, the wooing o't,
Meg was deaf as Ailsa Craig,
    Ha, ha, the wooing o't.
Duncan sigh'd baith out and in,
Grat his een baith bleer't and blin',
Spak o' lowpin o'er a linn;
    Ha, ha, the wooing o't.

Time and chance are but a tide,
    Ha, ha, the wooing o't,
Slighted love is sair to bide,
    Ha, ha, the wooing o't.
Shall I, like a fool, quoth he,
For a haughty hizzie die?
She may gae to—France for me!
    Ha, ha, the wooing o't.

How it comes let doctors tell,
    Ha, ha, the wooing o't,
Meg grew sick as he grew haill,
    Ha, ha, the wooing o't.
Something in her bosom wrings,

For relief a sigh she brings;
And O, her een they spak sic things!
    Ha, ha, the wooing o't.

Duncan was a lad o' grace,
    Ha, ha, the wooing o't,
Maggie's was a piteous case,
    Ha, ha, the wooing o't.
Duncan couldna be her death,
Swelling pity smoor'd his wrath;
Now they're crouse and cantie baith!
    Ha, ha, the wooing o't.

ROBERT BURNS

SONG

THE merchant to secure his treasure,
   Conveys it in a borrowed name:
Euphelia serves to grace my measure;
   But Chloe is my real flame.

My softest verse, my darling lyre,
   Upon Euphelia's toilet lay;
When Chloe noted her desire
   That I should sing, that I should play.

My lyre I tune, my voice I raise;
   But with my numbers mix my sighs:
And while I sing Euphelia's praise,
   I fix my soul on Chloe's eyes.

Fair Chloe blushed: Euphelia frowned:
   I sung, and gazed: I played and trembled:

And Venus to the Loves around
  Remarked, how ill we all dissembled.

MATTHEW PRIOR

TO A LADY

*She Refusing to Continue a Dispute with Me and
Leaving Me in the Argument*

SPARE, generous Victor, spare the slave
  Who did unequal war pursue,
That more than triumph he might have
  In being overcome by you.

In the dispute whate'er I said,
  My heart was by my tongue belied;
And in my looks you might have read
  How much I argued on your side.

You, far from danger as from fear,
  Might have sustained an open fight;
For seldom your opinions err,
  Your eyes are always in the right.

Why, fair one, would you not rely
  On reason's force with beauty's joined?
Could I their prevalence deny,
  I must at once be deaf and blind.

Alas! not hoping to subdue,
  I only to the fight aspired:
To keep the beauteous foe in view
  Was all the glory I desired.

489

But she, howe'er of victory sure,
   Contemns the wreath too long delayed;
And, armed with more immediate power,
   Calls cruel silence to her aid.

Deeper to wound, she shuns the fight:
   She drops her arms, to gain the field:
Secures her conquest by her flight,
   And triumphs when she seems to yield.

So when the Parthian turned his steed,
   And from the hostile camp withdrew,
With cruel skill the backward reed
   He sent; and as he fled, he slew.

MATTHEW PRIOR

SHE'S ALL MY FANCY
PAINTED HIM

SHE's all my fancy painted him
   (I make no idle boast);
If he or you had lost a limb,
   Which would have suffered most?

He said that you had been to her,
   And seen me here before:
But, in another character
   She was the same of yore.

There was not one that spoke to us,
   Of all that thronged the street;
So he sadly got into a 'bus,
   And pattered with his feet.

They told me you had been to her,
    And mentioned me to him;
She gave me a good character,
    But said I could not swim.

He sent them word I had not gone
    (We know it to be true);
If she should push the matter on,
    What would become of you?

I gave her one, they gave him two,
    You gave us three or more;
They all returned from him to you,
    Though they were mine before.

If I or she should chance to be
    Involved in this affair,
He trusts to you to set them free,
    Exactly as we were.

My notion was that you had been
    (Before she had this fit)
An obstacle that came between
    Him, and ourselves, and it.

Don't let him know she likes them best,
    For this must ever be
A secret, kept from all the rest
    Between yourself and me.

LEWIS CARROLL

A GENTLE ECHO ON WOMAN

Shepherd.	Echo, I ween, will in the woods reply,
	And quaintly answer questions: shall I try?
Echo.	*Try.*
Shepherd.	What must we do, our passion to express?
Echo.	*Press.*
Shepherd.	What most moves women when we them address?
Echo.	*A dress.*
Shepherd.	Say, what can keep her chaste whom I adore?
Echo.	*A door.*
Shepherd.	If music softens rocks, love tunes my lyre.
Echo.	*Liar.*
Shepherd.	Then teach me, Echo, how shall I come by her?
Echo.	*Buy her.*
Shepherd.	But what can glad me when she's laid on bier?
Echo.	*Beer.*
Shepherd.	What must I do when women will be kind?
Echo.	*Be kind.*
Shepherd.	What must I do when women will be cross?
Echo.	*Be cross.*
Shepherd.	Lord, what is she that can so turn and wind?
Echo.	*Wind.*

Shepherd.	If she be wind, what stills her when she blows?
Echo.	*Blows.*
Shepherd.	Is there no way to moderate her anger?
Echo.	*Hang her.*
Shepherd.	Thanks, gentle Echo! Right thy answers tell
	What woman is and how to guard her well.
Echo.	*Guard her well.*

JONATHAN SWIFT

THE KISS

I saw you take his kiss!' ' 'Tis true.'
'O modesty!' ' 'Twas strictly kept:
He thought me asleep—at least, I knew
He thought I thought he thought I slept.'

COVENTRY PATMORE

THE SORROWS OF WERTHER

WERTHER had a love for Charlotte
Such as words could never utter;
Would you know how first he met her?
She was cutting bread and butter.

Charlotte was a married lady,
And a moral man was Werther,
And for all the wealth of Indies,
Would do nothing for to hurt her.

So he sighed and pined and ogled,
And his passion boiled and bubbled,

493

Till he blew his silly brains out,
   And no more was by it troubled.

Charlotte, having seen his body
   Borne before her on a shutter,
Like a well-conducted person,
   Went on cutting bread and butter.

WILLIAM M. THACKERAY

I NEVER EVEN SUGGESTED IT

I KNOW lots of men who are in love and lots of men who
   are married and lots of men who are both,
And to fall out with their loved ones is what all of them
   are most loth.
They are conciliatory at every opportunity,
Because all they want is serenity and a certain amount
   of impunity.
Yes, many the swain who has finally admitted that the
   earth is flat
Simply to sidestep a spat,
Many the masculine Positively or Absolutely which has
   been diluted to an If
Simply to avert a tiff,
Many the two-fisted executive whose domestic conver-
   sation is limited to a tactfully interpolated Yes,
And then he is amazed to find that he is being raked
   backwards over a bed of coals nevertheless.
These misguided fellows are under the impression that
   it takes two to make a quarrel, that you can side-
   step a crisis by nonaggression and nonresistance,
Instead of removing yourself to a discreet distance.
Passivity can be a provoking *modus operandi*;
Consider the Empire and Gandhi.
Silence is golden, but sometimes invisibility is golder.

Because loved ones may not be able to make bricks
 without straw but often they don't need any straw
 to manufacture a bone to pick or blood in their eye
 or a chip for their soft white shoulder.
It is my duty, gentlemen, to inform you that women are
 dictators all, and I recommend to you this moral:
In real life it takes only one to make a quarrel.

OGDEN NASH

MAN, MAN, MAN

MAN, man, man is for the woman made,
And the woman is made for man;
As the spur is for the jade,
As the scabbard for the blade,
As for digging is the spade,
   As for liquor is the can,
So man, man, man is for the woman made,
   And the woman made for man.

As the sceptre's to be swayed,
As for Night's the serenade,
   As for pudding is the pan,
   As to cool us is the fan,
So man, man, man is for the woman made,
   And the woman made for man.

Be she widow, wife, or maid,
Be she wanton, be she staid,
Be she well or ill-arrayed,
   Shrew, slut, or harridan,
Yet man, man, man is for the woman made,
   And the woman is made for man.

ANONYMOUS

Appendix

Index of First Lines
Index of Authors & Titles

INDEX OF FIRST LINES

A

B

499

Index of First Lines

500

F

G

Index of First Lines

Index of First Lines

504

Index of First Lines

M

N

O

Index of First Lines

507

Index of First Lines

509

Index of First Lines

510

Index of First Lines

Index of First Lines

Y

INDEX OF AUTHORS & TITLES

513

Index of Authors & Titles

518

520

Index of Authors & Titles

522

523